English and English Linguistics

English and English Linguistics

Randal L. Whitman

Temple University

Holt, Rinehart and Winston, Inc.

New York   Chicago   San Francisco   Atlanta
Dallas   Montreal   Toronto   London   Sydney

To the Doctor
in Simsbury

Library of Congress Cataloging in Publication Data

Whitman, Randal L.
  English and English linguistics.

   1. English language—Grammar, generative.
2. Language and languages. I. Title.

PE1106.W48   425   74–19403

ISBN 0–03–010391-6

Copyright © 1975 by Holt, Rinehart
and Winston, Inc.
Printed in the United States of America

5 6 7 8 9   090   9 8 7 6 5 4 3 2 1

Preface

This book has two goals: it provides an introduction to transformational-generative grammar, placing it into a historical and philosophical context with other earlier linguistic traditions, and it provides a survey of the elements of English grammar—from a transformational point of view—intended to function as an elementary resource grammar.

The text is intended for anyone who wishes or needs to know the basis of transformational grammar, but it is especially intended for those who have a professional or personal need for a better acquaintance with English grammar—in particular, for prospective English teachers. Considerable portions of the text, especially in the first part, trace the impact of linguistic theories on English teaching, and there is continuous commentary throughout the text concerning issues that are relevant to English teachers; in addition, many of the exercises in the second and third parts are directed to them specifically.

With so much intended, the text has always threatened to mushroom out of all control. There is so much that one can say about generative grammar and so much about English that extreme effort was required to keep it simple, keep it short. The result is that in both directions the text is elementary. I trust that the introductory transformational grammar will equip readers to develop further on their own, or to follow others intelligently, but in particular to be able to formulate sensible notions about the basis of English sentences that they encounter. At the same time, I hope that the rest of the text can be used as a resource to English grammar by providing an elementary sketch of most points that arise in simple English sentences. It is essential, however, that readers go on to complement the discussions of those points contained herein and to supplement the material with points not covered.

In the course of the text, frequent reference is made to three other books: Robert Krohn's *English Sentence Structure* (Ann Arbor: University of Michigan

Press, 1971), Robert Lado and Charles C. Fries' *English Sentence Patterns* (Ann Arbor: University of Michigan Press, 1957), and J. M. Walsh and A. K. Walsh's *Plain English Handbook* (Cincinnati: McCormick-Mathers, 1972). The Lado and Fries book has been allowed to go out of print (to be replaced by the Krohn text), but it might be well worth while for readers to obtain copies of the other two for reference purposes. Otherwise, it would certainly be advisable to obtain one or another of the many available English reference grammars.

Acknowledgements

I am indebted to my students at the University of Hawaii, who field-tested this text, in the process offering many comments and criticisms that made themselves felt in successive revisions. To a considerable degree, it is difficult to tell which of the ideas found herein are mine and which theirs. Indeed, but for them, the text would never have been begun in the first place.

I wish also to express particular thanks to my friend L. Ben Crane of Temple University, who read the manuscript and argued over practically every point in it. I was forced to sacrifice some rather precious positions in the face of his intransigent opposition; I fear that this materially improved the book.

Finally, I would like to give special appreciation to my wife Leanna, who arranged life and children to keep me uninterrupted during periods of work and who in addition read and criticized the manuscript for style.

R.L.W.

Contents

Appendix: Summary of Rules

English
and
English
Linguistics

1

THEORIES IN LINGUISTICS

1.0   Linguistics Is a Science!

One of the principal goals of the structural linguist was to "establish linguistics as a science." This was an eminently laudable goal, but it meant different things to different people. To some, it meant that linguistics had to be quantified, and made susceptible to statistical treatment. To others, it meant that language should be characterized by laws and formulas. Numbers and formulas, after all, are certainly characteristic of the "hard" sciences—physics, chemistry, and the like—so why not linguistics? However, numbers, formulas, tables, graphs, and laws are merely the trappings of science; they are by no means what make a science scientific. What does? As it turns out, there is no specific defining characteristic of science that would satisfactorily distinguish between the sciences and the nonsciences. We thus have a rough system in which it is simply agreed that certain fields of study are sciences, other fields are definitely not sciences (such as English literature), and quite a few occupy a never-never land in between (such as sociology). The position of linguistics is generally considered to be in this indeterminate area, an inexactness that galled the linguistic academic of the first half of this century—he wanted to be a scientist.

The structural linguist attempted to solve his problem in the following way: he first defined the nature of a science and then defined linguistics to conform to that description. To the structuralist, science involved the following steps:

1. The observation of facts—real, "hard" facts, whose existence could not be disputed. These he called data;
2. The analysis of the data to form a hypothetical pattern, a description of this pattern being then a hypothesis of the phenomenon under study;
3. The extrapolation of the pattern to make predictions of new, as yet unobserved, occurrences;
4. The testing of these predictions to determine their accuracy.

The structuralist then defined what he considered to be the real hard facts of language, or linguistic data. Quite simply, they were any recorded act of speech and any preserved act of writing. If the speech was not recorded (by a tape recorder or perhaps a stenographer), it had the status of hearsay, which is to say not much status as data at all. Since the language data existed principally on pieces of paper, this led to a sense of language itself having an existence on paper quite independent of the speaker. Certainly, language was considered to have an existence independent of the speaker's mind, for the concept of "mind" was quite alien to the structuralist in so far as "mind" was exquisitely unobservable.

Here we come to the nub of the linguistic controversy of the 1960s. The newly emergent generative linguist claimed that language, far from being independent of the mind, was so inextricably tied to the mind that the study of language was virtually the study of the human mind. As an immediate result, the structuralist accused the generativist of fomenting unscientific endeavor (among other things), because nothing to do with the mind could be observed objectively. The generativist responded that objective observability was not a *sine qua non* of science as far as he was concerned and that, furthermore, by so believing, the structuralist had straight-jacketed himself into unproductive work. The basic difference between the two positions lies in a redefinition of science by the generativist. Where the structuralist claimed that science began with the analysis of data to deduce hypothetical models, which could then be tested, the generativist said that the hypotheses need not themselves be products of any sort of objective procedure, but could instead derive from the imagination of the scientist. Science consisted of testing these hypotheses. Thus both the structuralist and the generativist believed themselves to be engaged in science, even though the two could hardly speak together without each accusing the other of pseudo-science or null-science. In the long run, of course, it hardly matters, for it is not we, but "scientists" of the future who will have the last word in the matter.

1.1   Traditional, Structural, and Transformational-Generative Linguists

There are three broad categories of linguists that will concern us here, although it is not necessarily easy to identify individual linguists as belonging purely to one category or another. The three are usually labeled traditional, structural, and transformational-generative (henceforth TG) linguists. The three have important historical relationships, for each of the latter two revolted against its predecessor.

1.11   TRADITIONAL LINGUISTICS

Of the three, the "traditionalist" is the most misunderstood, for he is the least well defined. As a functional definition, we will say that a traditionalist is any linguist who worked before the structural revolution, or before about 1930, and this definition covers a considerable variety of grammatical philosophies and approaches. There are, however, several sorts of traditionalists who are of particular interest to us.

The first is the "universalist" grammarian—Roger Bacon (1214-1294) is perhaps the best known—who felt that there was an ideal, or universal, grammar in whose terms the rules of all particular grammars could be discussed. To many universalists, the classical languages Greek and Latin appeared to conform best to their concept of ideal grammar. English, then, would be described in terms of Latin forms and as if subject to Latin grammatical constraints. A noun, for example, would be presented in the form of the Latin noun paradigm:

Nominative:	the house
Genitive:	of the house
Dative:	to the house
Accusative:	the house
Ablative:	in, at, by, or from the house
Vocative:	O house

This approach is fairly evidently an unproductive one, and the universalist didn't last out the medieval period. His influence on English was, however, profound, and is still evident in today's schoolroom. One of his dicta, for example, was that a sentence should not end with a preposition—for they don't in Latin. Such a rule was never true of English; even in Old English you could find sentences ending with prepositions. English, in fact, provides mechanisms for piling up a number of sentence-ending prepositions, as Morris Bishop's poem shows:

I lost a naughty preposition
He lived, I think, beneath my chair.
I cried aloud to him, "Perdition!"
"Come on up out from down under there!"

Now language is my vade mecum
And straggling phrases I abhor:
And yet I wonder, what should he come
On up out from down under for?[1]

Another familiar restriction that the universalist applied to English was the Latin constraint against the use of the accusative form of a noun after the verb *esse* (to be). Since *me* is the "accusative" form of the first person pronoun (as in the paradigm),

Nom.: I
Gen.: my
Dat.: to me
Acc.: me
Abl.: by me
Voc.: O me

it became wrong to say *It's me*, and school teachers have taught us to say *It's I* instead ever since.

The second major kind of traditionalist was the "prescriptivist," who viewed language moralistically: there was "good grammar" and there was "bad grammar." This may sound somewhat familiar to you as a contemporary phenomenon, and of course it is. It is a very human trait to feel that there are right and wrong ways of doing things—including speaking—and as a consequence it is fair to say that prescriptivism in grammar has been around as long as there have been grammarians. The prescriptivist tends to be conservative, and to regard language change as corruptive; the language of his ancestors had beauty, but the language of his contemporaries is always diminished.

The authority of the prescriptivist came to a peak in the middle of the eighteenth century, with the publication in 1755 of Samuel Johnson's *A Dictionary of the English Language* and in 1762 of Bishop Lowth's *A Short*

[1] "The Naughty Preposition," from Morris Bishop, *A Bowl of Bishop* (Dial Press, 1954). Copyright 1954 by Morris Bishop. Reprinted by permission of Alison M. K. Bishop. Originally published in *The New Yorker*.

Introduction to English Grammar. Both of these works had an immense and continuing impact on the structure of English. Some of Lowth's decisions as to the rightness and wrongness of locutions were arbitrary, and violated the custom of his day, yet still stand today. For example, writers of Lowth's era used both *better than he* and *better than him*; Lowth determined that the former was correct and the latter wrong, because of what might follow, that is, *better than he is*. His decision, and his reasons, continue to be observed today.

One present complaint about prescriptivists is that they had a tendency to account for discrepancies between English and their rules by inventing new labels on an *ad hoc* basis. For example, we find the following in Walsh and Walsh (1939:19):

> The RETAINED OBJECT is in the objective case:
> I was given a *watch* by my father.
> A retained object is one that has been retained after a verb has been changed from active to passive.
> My father gave (active) me a *watch*. (direct object)
> I was given (passive) a *watch* by my father. (retained object)
> This is called RETAINED OBJECT because a verb in the passive voice does not take a direct object.[2]

The key to the concept of the "retained" object lies in the discrepancy between the rule that passives do not take objects and the obvious fact that they do sometimes. The modern linguist would say that it is wrong to invent the "retained" object when what is clearly necessary is a better understanding of the rules concerning the passive.

The prescriptivist's appreciation of his rules was so great that, on rare occasions, he appeared to be unable to see the discrepancy between his claims and the realities of English. In Walsh and Walsh (1972:53-54), we find, for example:

> The subject of an infinitive is in the objective case:
> We asked *him* to go. (*Him* is the subject of *to go*.)
> In an infinitive clause, a predicate noun ... used after *to be* is in the objective case to agree with the subject of the infinitive:
> They took me to be *her*.
> If the infinitive *to be* has no subject, the predicate noun ... following it is in the nominative case:
> He was thought to be *I*.

Clearly something is wrong with the principle of subject-predicate noun agreement as implied above. What is amazing, of course, is that the Walshes saw nothing wrong about the example they used to illustrate their rule.

The conservatism of the prescriptivist shows up best when there is competition between an older form and a more recent alternative. Perhaps a hundred years ago there would have been no competition between *may* and *can* in the sentences

---

[2] Also in Walsh and Walsh, (1972:18), but with the final observation deleted.

You would not say

Mother, CAN I have an apple?

Everybody knows that you are old enough, and big enough, and strong enough to have an apple.

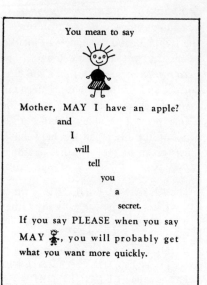

You mean to say

Mother, MAY I have an apple? and

I

will

tell

you

a

secret.

If you say PLEASE when you say MAY 🏃, you will probably get what you want more quickly.

From *Grammar Can Be Fun* by Munro Leaf; copyright 1934 by Munro Leaf; copyright © renewed 1962 by Munro Leaf; reprinted by permission of J. B. Lippincott Company

May I have a cookie? and *Can I have a cookie?* for the latter simply did not exist. At some point, however, *can* began to compete with *may*, gained favor over the years, and today finds itself in a dominant position—nine out of ten people will use *can* rather than *may*. The prescriptivist position is well illustrated by two pages shown here from Munro Leaf's *Grammar Can Be Fun* (1934)—only a donkey would say *can*. However, the prescriptivist's position has eroded somewhat and is today a subject of humor (albeit slightly)—see the cartoon "Hi and Lois" by Mort Walker and Dik Browne.

I would not like to give the impression that prescriptivism is on the run, however. When Merriam-Webster published the third edition of its *International Dictionary of English* in 1958, there were howls from all sides that the dictionary had abrogated its instructional (that is, its prescriptive) purpose by not telling how the words in it *should* be used, but instead telling how they *were* used. One of the many sins in Webster's Third that excited special comment and condemnation was the listing of *infer* as a synonym for *imply*. We all know that English teachers insist that *infer* and *imply* are different, and many of us remember special instruction on the point. At the same time, it is obvious that the distinction is difficult for many to grasp, and such people may unpredictably misuse the two. In other words, for all practical purposes they may use *infer* and *imply* interchangeably, which is to say as synonyms. A prescriptive dictionary editor would have no difficulty in deciding what to do: the two words have different meanings. The editors of Webster's Third, however, felt obligated to reflect—at least somewhere in the entry—the fact that some people do use the

HI AND LOIS
By Mort Walker and Dik Browne

two words as synonyms. The principal definitions, however, remained as they always had been. Poor Webster's Third was denounced right and left, burned by Nero Wolfe, and banished from the editorial desks of many magazines, newspapers, and publishers.

The rejection of the prescriptive ethic slightly predated the structural revolution with the advent of the "descriptivists." The descriptivist had his heyday between 1900 and 1930 and was at his best in Otto Jespersen. The basic tenet of descriptivism was that the grammarian's purpose was to describe language as he found it rather than in some idealized form. Jespersen's *Essentials of English Grammar* (1933) is a model of lucidity that has not been matched since. It is a faithful portrait of real English.[3]

The Reed-Kellogg (RK) diagram was the principal tool of sentence description for the pre-descriptive traditionalist, and most Americans who learned English in school before 1960 probably can remember parsing sentences with RK diagrams. In case the details are vague, a brief review might be in order:

The basic part of the RK diagram is the base line, a horizontal line divided into two parts by a short vertical line. Here we find the subject and the predicate of the sentence, as in *Fish swim*. (Figure 1.1).

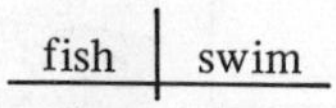

fish | swim

Figure 1.1

If the predicate consists of a verb and a direct object, they are separated by a shorter vertical line that does not extend below the base line, as in *Dogs chase cats*. (Figure 1.2).

dogs | chase | cats

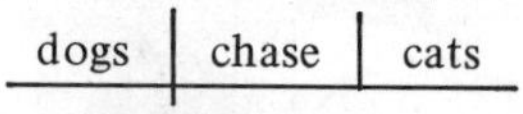

Figure 1.2

Modifiers appear on slanted lines below the word modified, as in *The little boy hit his sister in the garden*. (Figure 1.3).

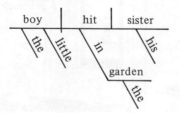

Figure 1.3

And so on. Further examples may be found in Walsh and Walsh (1972).

---

[3] For an excellent discussion of Jespersen, see the Introduction in Lester (1971).

Exercise 1.11

Draw Reed-Kellogg diagrams for the following:
1. Mary saw a piano in her teacher's house.
2. The child was miserable.
3. The boy whom you saw is named Charlie.
4. A dog ran under the fence.

1.12 STRUCTURALISM

It is not easy to establish the precise beginnings of the structural revolution, but Leonard Bloomfield is usually called the father of American structuralism and is frequently quoted with respect to the status of meaning in structural linguistics, for this sums up the principal difference between the structuralist and the descriptivist.

The study of language can be conducted . . . only so long as we pay no attention to the meaning of what is spoken. (1933:75)

The problem with meaning (as the structuralist saw it) was that there was no way to get a firm analytical grip on it; meaning was intrinsically unobservable. As was previously mentioned, the structuralist was committed to the study of objective data, so meaning fell outside the scope of his science.

The consequences of the elimination of meaning from the analysis of a language cannot be appreciated until you consider what a structuralist was then required to do. Imagine that someone has given you a hundred hours of tape-recorded Mixabese, perhaps in the region of a million words of connected speech. You have been asked to prepare a grammar of the language. It goes without saying that this is the first time you have ever heard of the language, that you have no fraction of an idea what the tapes might be about, and of course there are no speakers of Mixabese around who might help you with your problem. Nevertheless, the structuralist's carefully worked-out discovery procedures, as spelled out in Harris (1951), for example, would provide you with your approach.

Your hundred hours of tapes represents what was called "primary linguistic data" (PLD). Any analysis had to begin with an amassed corpus of PLD of sufficient length to give statistical significance to the study. For a syntactic study, a million words would be considered quite adequate. The essential characteristic of a corpus was that it be representative of the language as a whole, for the analyst was allowed no information about the language that he could not draw from the corpus itself. Ideally, the structural analyst functioned as an unthinking computer, dependent solely on his data and his programmatic set of procedures. The ensuing analysis was not, therefore, really an anlysis of a language; it was an exhaustive analysis of the corpus. Thus, the degree to which the corpus was *not* representative of the language was exactly matched by the failure of the analysis to describe the language.

From a sufficient corpus of continuous speech, the structuralist could deduce the phonological structure of the language, ultimately producing a phonemic transcription of the entire corpus. This transcription would serve, in turn, as the corpus for a morphological investigation of the language, or the segmentation of the corpus into its morphemes. A morpheme was defined as the smallest meaningful unit of language, or a unit which could be consistently associated with some meaning but which could not be broken down into smaller consistently meaningful units. Some morphemes were meaningful in the ordinary sense of the term, such as *cat*, while others had "syntactic meaning," such as the plural *-s*, which had the meaning "plural." Thus the word *cats* consisted of two morphemes, *cat* and *-s*. The problem of determining the morphemic inventory of a language was a considerable one, but paled into insignificance when compared to the problem of determining the morphology of a language whose meanings were quite unknown. Nevertheless, Harris (1951) tells you how.

Having completed the morphological analysis of the language, the structuralist then proceeded with a syntactic analysis. His corpus, at this point, probably resembled an ordinary printed text, for a good morphological analysis would probably have provided sufficient information to determine where word boundaries and—more important—sentence boundaries lay. The purpose of a syntactic analysis was twofold: (a) to categorize words into a limited set of word classes, and (b) to categorize sentences into a limited set of sentence patterns.

The categorization of words was already partially completed in the course of the morphological analysis, for one aspect of a word class involved the affixes that could be associated with a particular class of words. For example, the words *cat*, *dog*, and *idea* could be assigned to the same class of words by virtue of the morphological criterion, that all could occur with the plural morpheme *-s*. Categorization was completed by an analysis that determined the specific relationships that word classes could have with each other in specific sentence types. The procedure was somewhat complex, however, as all relevant information had to be derived from the corpus.

Step 1 would involve taking a word at random from the corpus along with the sentence in which it occurred, for example, *cat* in *The cat ate a fish*. The word *cat* would be deleted, leaving a Sentence Frame (SF): *The . . . ate a fish*. The word *cat* would then be assigned to a particular word class, say Class I, and at this moment *cat* and only *cat* would be a member of Class I. The SF *The . . . ate a fish* would be simultaneously defined to be a Class I SF, such that any single word found occupying the frame in the position where *cat* was found would be known to be a Class I word also. One can think of dozens, perhaps hundreds of such words immediately. The structuralist, however, was not allowed to "think up" additional membership in the word class; he had to search through his corpus for other instances of the SF and find his Class I words there. In a corpus of a million words there are likely to be upward of 100,000 sentences, and thus a fair chance of finding perhaps three or four additional cases of the SF,

The . . . ate a fish, and within them a few additional Class I words to add to *cat*, let us say *man* and *dog* (the other cases being repeats of *cat*).

Step 2 would involve a dramatic widening of the search. All additional SFs with *cat* would be located, along with all SFs with *dog* and *man*. The analyst would now have a considerable stock of Class I SFs, and by exhaustively culling through his corpus again should proportionally increase his collection of Class I words. The process would be repeated as many times as necessary to exhaust the corpus of Class I words, at which point the investigator would begin anew with his initial Class II word *ate*, and so on until all words in the corpus were accounted for.

Given a million words of text, the entire analysis might not take more than several lifetimes to complete without a computer, and even with a computer the chances are that the time involved would be prohibitively expensive. As a matter of practicality, no structuralist ever did analyze a language with which he was unfamiliar, and it seems fair to suppose that, in fact, he made considerable use of his knowledge of the meanings of his data, and in particular his knowledge of the traditional classifications of the words. Class I (cf. Fries, 1952) is coextensive with nouns, Class II with verbs, Class III with adjectives, and Class IV with adverbs. The substitution of labels came about because the structuralist—Charles C. Fries, in particular—felt that the traditional labels were so contaminated with nonscientific connotation that it was better to scrap them entirely. What, after all, is a "noun"? The traditional definition was that it was a "person, place, or thing"; whatever else might be wrong with this definition, it was totally semantic, a property strictly disallowed by the structuralist. As far as he was concerned, the only allowable definition of a noun—that is, a Class I word—was that it could occur with the plural morpheme on the one hand and that it occurred in Class I Sentence Frames on the other.

Fries' displeasure with the terminology "noun," "verb," and so on, was carried through to its practical application in the English materials with which Fries is associated, the Michigan English Series. If you examine Lesson I of Lado and Fries' *English Sentence Patterns* (1957) as an example, you will find that the grammar of statements with *is* is presented with numbers above the words (Figure 1.4), with a note to the student following:

1	2	3
The lesson	IS	interesting
The lesson	IS	important
The class	IS	important
The student	IS	intelligent

Figure 1.4

NOTE: LESSON, CLASS, STUDENT, etc., are Class 1 words. IS is a Class 2 word. INTERESTING, IMPORTANT, INTELLIGENT, etc., are Class 3 words.

The learner had no access to the terms "noun," "verb," or "adjective" at all. It is my understanding that even the teachers at Michigan corrected the terminology to the traditional terms. When *English Sentence Patterns* was replaced in 1971 by *English Sentence Structure* (by Robert Krohn), the use of the traditional terminology in the grammatical presentations was one of the most evident changes.

Having fully classified the words of the corpus, the sentences were then classified into types according to the sequences of word classes they contained. Thus, for example, Sentence Pattern I might be

Group A–Class I–Class II–Group A–Class I

as exemplified by the sentences, *The cat ate a fish, My uncle married a teenager*, and *A horse is a mammal*. It was assumed that with a sufficiently large corpus, all of the major sentence patterns would be elicited. It was taken for granted that no corpus could ever totally exhaust the language of sentence patterns absolutely, just as it was assumed that no corpus could ever account for the total vocabulary of a language. Absolute description, however, was never the purpose of the structuralist; he knew his limits.

Since mere sequences are not especially informative of the internal structural relationships of sentences, a form of analysis was developed for dealing with sentences of known meaning: "immediate constituent analysis" (ICA). ICA was intended to provide a means for establishing the internal mechanics of sentences and is, in effect, the structural equivalent to the traditionalist's parsing: the IC diagram is to the structuralist as the Reed-Kellogg diagram was to the traditionalist.

IC diagrams are reasonably easy to construct. The shortest sentence type (in the statement class) consists of two words, such as *Fish swim, Mary cried*, etc. The ICA process consists of making successive cuts in a sentence until all the words of that sentence are separated from each other. In a sentence like *Fish swim*, the process entails one cut only (Figure 1.5). In so far as the sentence represents the shortest, and therefore, perhaps, the most basic sentence type in English, the IC cut (called the "A" cut in the IC diagram in Figure 1.5) is attributed some significance: it should be found in all sentences. In fact, we may recognize the old familiar subject/predicate division in cut "A," which will always be the first cut in a sentence.

Three-word sentences come in several types, one of which is represented by *Cats eat mice*. Cut "A" will divide *cats* from *eat mice*, leaving *eat* and *mice* to be divided by cut "B" (Figure 1.6). While cut "A" might be necessary to all

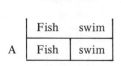

	Fish	swim
A	Fish	swim

Figure 1.5

	Cats	eat	mice
A	Cats	eat	mice
B	Cats	eat	mice

Figure 1.6

statements, cut "B" would not, and would not be found, for example, in *Cats are queer* (Figure 1.7). Articles and auxiliary verbs may be added (Figure 1.8). Note that cut "H" involved two cuts simultaneously, both between the article and the noun it governs.

Modifiers may be accounted for, as in Figure 1.9, which would be more conventionally represented as in Figure 1.10. The IC diagram is most familiar, however—at least to many contemporary school children—in the form of the boxed diagram shown in Figure 1.11.

	Cats	are	queer
A	Cats	are	queer
C	Cats	are	queer

Figure 1.7

	The	cat	has	eaten	the	mouse
A	The	cat	has	eaten	the	mouse
B	The	cat	has	eaten	the	mouse
G	The	cat	has	eaten	the	mouse
H	The	cat	has	eaten	the	mouse

Figure 1.8

	The	cat	in	the	garden	has	eaten	the	little	mouse
A	The	cat	in	the	garden	has	eaten	the	little	mouse
B	The	cat	in	the	garden	has	eaten	the	little	mouse
D	The	cat	in	the	garden	has	eaten	the	little	mouse
E	The	cat	in	the	garden	has	eaten	the	little	mouse
F	The	cat	in	the	garden	has	eaten	the	little	mouse
G	The	cat	in	the	garden	has	eaten	the	little	mouse
H	The	cat	in	the	garden	has	eaten	the	little	mouse

Figure 1.9

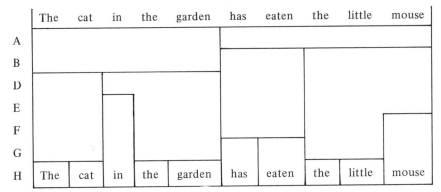

Figure 1.10

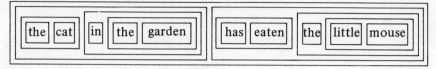

Figure 1.11

Exercise 1.12

Draw boxed diagrams of the following sentences. You may wish to consult Francis (1958, chap. 6) as you do these sentences.
1. Mary saw a piano in her teacher's house.
2. The child was miserable.
3. The boy whom you saw is named Charlie.
4. A dog ran under the fence.

1.13 THE STRUCTURALIST AND THE AUDIO- LINGUAL METHOD

The "audio-lingual" (henceforth AL) method of language teaching became the dominant method of language instruction in the United States during the 1950s and probably continues to occupy a dominant position today, although in somewhat modified form. While details of the AL method go back to the middle ages (at least), its resurgence and formalization was almost entirely due to the structural linguist.

The AL method embodies a number of structuralist principles, the most general of which is reflected in the method's name: language is primarily speech, with writing a secondary system of speech representation. Thus hearing (audio-) and speaking (lingual) are the main linguistic skills to be learned in a language class, reading and writing to come later. This ordering of language skills was a cardinal principle of the applied structuralist, and proved to be one of the earliest points of conflict between language teaching theoreticians of the structural and transformational camps.[4]

Just as the structuralist began his analysis of a language with a complete phonological analysis, so did he feel that the language learner should begin by mastering the target sound system. In its purest form, the AL method required phonological drills *ad nauseam* until such time as the learners demonstrated an adequate mastery of target pronunciation. Only then might the teacher move on to grammar.

The form of the most common phonological drill, the "minimal pair drill," came straight from the structuralist's desk. One of the most powerful analytic

[4] Lado, for example, did not give way on the ordering of skills until quite recently (1972).

tools in the structuralist's armory was the "minimal pair." The phoneme was the basic organizational unit of sound, but was nevertheless abstract, representing a class of allophones. Since it was abstract, there was no way to hear it directly, and an indirect tool was required with which phonemes could be identified. This was the minimal pair. Very loosely stated, a minimal pair consists of two words whose pronunciation is almost the same, in fact differing in only one respect. As long as the two words are different in meaning, the difference in pronunciation is evidence of a phonemic difference. Thus we know that aspirated and unaspirated p's are not phonemically different in English, for there is no minimal pair for them (they are phonemically different in Danish, however). The minimal pair *sip, ship,* on the other hand, suggests a phonemic difference between the sounds "s" and "sh" (which are not phonemically different in Japanese). Minimal pair drills consisted of little more than having learners pronounce minimal pairs. Certain national groups would be diagnosed as having a certain phonemic problem, thus requiring more minimal pair drills with those particular phonemes. The Spanish-speaking peoples, for instance, would be advised to have a heavy dose of "s," "sh" drills, "sh," "ch" drills, "ee," "i" drills, etc., while the Japanese would be given extra doses of "lip," "rip"; "play," "pray"; "lewd," "rude," and so on.

Exercise 1.13

Which of the following are minimal pairs, and what phonemic differences do they support?

1. coughed, soft
2. cows, cause
3. muse, muss
4. mew, moo
5. liver, diver
6. lag, lamb
7. mother, mutter
8. cot, caught
9. maid, made
10. brought, broth

Once the learner had adequate control of target pronunciation, he was introduced to "pattern" drills. The term "pattern" and the concept it represented was purely structural in origin. Within any one pattern drill, the sequence of word classes is held invariant, while the words themselves might change freely.

In addition to establishing the contents of an AL textbook, the structuralist also established the way in which this text should be used, that is, the behavior on the part of the teacher.

From the beginning, the structuralist tied his theory of language to the then-current behavioral theory of learning. Bloomfield discussed the phenomenon of first language learning in terms of a straightforward stimulus-response model (1933:23ff). In essence, the stimulus-response (S → R) model begins with the basic assumption that language is a complex set of mechanical, ingrained habits, and that language learning consists of the establishment of these habits. In general, the structuralist saw the learning of language as being little different from learning how to drive, which involves the voluntary, conscious practice of integrating the hand, foot, and eye until it is no longer voluntary or conscious—that is, until it has become a habit. Just as it was necessary to practice driving to reach this state, it was necessary to practice language. Since grammar consisted of sentence patterns, one had to practice the patterns until their use became automatic. The type of repetitive practice required to achieve this automaticity was supplied by the pattern drill.

To understand fully the import of this assumption, one must realize that, in theory, the establishment of sentence pattern habits was quite divorced from any consideration of meaning. For instance, there would have been no theoretical argument against the use of nonsense words in a substitution drill (nor, of course, any arguments in their favor, either). Just as learners were not encouraged to ask about the meanings of words used in pronunciation drills (and nonsense words might easily creep into those), learners would not be encouraged to ask about the meanings of the sentences they were practicing. Certainly, there was no felt need to provide any sort of context for a sentence in a pattern drill. After all, the learner was engaged in incising upon his mind a pattern, and whether or not he understood the meanings of individual sentences in the drill, he had the same access to the pattern. In behavioral theory, at least, if you are trying to instill a Class 1–Class 2–Class 1 habit, you get as much out of *The wugs wimbled the worrats* as you do from *The students read the books.* However, it is not likely that many practicing teachers *did* discourage considerations of meaning in their classrooms. Probably not too many really understood the full import of the mechanistic theory underlying the structure of the drills, anyway.

A secondary aspect of the behavioral model was that "bad" habits had to be avoided. If a student made a mistake, it had to be instantly corrected, for a mistake constituted practice of an undesirable habit.

A full statement and defense of the AL method can be found in Wilga Rivers' *The Psychologist and the Language Teacher* (1964).

1.14 THE TRANSFORMATIONALIST AND THE AL METHOD

In addition to rejecting structural linguistic theory (we will return to this in the next section), the TG theorist also embraced cognitive psychology rather than behavioral psychology, thus rejecting the structuralist's assumptions about language learning as well. Oddly enough, however, this does not mean that the TG theorist rejected the utility of the AL texts or the effectiveness of the AL method. There is a great deal of understandable confusion that results from separating the method from the theory that created the method—part of the confusion resulting from the belief that the structuralist did invent the AL method (as was said previously, he didn't invent the method; audio-lingualism, as a method, has a long history). The contribution of the structuralist was to attribute theoretical validity to the method, and at the same time to specify the particular form of the texts used and the behavior of the teacher. In a sense, the structuralist specified a particular bit of an older and broader tradition, saying that this bit had theoretical validity. Most teachers, however, probably out of a compound of instinct and ignorance of structuralism, taught in the broader tradition rather than the closely restricted theoretical one. There are actually two AL methods: the classroom teacher's version and the structuralist's version. The former has always had a fair degree of empirical success attributed to it, which has usually been taken as evidence of the empirical success of the latter. In reality, the structuralist's version has probably never received anything like a widespread test at all.

It may even be claimed that the success of the AL method has nothing to do with structural and behavioral theorizing at all, but has been, rather, successful to the degree that the classroom version has differed from the theoretical one. A TG theorist would claim, in fact, that the success of the AL method is due to the fact that it is reasonably consonant with cognitive assumptions about rule internalization. The presentation of large numbers of grammatical sentences with similar deep structures may promote learning of the type that cognitivists claim to be necessary in language acquisition. Thus there is nothing inconsistent with the fact that Krohn's *English Sentence Structure* (1971) contains drills that are virtually identical with the Lado/Fries drills. Where Lado and Fries assumed that drills led to the formation of habits, Krohn assumed that they led to rule internalization.

1.15 TRANSFORMATIONAL-GENERATIVISTS[5]

Back in 1957, Noam Chomsky inaugurated the "transformational revolution" with the publication of *Syntactic Structures*.[6] By 1965, when his *Aspects of the Theory of Syntax* appeared, TG theory was ascendant, with only a few major structuralists holding out.

In principle, the TG theorist rejects the structuralist's purely empirical approach to language. This has two aspects: the rejection of description as the general purpose of linguistic practice, and the rejection of "primary linguistic

---

[5] The newcomer to the field may be somewhat justifiably confused by the numerous terms that describe the modern linguist: transformationalist, generativist, and transformational-generativist (TG). The terms are not quite all the same, for reasons quite beyond the scope of this text, although they are often used almost interchangeably.

[6] It is my understanding that this small tome was rejected by a number of publishers before Mouton took it on.

data" (cf. p. 11) as the necessary starting point. Thus the structuralist's carefully worked-out segmentation and categorization procedures were dismissed as unnecessary to linguistic pursuits.

The TG grammarian instead concerned himself with the proposition that grammar entails a psychological reality on the part of the speaker/hearer, and that it was his job to work out the details of that reality. He did not concern himself with what *had* been said, as did the structuralist, but with what *could* be said, and why.

1.16 INTUITIONS

One of the most interesting aspects of the mentalistic orientation of the TG theorist is his use of speaker intuitions as his data. His argument takes the following form:

1. Language is rule-governed behavior; that is, speech is not "free," but is controlled by mental rules of grammar.
2. The speaker knows these rules, but knows them only unconsciously; the rules are part of his unconscious mind, so he has no *direct* access to them.
3. An individual has *indirect* access to his unconscious knowledge; a speaker has *intuitive* access to the rules of his language.
4. There being no other form of access to the unconscious mind, intuitions about language are the only available information concerning the mental processes of language.

The term "intuition" itself tends to lead one to notions of "female intuition," on the one hand, and clairvoyance on the other, which is unfortunate, for this is not at all what the TG linguist means when he talks about an intuition. An intuition is best seen as a bit of information that springs from the unconscious rather than the conscious mind. It has, therefore, a peculiarly indefensible property: you cannot say just why you know or believe that the information is true. There are several sorts of linguistic intuitions that we may discuss: intuitions of grammatical categorization, of grammaticality, of semantic well-formedness, and so on. For example, the TG theorist claims that any speaker can identify the part-of-speech of a word like *cat* (so long as he knows the term "noun" for use in such an exercise). They claim, furthermore, that a speaker will not work out this categorization inductively, but will categorize the word immediately from the unconscious knowledge that *cat* is a noun. Again, the linguist claims that any speaker can respond to the type of question: "Is such-and-such a sentence grammatical?", and that his response is based on the unconscious knowledge that he has of his grammar. In other words, if the rules of your grammar specifically permit you to form a certain sentence, then you would always recognize that sentence to be grammatical, and vice versa. It has always been recognized that there are dialectal differences in grammar as well as pronunciation, so that it is expected that there will be some sentences that will be accepted as grammatical by some speakers of English but not others. One such may be *Not many people don't like John*. What is interesting is the frequent mutual inability of disagreeing speakers to believe that the other seriously means what he says. On more than one occasion I have heard arguments whose substance ran: "How can you say that that sentence is grammatical?" "Because it *is*!" "But it *isn't*!" Intuitions have sometimes been accurately described as "gut-level reactions"; one property of such reactions is that they are generally nonintellectual and therefore nonarguable.

The TG linguist uses intuitions to test his hypotheses about language. First he invents (hypothesizes) a rule; then he creates sentences that obey the rule and others that break the rule. He tests all of the sentences on speakers (sometimes only himself, regrettably), and if their judgments accord with the grammaticality values predicted by the hypothesis, he feels that the hypothesis is supported.

The linguist is hardly embarrassed by this reliance on such insubstantial stuff. Chomsky, in fact, implies that this is what linguistics should be all about. Concerning an ideal generative grammar, he says, "such a grammar could probably be called an explanatory model, a theory of the linguistic intuition of the native speaker" (1962:533). He goes on to defend the position:

> There is a certain irreducible vagueness in describing a formalized grammar as a theory of the linguistic intuition of the native speaker. It is sometimes claimed that operational, i.e., objective tests for degree of grammaticalness and the like can guarantee both objectivity and significance for the theory of grammar, but this is a misconception. If an operational test for grammaticality were devised, we would have to test it by determining how well it accords with the linguistic intuition of native speakers. In exactly the same way, we judge the adequacy of a proposed theory of English structure (an English grammar). . . . Optimally, we would like to have both, and we would like to have them converge, but they must, for significance, converge on the linguistic intuition of native speakers (1962:533).

It is the unabashed dependence on (not to mention active purpose to account for) intuitions that, perhaps more than anything else, causes the structuralist to climb the walls in an agony of moral outrage.

Exercise 1.16

What part of speech is the word *cat*? How would a traditionalist, a structuralist, and a TG grammarian answer, and how would they justify their answers?

1.2   Language Is Innate, Universal, Abstract, and Creative

There are four claims that the TG grammarian makes about language: it is innate, universal, abstract, and creative.

1.21 LANGUAGE IS INNATE

The TG grammarian maintains that language is innate in humans. There may be a certain amount of confusion encountered when considering this claim, some of which stems from differences among TG linguists in the meanings they place on it in the first place.

At the very least, all TG grammarians seem to agree on one aspect: the capacity for language is innate in *Homo sapiens* and is a part of his genetic heritage. This is understood to be different from merely being born with the physical capacity (that is, with the appropriate vocal organs); what you are born with is a mental predisposition to language.

This does not mean that a child has a predisposition toward any particular language. All human babies may be said to have the same predisposition, and if one baby eventually learns Chinese and another French, it is because their linguistic environments are Chinese and French, respectively.

A fractionally more ambitious notion of the innateness of language is that of an innate language "faculty," in which it is claimed that this proclivity to language is not part of a general mental capacity to process perceptual data, but instead has its own specific mental niche where language data is processed and rules formed. The notion of a "language acquisition device," or LAD, would conform to the idea of an innate language faculty.

Then, in varying detail, there is the rationalist's more extreme position, that certain general aspects of language itself are innate.[1] Chomsky is probably the most important linguist of this pursuasion, and argues, for example, that certain basic linguistic concepts like "noun" and "verb" are themselves innate—that part of the processing system involves use of these preexisting categories rather than their evolution.

In the course of this text, the middle position—that of an innate faculty of language—will be adopted.

In general, the LAD is conceived of as being a set of rules for the induction and processing of environmental human language data. The LAD responds to this data by inducing language rules, a grammar, which the child then uses in turn to produce *his* acts of speech. In general, the LAD is sufficiently efficient that the child will induce approximately correct rules (that is, approximately the same as those possessed by the people in the environment). In so doing, the child "learns" his language, and in turn becomes part of the environment for the next generation of children. The LAD is such that it would be impossible for the normal child to induce Chinese rules from French data. If the environment offers two sets of data—say both French and Chinese—the child cannot be expected to recognize this. However, his LAD will almost infallibly distinguish between the two intermixed sets of data, either rejecting one or providing rules for both, in which case the child grows up bilingual.

One consequence of the innateness hypothesis may have more than passing interest for the science fiction buff. It is assumed that LAD is species-specific. A human child can learn any human language, but his LAD will not tolerate any other data. If we accept that, for instance, porpoises have a real language (that is, can genuinely converse with each other on an intellectual, rather than an instinctive basis), then we should also have to accept that porpoises have a porpoise LAD. However, many TG grammarians would assert that the structure of the porpoise LAD is genetically different from that of the human LAD, with the result that each one's LAD would be incapable of inducing the rules of the other's language. In other words, interspecies communication is impossible. As yet, there is no evidence that any two species do intercommunicate, and the hypothesis stands.

The entire innateness hypothesis is in contrast to the structuralist's notions of how language is learned. He was attuned to the behaviorist's idea that learning is best described through a stimulus-response paradigm, that is, that specific utterances were learned as responses to particular stimuli/situations. Instead of having genetic equipment that "caused" humans to learn language, as it were, the structuralist claimed that the human organism was simply complex enough to organize complicated responses to complicated stimuli.

---

[1] There is evidence accumulating that suggests that certain aspects of language patterning are, in fact, innate (cf. Eimas, 1971).

1.22 LANGUAGE IS UNIVERSAL

Because of the innate nature of the human language capacity, and the LAD in particular, the TG grammarian makes a second general claim about language: it is universal. This claim goes far beyond the trivially true observation that all humans (normal ones, anyway) speak language—although in fact this can certainly be attributed to the universal LAD. The claim is much stronger: that the forms of all grammars are, at bottom, identical. The rules of Chinese, the rules of French, and the rules of English all have a hidden, underlying sameness. All languages, after all, take form in the human mind as a result of the workings of the LAD. Since the LAD is identical in all humans, surely the form of the languages that issue from it will reflect this identity. Well, surely perhaps. There is no evidence that can be brought forth to support the contention unambiguously, and there are no necessarily evil consequences to the theorist should the claim prove to be false.

The claim is quite antithetical, however, to the structural assumption that different languages should be treated as if they were completely and absolutely different. Nevertheless, even structuralists talked about linguistic universals, although, as it turns out, their notion of universals is quite different from the TG notion.

In Greenberg's *Universals of Language* we find the admonition, "we do not want to invent language universals, but to discover them" (1963:1), which immediately gives us the needed clue that the structuralist's search for universals involved discovery procedures. Hockett (1963) further spelled out a set of ten governing propositions, three of which are worthy of comment.

1. The assertion of a language universal must be founded on extrapolation as well as on empirical evidence (1963:2).

In other words, if the weight of the empirical evidence clearly establishes a pattern, then one may generalize the pattern without further empirical evidence. If a feature is found in 100 languages without exception, there is a good chance that it will probably be found in the next hundred as well. This proposition is significant because it implies that the search for universals is basically tied to statistical analysis.

2. The distinction between the universal and the merely widespread is not necessarily relevant (1963:3).

In other words, a "universal" need not be universal to be meaningful. A feature present in merely a large number of the analyzed languages may be of substantive interest.

3. The problem of language universals is not independent of our choice of assumptions and methodology in analyzing single languages (1963:6).

In other words, the procedures for finding universals is essentially the same as the procedures for analyzing languages.

Thus the search for universals was conducted independently of meaning and was based on primary linguistic data. The universals they found were principally statistical ones. For example, Greenberg's first universal is:

Universal 1. In declarative sentences with nominal subject and object, the dominant order is almost always one in which the subject precedes the object (1963:61).

The discovery of a universal was not quite an end in itself, but the structuralist was prevented from speculating on the significance of such observations by his view of science. Universals had some application to making sense of certain problems of language classification, but otherwise there did not seem much that you could do with them. The TG grammarian, on the other hand, regarded universals as potential evidence as to the structure of the LAD and the language faculty. If, for example, Greenberg's Universal 1 were taken as a genuine universal, the next step would be to worry over the question "Why?", to see if the fact could throw any light onto the relationship between human mind and human language.

1.23 LANGUAGE IS ABSTRACT

Almost all linguists—traditionalists, structuralists, and TG theorists alike—agree that the relationship between form and meaning (words and their referents, etc.) is abstract, on the grounds that, in most cases, the relationship is highly arbitrary. However, this is not what the TG grammarian is talking about when he says that language is abstract. His point is that language is in the mind, and the mind deals with abstractions. Put another way, the moment I write down a sentence on this page, it assumes a physical reality. At this point, the sentence is not abstract in the least. However, as I sit here formulating my next sentence, that sentence is real only within the confines of my mind, and we say that it has abstract reality. There are, moreover, levels of abstractness involved. The TG grammarian thinks of the process of producing a physically real sentence as starting with extremely abstract concepts, gradually working up through less and less abstract concepts and organization, until finally it emerges in all its finery. The TG grammarian conceives his purpose in charting the course of these successive abstractions, so as to get to the deepest and most abstract formulations of language-in-the-mind. One of his greatest problems is that he is forced to use formal, concrete notation to represent things that are quite unconcrete. For example, to represent the abstraction that underlies the word "cat," he uses the notation *cat,* adding the caution that *cat* has neither pronunciation nor spelling in its abstract form. This is sometimes confusing, and we will return to the point toward the end of the chapter, as it concerns sentences as well.

1.24 LANGUAGE IS CREATIVE

The fourth general characteristic of language claimed by the TG theorist is that it is creative. In the 1950s, the Italian neolinguists took violent issue with the structuralists on the same ground, but they meant "creative" in its artistic sense, while the TG grammarian is referring to the nonlimitedness of language. There are a number of ways in which we can explore this sense of the creativity of English. There are an infinite number of sentences which can be called English sentences, and the proof of this is trivial. As long as *I have forty-seven billion and ninety-six dogs.* is a sentence of English, it is child's play to demonstrate that there is potentially an infinite number of such sentences. What is much more important, however, is that our creativity is individual, in that any one of us can produce and/or understand completely novel utterances. (This is not, mind you, a claim that you can understand *any* novel sentence, and I would be willing to bet that at least half of you do not understand the sentence, *Eggs contain lipid.*). These novel utterances may have quite commonplace words in novel juxtapositions. To my mind, creativity is best understood in realizing that people can understand, and perhaps appreciate, jokes like:

What's purple and buzzes?
An electric grape.

The TG grammarian sees creativity in English syntax as well, in the unlimitedness of structures that you can produce and understand. There is, however, a finite number—and a surprisingly small number, for that matter—of syntactic rules with which these structures can be generated. The way that you can get from this small set of rules to the infinitely large set of structures is through the existence and use of recursive rules.

A recursive function is one that manages to build into itself a cyclic step that goes on and on without end. A common-garden example of recursivity is the old Morton Salt shaker, which had a picture of a girl holding a Morton Salt shaker, which showed a picture of a girl holding a Morton Salt shaker, . . . , etc. Another example is the story that begins, "It was a dark and stormy night, and three men were sitting around a fire. One of them said, "Let's have a story!" So another began: "It was a dark and stormy night. . . . " These are examples of recursive systems in which the recurring elements are unchanging. There is little difference to the system if certain changes are built in. For example, if the Morton Salt shaker showed first a girl, then a monkey, then an Indian, etc., holding the Morton Salt shaker, no violence would have been done to the recursivity of the system, and we would get a little closer to the kind of recursivity that is found in language. A popular example of recursivity in English structure is the poem, "This is the maid that milked the cow that tossed the dog that chased the cat that killed the rat that ate the malt that lay in the house that Jack built." Recursivity in German is illustrated by the joke (popular among graduate students preparing for a reading examination) about the German professor who wrote a twenty-volume masterpiece with all the verbs in the last volume.

1.3   Patterns and Rules

As far as the structuralist was concerned, the substance of syntactic structure was patterning. The patterns of English ranged from the very simple +verb+ (*Go!*) to the more complex +article-adjective-noun-auxiliary-verb-preposition-article-noun+ (*The red book may be on the table*) and far beyond. Given a fairly large corpus, the structuralist felt that he could isolate all of the important patterns and probably most of the less important ones as well. The emphasis on patterns shows up explicitly in the Lado/Fries text, in which each lesson introduces a new pattern, contrasting it to an old one with which it shares numerous characteristics but differs in some essential detail. For example, Lesson XIII begins:

Observe PLANS TO, HAS TO, LEARNING TO, etc.

Previous Pattern (Lesson XI):

He doesn't	study every day,	but he	should.

New Pattern:

STATEMENTS

He didn't	go	but he	PLANS TO
He doesn't	want to go	but he	HAS TO
He can't	speak English	but he's	LEARNING TO
	(etc.)		

In rejecting the assumption that there is fun or profit in discussing English in terms of patterns of this sort, the TG grammarian rediscovered the "rule." Heretofore, English rules had been considered the province of the prescriptivist. The following list, abridged from Feinstein (1960), is both typical of the kinds of rules that prescriptivists provided as well as the somewhat cavalier attitude that we have toward them today.

27

A LIST OF GOOD GRAMMAR RULES

(Memorize quick, like a good writer should)

1. Don't use no double negatives.
2. Make each pronoun agree with their antecedent.
3. Join clauses good, like a conjunction should.
4. About them sentence fragments.
5. When dangling, watch your participles.
6. Verbs has to agree with their subjects.
7. Just between you and I, case is important too.
8. Don't write run-on sentences they are hard to read.
9. Don't use commas, that aren't necessary.
10. Try to not ever split infinitives.
11. Its important to use apostrophe's correctly.
12. Proofread your writing to see if any words out.
13. Correct spelling is esential.

One could add to this list indefinitely. Funny or not, all of the above rules have a certain validity. None of us have trouble in perceiving that each sentence is ungrammatical, and ungrammatical in the specific way that it is intended to be. And yet, we also know that the rules are inadequate to describe or explain English. First of all, all of the rules are oriented toward the avoidance of mistakes, rather than the production of good sentences. Second, many of the rules are not always correct as given. Consider the first. We know that multiple negatives occur quite regularly in "substandard" English, so that the rule does not apply to English-as-a-whole, but to some concept of "desirable" English. Then too, even in "good" English there may be circumstances where multiple negation is permitted, as in our earlier example (p. 21), *Not many people don't like John.*

To the TG grammarian, in any case, the notion of "rule" has nothing to do with prescriptive rules. To the transformationalist, a rule is, in essence, a chunk of knowledge that a person has, deep down inside, about his language. In order to understand better what he means by "rule," however, we have to understand his model of language in general.

1.4   The TG Model
of Language

You may have previously heard the terms "competence" and "performance" bandied about; these terms and the concepts they represent lie at the heart of the generative model of language. It seems, however, that no two linguists have precisely the same understanding of the difference between competence and performance, and the discussion below will differ in varying amounts from accounts given by other linguists. Some linguists have suggested that the problem with the distinction lies in the label "competence," and to a certain extent I tend to agree. It does not mean what people think it ought to mean, as you will see. All linguists, at any rate, agree that competence is part of performance, that performance wholly includes competence. We will start with the larger concept.

1.41 PERFORMANCE

The real act of saying (or writing) something is an act of performance. Virtually everything that is involved in such an act must be accounted for in a full theory or model of performance.

Among the most obvious aspects of linguistic acts are the motor properties: the movements and shapes of the vocal tract.[1] However, motor control and motor properties are not usually considered part of performance, for movements of the lips, etc., are not considered "mental." Motor properties are, however, conceived of as being "driven" by complex coded signals from the brain, and it is what goes into the coding of these signals that belongs in a theory of

---

[1] And, by analogy, the movements of the fingers in writing; for the rest of this text we shall not consider writing further.

performance. There are a number of personal factors that presumably influence the coding of signals—beliefs, memory limitations, mood, etc.—but we know very little about how these things affect speech acts and assume that their influence is unpredictable and transitory.

There are, on the other hand, at least four major factors that probably do play important roles in the formation of performance: intentions, presuppositions, knowledge of grammar (competence), and knowledge of grammar use (heuristics).

Intentions are—perhaps—coextensive with thought. By and large, we do not speak without intending to communicate something or other, and it seems plausible to assume that one's intentions provide the motivation for speech. Intentions may be hidden—we say things that we "didn't intend to"—or they may not; but in the course of speech we are probably not particularly conscious of what we are about to say, although at the same time we are seldom surprised by what we have just said. Sometimes we stop to think things out, and carefully "choose our words," but more frequently it seems that the intention hardly precedes the performance. Our intentions presumably lead us to say things one way rather than another. If we intend to withhold certain bits of information, our language provides means for doing so, and we may say *The cookies all got eaten, Mommy,* rather than *I ate all the cookies, Mommy.* In general, however, linguists have not yet gotten around to a theory of intentions, or a theory of their relationship to performance.

Presuppositions, on the other hand, are much discussed in recent linguistic literature. Presuppositions are assumptions on the part of the speaker concerning the truth or value of certain aspects of the content of his speech. For example, *John got blamed for doing that* involves the presupposition that "doing that" was somehow bad, whereas *John got praised for doing that* involves the opposite presupposition. Now there is nothing about the words *doing that* which makes goodness or badness self-evident, so such presuppositions must come from within the speaker (Fillmore, 1969). In discussing the use of *some* and *any,* Robin Lakoff (1969) makes the point that presuppositions of value are involved.

1 a. If you eat some more bread, I'll give you a penny.
   b. If you eat any more bread, I'll give you a spanking.

   c. If you eat some more bread, I'll give you a spanking.
   d. If you eat any more bread, I'll give you a penny.

Lakoff claims that sentences 1a and 1b appear to be more natural than 1c and 1d, because *some* seems to be associated with presuppositions of the desirability of eating more bread, while *any* is the opposite. Thus *some* should go with the promise of reward (presupposing that a penny is a reward), and *any* with the threat of punishment. Sentence 1c, of course, would be perfectly normal for a sadist speaking to a masochist, in which case a spanking would be a reward, and *some* therefore appropriate. The theory of presuppositions, for all the attention it has received, is still in an exceptionally rudimentary state.

Knowledge of grammar, or **competence**, is the unconscious but encyclopedic grasp that the speaker has of the rules underlying his language. Linguists attempt to specify this knowledge by making hypotheses about these rules, under the assumption that "knowledge" of the rules of language means "possession" of the rules. Thus, if you have a rule, you must know it, and vice versa. All such knowledge is, as has been said before, quite unconscious; your only access to this knowledge is through your intuitions.

These rules, however, don't *do* anything; they are static, simply existing for you to use. An analogy may help you to understand this point: a dictionary embodies a great deal of knowledge about words—their spelling, pronunciation, history, use, etc.—but a dictionary itself does not spell, pronounce, or use the words it contains; you do that. The dictionary is a static repository of knowledge that is available for you to use. Your competence, similarly, is a repository of language rules that is available for you to use.

If you don't know how to use a dictionary, however, you cannot use it. Many of you probably do not know how to use a Chinese-character dictionary, for example, rendering the knowledge it contains largely inaccessible to you. *Knowledge of grammar use*, or **heuristics**, is what makes it possible for you to use your competence. This sort of knowledge involves rules, too, but of a dynamic nature. These rules will relate your intentions and presuppositions to the forms that are available for their expression in your competence.

A model of performance might look something like Figure 1.12.

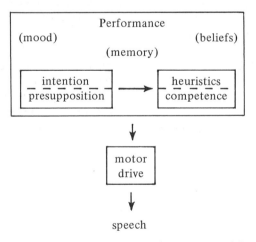

Figure 1.12   A possible performance model.

1.42 COMPETENCE

What the TG grammarian is mostly interested in is the competence compartment, and he defines competence to be the proper domain of a linguist's interests (everything else being someone else's interests).[2] Theories and models of competence abound, although all share the central characteristics outlined above, that competence is unconscious and encyclopedic, and that it consists of rules. Most models also agree that competence itself consists of three subsidiary domains: semantics, syntax, and phonology.

The Chomskyan model (Figure 1.13) assumes that syntax is central to competence, and that semantics and phonology are subsidiary systems that "interpret" the output of the syntactic component. ("Interpretation" is here a rather complex notion; very roughly, the semantic and phonological components determine the appropriate semantic and phonological representations of the "sentence" that the syntactic component generates.)

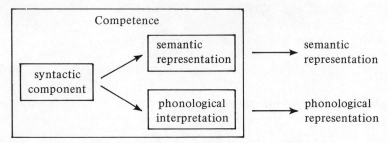

Figure 1.13 Model of Chomskyan competence.

Because he claims that the Chomsky model does not really explain how people get from idea to speech (or vice versa), Steinberg (1970) offers a variant of the competence model in which syntax is not central, but in which all three components operate equally and simultaneously to intercede between idea and speech (Figure 1.14). There are still other models of competence, in which the internal components are rearranged, but perhaps Chomsky is right when he claims that all models are just "notational variants" of his theory. In this spirit, we will follow Chomsky's lead in calling his theory the **Standard Theory**. In any case, we are here interested only in the syntactic component.

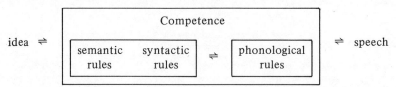

Figure 1.14 Model of Steinbergian competence.

As might be expected, there are a number of variations in the ways in which the syntactic component may be modeled. We will discuss here only Chomsky's "standard" model of the syntactic component (Figure 1.15).

---

[2] This assertion is hotly disputed by the more recent generation of "generative semanticists," who say that the position is needlessly restricted.

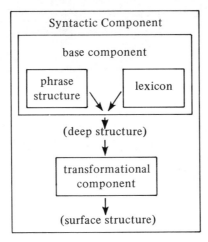

Figure 1.15   Standard Model of syntax.

As can be seen, the syntactic component consists of a **Base** component and a **Transformational** component. The Base component consists in turn of a **Phrase Structure** component and a **Lexicon**. The Phrase Structure component and the Transformational component both consist of rules, and it is the nature of these rules that will occupy us in the succeeding chapters.

As is implicit in the model, the base component produces things called "deep structures," which feed into the transformational component, which produces other things called "surface structures." In order to understand the distinction between deep and surface structure, it is necessary first to understand one of the primary justifying features of the transformational approach to language: its explanation of paraphrase and ambiguity in language.

1.5 Paraphrase and Ambiguity

Paraphrase and ambiguity are essential, twin concepts that lead to the conclusion that there are two real levels of structural description—deep structure and surface structure.

Let us take it for granted that the principal purpose of obtaining descriptions of sentences is to explain what they mean, that is, that linguistic descriptions account for the relationship between sentences and sentence meanings. What can one infer from the fact that a sentence has one description? If this description is supposed to account for both the form and the meaning of the sentence, as indicated in Figure 1.16, then one must conclude that each sentence has one meaning and each meaning has one sentence. But it doesn't work out this way, at least not according to the TG theorist.

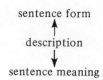

Figure 1.16

Some sentences may be paraphrases of other sentences—that is, more than one sentence may exist for one meaning; some sentences may be ambiguous—that is, more than one meaning may exist for one sentence. In other words, the linguist must account for both situations (Figure 1.17). Since a single description can account for only a single sentence-to-meaning relationship, it will require more than one description to account for cases of paraphrase or ambiguity. The TG grammarian posits the two levels of description, deep and surface structure, to do just that.

PARAPHRASE   AMBIGUITY

Figure 1.17

Deep structures are defined to represent individual meanings. In other words, every different sentence meaning can be represented by a different deep structure, on a one-to-one basis.

Surface structures are defined to represent individual sentence forms, again on a one-to-one basis. Every formally different sentence has its own unique surface structure.

Thus meaning is uniquely represented by deep structure, and sentence forms are uniquely represented by surface structure (Figure 1.18).

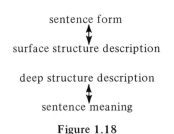

Figure 1.18

Paraphrase, then, is a case where several surface structure descriptions relate to one deep structure, and ambiguity is an instance of one surface structure relating to several deep structures. The transformational component consists of rules that relate the two levels of description.

1.51 PARAPHRASE

Within the context of TG theory, however, the notion of paraphrase is somewhat technical and not as broad a concept as it is in ordinary English. Paraphrases must certainly mean the same thing, but they must also involve the same content words[1] or principal lexical items. Thus, for example, consider

John bought the book from Mary.
Mary sold the book to John.

While they may mean the same thing, they cannot be considered grammatical paraphrases within the context of TG theory, because different content words

[1] That is, nouns, verbs, adjectives, and adverbs.

are involved—*buy* and *sell*. Beyond that, the problems of asserting a paraphrase relationship are peculiarly difficult. The four sentences below illustrate the difficulty.

1 a. John gave the apple to Mary.
   b. John gave Mary the apple.
   c. Mary was given the apple by John.
   d. It was Mary who was given the apple by John.

While many TG grammarians would assert that all four are paraphrases, deriving from a single deep structure, others would claim that while 1a and 1b are paraphrases on the one hand, and 1c and 1d are paraphrases on the other, 1a and 1b are not paraphrases of 1c and 1d; thus, two deep structures would be involved. Finally, numerous linguists would claim that three deep structures are evidenced, for only 1a and 1b are paraphrases. Each set of grammarians has necessarily different phrase structure grammars, to account for the differing inventory of deep structures, although it may be true that the differences are minor. There can be no ultimate authority as to the correctness of assertions of paraphrase-hood, of course, and so no means for resolving this kind of dispute.

Exercise 1.51

Which of the following pairs are paraphrases in the TG sense, and which are not?

1. John kissed Mary and Bill kissed Mary.
   John kissed Mary and so did Bill.

2. John handed Mary a letter.
   John handed a letter to Mary.

3. It's ten past four.
   It's ten after four.

4. To fly planes is easy.
   It's easy to fly planes.

5. The bouncing ball is mine.
   The ball that's bouncing is mine.

1.52 AMBIGUITY

Ambiguous sentences are much easier to deal with, although here, too, you get conflicting assertions about the number of interpretations a sentence may receive. Most cases, at least, are fairly clear.

Probably the best-known (in linguistics) example of an ambiguous sentence is *Flying planes can be dangerous,* which has the meanings (given in terms of paraphrases):

2 a. To fly planes can be dangerous.
   b. Planes which are flying can be dangerous.

While both 2a and 2b are paraphrases of the original sentence, they are not paraphrases of each other. The situation is roughly depicted as in Figure 1.19. That there is a set of rules A that will take you from deep structure I to surface structure 1, and another set of rules C that will take you from a different deep structure II to the same surface structure 1 is best described as a gigantic coincidence, a horrible accident, and so on, that strikes quite unpredictably in human languages. While *flying planes* is ambiguous in English, its translation into other languages is not ambiguous—that is, there will always have to be two distinct translations. With occasional exceptions, the ambiguities of one language will not be shared by another.

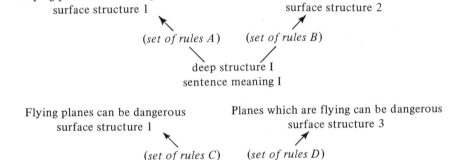

Flying planes can be dangerous
surface structure 1

To fly planes can be dangerous
surface structure 2

(*set of rules A*)   (*set of rules B*)

deep structure I
sentence meaning I

Flying planes can be dangerous
surface structure 1

Planes which are flying can be dangerous
surface structure 3

(*set of rules C*)   (*set of rules D*)

deep structure II
sentence meaning II

Figure 1.19

Exercise 1.52

Which of the following sentences are ambiguous? What are their meanings? Distinguish between cases in which a sentence is ambiguous on grammatical grounds and on lexical grounds.
1. Hunting tigers can be dangerous.
2. Crouching leopards can be dangerous.
3. The lamb was too hot.
4. The eating of the pigs was disgusting.
5. It was too cold to drink.

1.53 AMBIGUITY IN THE OTHER SCHOOLS

The ability to enstructure ambiguous sentences explicitly was well within the reach of the traditional linquist. There are, for example, two Reed-Kellogg diagrams (Figure 1.20) for the two meanings of *Flying planes can be dangerous*, corresponding to the interpretations 2a and 2b previously discussed (cf. Walsh and Walsh, 1972:51-52).

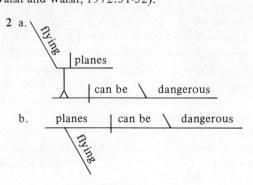

Figure 1.20

It has long been claimed that the structuralist could not distinguish between the meanings of ambiguous sentences as long as he used ICA diagrams, since the diagrams simply noted surface structure order rather than relationships. This is not entirely true, however. The augmented ICA diagram, as found in Francis (1958), was perfectly capable of distinguishing the two meanings of our sentence (Figure 1.21; the notation C represents a verb-complement relationship; P represents a subject-predicate relationship; → represents a modifier-modifiee relationship). Thus the ability to handle ambiguity was by no means the special talent of the TG grammarian. Any traditionalist could do the same thing, and many structuralists were capable of it too.

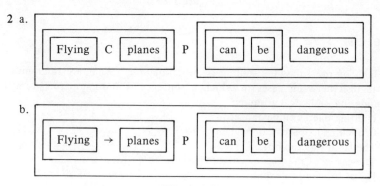

Figure 1.21

1.54 QUASI-AMBIGUOUS SENTENCES

If identical sentences may have different deep structures, then structurally similar sentences may also. I call such sentences "quasi-ambiguous" (no one else calls them anything). Consider the pair:

3 a. John is easy to please.
   b. John is eager to please.

According to both traditional and structural grammarians, these sentences are structurally identical, with the RK and ICA diagrams shown in Figure 1.22. The TG grammarian claims, however, that the underlying relationships between *John* and *please* in the two sentences are totally different, and that the two have equally and correspondingly different deep structures. In *John is easy to please, John* is the deep structure object of *please*, as in the paraphrase, *It is easy to please John*. In *John is eager to please*, on the other hand, *John* is the deep structure subject of *please*, in that he will do the pleasing. For exemplary purposes only (since you don't know enough to understand them yet), the two, highly abridged deep structures are given in Figure 1.23, in which, by inspection, you can see that in 3a, *John* is the object of *please* (comes after *please*), whereas in 3b, *John* precedes, or is the subject of *please*.

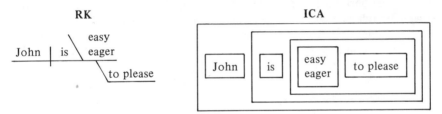

RK   **ICA**

Figure 1.22

3 a. John is easy to please   b. John is eager to please

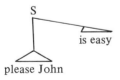
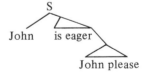

Figure 1.23

The discovery of these relationships was rather a triumph for the TG grammarian, for it represented a truth about English that had not been suspected previously (at least not in print), and an obvious inadequacy of structuralism by inference. Here, finally, was an instance in which TG grammar was unquestionably superior to structural grammar. One may pardon the TG theorist for being smug about it.

Exercise 1.54

Which of the following pairs of sentences are quasi-ambiguous, that is, have similar surface structures but dissimilar deep structures?
1. It's falling.
   It's interesting.

2. Eating candy may be fattening.
   Falling stars can be beautiful.

3. The boy was too cold to drink.
   The toast was too hot to eat.

4. John called up the hospital.
   He sat on the couch.

1.55 INTERMEDIATE STRUCTURES

If deep structures are what are "fed into" the transformational component, and surface structures are what come out, then one can talk usefully about intermediate structures as well. As it will turn out, the transformational component consists of a large number of transformational rules. The rules are applied in sequence, each rule applying to the result of the previous rule. The first transformational rule applies to the deep structure, modifying it into a temporary transitional structure which we will call an intermediate structure. The second rule applies to this intermediate structure, modifying it into another intermediate structure, and so on, until the final transformational rule is applied, resulting in the surface structure. Intermediate structures are "holding patterns" in a sense, and have no specific importance to the language as a whole. They may, however, be discussed by linguists as if they were as real as deep and surface structures.

1.6 Deep Structure, Surface Structure, and Sentence

A frequent source of confusion involves the meaning of the term "sentence." The idea of "sentence" means various things, ranging from a highly abstract concept to the sentence-as-we-say-it.

In the beginning, there is "sentence" as a single, totally abstract unit symbolized by S. We might call this the sentence concept.

The base component takes S, and through the application of phrase structure rules and the addition of words from the lexicon, produces an ordered string of terms and words called a deep structure (for example, *please John is easy*).[1] This is sometimes called an "underlying sentence." A deep structure is highly abstract, having neither pronunciation nor spelling, although to represent it formally, as above, we *use* spelling.

The transformational component takes the deep structure and applies transformational rules to it, each rule producing an intermediate structure, the last rule producing the surface structure (for example, *it is easy to please John*). While the surface structure is less abstract than the deep structure, it still has neither spelling nor pronunciation. Surface structures are occasionally (but incorrectly) called "surface sentences."

The phonological component now takes over and cloaks the terms of the surface structure with an appropriate phonological representation and, in the process, establishes appropriate phonological forms for all the words. These are ultimately produced in the form of coded signals to the mouth, lips, etc., and the "real sentence" emerges.

---

[1] As it will turn out, this is not a proper representation of a deep structure. The proper one would have done you no good, however, and would have been more difficult to understand for this discussion.

To summarize:

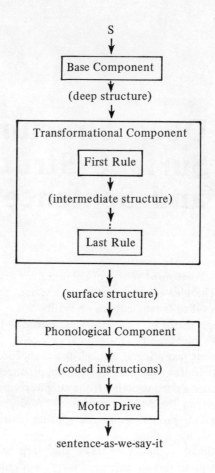

References: Part 1

Bloomfield, Leonard. 1933. *Language*. New York: Holt, Rinehart & Winston.

Chomsky, Noam. 1957. *Syntactic Structures*. The Hague: Mouton.

Chomsky, Noam. 1962. "Explanatory models in linguistics." E. Nagel, P. Suppes, and A. Tarski, eds., *Logic, Methodology, and Philosophy of Science*. Stanford, Calif.: Stanford University Press.

Chomsky, Noam. 1965. *Aspects of the Theory of Syntax*. Cambridge, Mass.: M.I.T. Press.

Eimas, Peter. 1971. "Speech perception." *Science* 171:303-306.

Feinstein, George. 1960. "Letter from a triple-threat grammarian," *College English*, XXI/7:408.

Fillmore, Charles. 1969. "Verbs of judging." *Papers in Linguistics*, I/1:91-117.

Francis, W. Nelson. 1958. *The Structure of American English*. New York: The Ronald Press.

Fries, Charles C. 1952. *The Structure of English*. New York: Harcourt Brace Jovanovich.

Greenberg, Joseph, ed. 1963. *Universals of Language*. Cambridge, Mass.: M.I.T. Press.

Harris, Zellig. 1951. *Methods in Structural Linguistics*. Chicago: University of Chicago Press.

Hockett, Charles. 1963. "The problem of universals in language." J. Greenberg, ed., *Universals of Language*. Cambridge, Mass.: M.I.T. Press.

Jespersen, Otto. 1933. *Essentials of English Grammar*. London: George Allen and Unwin.

Krohn, Robert. 1971. *English Sentence Structure*. Ann Arbor: University of Michigan Press.

Lado, Robert. 1972. "Evidence for an expanded role for reading in foreign language learning." *Foreign Language Annals*, V, May.

Lado, Robert, and C. C. Fries. 1957. *English Sentence Patterns*. Ann Arbor: University of Michigan Press.

Lakoff, Robin. 1969. "Some reasons why there can't be any *some-any* rule." *Language*, 45:608-615.

Leaf, Munro. 1934. *Grammar Can Be Fun*. Philadelphia: J. B. Lippincott.

Lester, Mark. 1971. *Introductory Transformational Grammar of English*. New York: Holt, Rinehart & Winston.

Rivers, Wilga. 1964. *The Psychologist and the Language Teacher*. Chicago: University of Chicago Press.

Steinberg, Danny. 1970. "Psychological aspects of Chomsky's competence-performance distinction." *Working Papers in Linguistics* (Honolulu: University of Hawaii).

Walsh, J. M., and A. K. Walsh. 1939, 1972 (6th ed.). *Plain English Handbook*. New York: McCormick-Mathers.

Webster. 1958. *International Dictionary of English, Third Edition*. Springfield, Mass.: Merriam-Webster.

2

PHRASE STRUCTURE GRAMMAR

PROLOGUE

It is an unfortunate but understandable fact that a great many people, linguists and nonlinguists, who might otherwise obtain something of value from transformational grammar, are repelled by the pseudo-mathematical gimcrackery of the TG approach. Such people may reject the possibility of learning TG grammar in much the same way that they reject the possibility of learning to operate a complex piece of equipment. This is quite unfortunate, for in fact transformational grammar is quite common-sensical once you penetrate its forbidding exterior and has more to offer than any other linguistic approach.

2.0   Introduction

Recall that the Standard Model of the syntactic component consists of a Base Component, which consists of a Phrase Structure Component and a Lexicon, and which produces "deep structures," and a Transformational Component, which produces "surface structures," as shown in Figure 2.1.

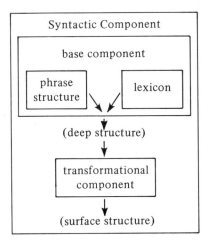

Figure 2.1

In this part of the text we will introduce and discuss those rules that belong to the Phrase Structure (PS) component, along with some discussion of the sorts of information that are provided by the Lexicon.

2.1   Phrase Structure Grammar

        The function of the phrase structure grammar, along with the lexicon, is to produce deep structures, or structures that correspond directly to the meaning that the speaker wishes to formulate (cf. pp. 33, 41). In practice, this works out to mean that the PS grammar produces structures that are nearly identical to elementary sentences. In the earliest days of transformationalism, in fact, the PS grammar was held to produce such elementary sentences, called "kernel sentences" (cf. Chomsky, 1957), from which more complex sentences were derived by transformational rules. For reasons we shall not get into, this approach was abandoned for the present one, although by and large it is still a good rule of thumb to test one's deep structures against a simple sentence for word order—we shall see how, in due course.

The starting point for all PS grammars is the sentence concept, symbolized by S. The first rule proposed in all such grammars is "S consists of . . . ," or "S → . . . ."

In Chomsky (1957, 1965), Jacobs and Rosenbaum (1967), and others,

S → NP + VP   (NP: noun phrase, VP: verb phrase)

In Lester (1971) and others,

S → NP + Aux + VP   (Aux: auxiliary verb phrase)

In DiPietro (1972) and others,

S → M + P   (M: modality, P: proposition)

The format of these rules is the format for all PS rules (sometimes also known as "rewrite rules"): some single constituent (in the above cases, S) is rewritten as or replaced by one or more other constituents. In ordinary terms, this constitutes a claim that the constituent on the left of the arrow consists of the constituents to the right of the arrow.

The (+) sign is used to mean "followed by"; some texts use a ligature (^) instead for this purpose, and others use no sign at all.

A PS rule has a straightforward relationship to a tree diagram, sometimes called a "phrase structure tree" (you have to turn the tree upside down to see why it is called a "tree"). For example, the rules

S → NP + VP   S → NP + Aux + VP   S → M + P

can be expressed in tree form as, respectively,

The symbol to the left of the arrow forms a tree node; the symbols to the right of the arrow are set out, in the same order, below the node, and connected by lines to the node. When drawing a tree, one must always be sure that the form of the tree corresponds exactly to the PS rules that it represents.

Let us look at a sample (and quite primitive) PS grammar of English. PS Grammar (One) will be but the first of a series of PS grammars, each of which, like a Last Will and Testament, will revoke all previous grammars. In fact, we will never get to the final and ultimate PS grammar. No one ever does.

2.11 PHRASE STRUCTURE GRAMMAR (ONE)

1 S → NP + VP
2 NP → Art + N   (Art: article; N: noun)
3 VP → Aux + V + Comp   (V: verb; Comp: complement)
4 Aux → Ten + (Mod) + (Perf) + (Prog)   (Ten: tense; Mod: modal; Perf: perfect; Prog: progressive)
5 Comp → $\left\{ \begin{array}{l} NP \\ Adj \\ Loc \end{array} \right\}$ (Adj: adjective; Loc: location)
6 Loc → P + NP   (P: preposition)
7 Ten → $\left\{ \begin{array}{l} present \\ past \end{array} \right\}$

Lexical Rules

8 Art → {∅, Lex[Art]} (for example, a, the)
9 N → Lex[N]   (for example, boy, girl, idea, stone, school)
10 V → Lex[V]   (for example, see, be, go)
11 Mod → Lex[Mod]   (for example, will, can)
12 Perf → have + -en
13 Prog → be + -ing

14 P → Lex[P]   (for example, to, from)
15 Adj → Lex[Adj]   (for example, good, happy, liquid)

The rules of PSG(One) give us enough to discuss the various notational conventions that are usually employed in writing such grammars.

The arrow and plus sign have already been discussed.

The parentheses in rule 4 indicate optionality. The auxiliary consists of tense, at least, followed by an optional modal, an optional perfect, and an optional progressive. There are eight different ways to realize this rule:

Aux → Ten
Aux → Ten + Mod
Aux → Ten + Perf
Aux → Ten + Prog
Aux → Ten + Mod + Perf
Aux → Ten + Mod + Prog
Aux → Ten + Perf + Prog
Aux → Ten + Mod + Perf + Prog

The braces in rules 5, 7, and 8 mean "choose one from among these." Rule 5, for example, Comp → {NP, Adj, Loc} can be realized in three ways:

Comp → NP
Comp → Adj
Comp → Loc

In other words, in this grammar a complement is either a noun phrase, an adjective, or a locative phrase.

Rule 8 includes the symbol $\emptyset$, the "zero" or "null" symbol. In this case, it represents a "null article." Null forms represent forms that have no overt appearance, but that are regarded as having an existence anyway, for various reasons.

Rules 12 and 13 include the symbols *-en* and *-ing*, standard representations for the past and present participles, respectively, as in *broken* and *breaking*. These symbols have been in use since structural times, despite the fact that only a small minority of verbs actually have a past participle that ends in *-en*.

We will discuss the form of the lexical rules shortly.

The PSG(One) can be responsible for a considerable number of deep structures (the natural output of a PSG). All deep structures will involve the first three rules identically, since there is no choice or optionality given in them (Figure 2.2).

With rule 4, however, Aux → Ten + (Mod) + (Perf) + (Prog), we must choose which, if any, of the optional constituents that we will "activate." Let us say that, in this instance, we will select

4 Aux → Ten + Mod + Prog

RULE	STRING	TREE

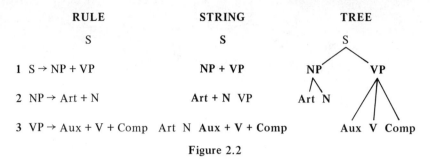

Figure 2.2

giving us the string

Art   N   **Ten + Mod + Prog**   V   Comp

and the tree shown in Figure 2.3.

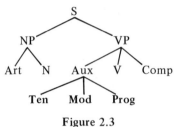

Figure 2.3

In rule 5, a complement must be chosen; let's take Comp → NP. The string is now *Art   N   Ten   Mod   Prog   V   NP* and the tree appears as in Figure 2.4.

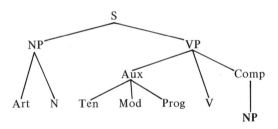

Figure 2.4

Because rule 5 gives us another NP to work with, we must return to rule 2, NP → Art + N for another go, achieving the string

Art   N   Ten   Mod   Prog   V   Art + N

and the tree shown in Figure 2.5.

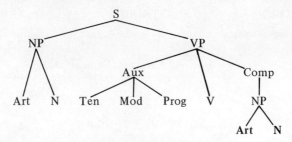

Figure 2.5

In rule 6, tense must be selected, here, the present tense:

Art N *pres* Mod Prog V Art N

and the tree as shown in Figure 2.6.

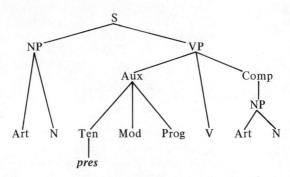

Figure 2.6

This leaves us with only the lexical rules. The rule

N → Lex[N][1]

means, in effect, that the place filled by the grammatical constituent N should now be filled by a lexical item, or word, marked [N] in the lexicon.

2.12   THE LEXICON

The Lexicon is comprised of words together with various sorts of information about them, including, among other things, their grammatical categories. For example, the word *boy* would be marked as being a noun, symbolized here by the feature [N].[2]

---

[1] All grammatical features are indicated by square brackets.

[2] Note, however, that the rules Prog → be + -ing and Perf → have + -en do not involve any lexical substitution. This reflects the fact that the verbals *be* and *have* have no independent meanings in their respective constructions.

If we select from our lexicon [as represented in the examples given in PSG(One)] the words *a, boy, will, go, the, stone* to fill in the indicated grammatical positions in our tree, we obtain the final deep structure tree, shown in Figure 2.7.

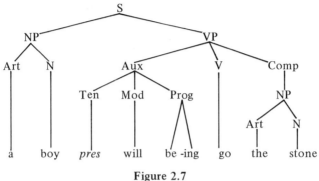

Figure 2.7

It is very important to realize that the deep structure is more than just the D.S. string

a boy *pres* will be -ing go the stone

it is the history of the string's derivation as well, as represented by the shape of the tree. This tree shape is called a **phrase structure marker**, and a deep structure is completely described by its D.S. string plus its PS marker.

The deep structure derived above underlies the sentence *A boy will be going the stone*, obviously a sentence of no great merit. We will take up what we can do to avoid such sentences in the next section.

It may appear, from the expression of the rules given so far, that the TG linguist is claiming that a speaker first generates the entire grammatical structure of a sentence, only then putting in its words as a final step in the process. This notion has provided the source of a good deal of contention, principally by linguists who claim that the speaker must know what words he is going to use in a sentence *before* he places them in particular structures. However, as long as we posit that the starting point of a sentence is an abstract complex of meaning, it is not necessary that specific words be selected to express various parts of that meaning prior to the selection of the structures that will meaningfully relate those words to each other. In other words, about all we can really say is that meaning is expressed by a combination of words and structure together, and an ordering of the two is beyond our present knowledge. Since competence—where the syntactic component is lodged—does not pretend to account for the actual formation of speech (which is the province of a theory of performance), the TG rules claim only that the PS rules and the lexicon are related at the point where they merge: at the deep structure. This might be more clearly represented in the grammar if we were to change the representation of the lexical rule

N → Lex[N]

to a form which suggested a more mutual dependence:

N ↔ Lex[N]

Exercise 2.12

1. Using PSG(One), draw trees for the deep structures that you suspect underlie the following sentences:
   a. The boy has seen the girl.
   b. School was good.
   c. The girl was going to school.
   d. A girl can be seeing the stone.
   e. The boy will have been in the school.

   Check, in each case, that each part of your tree diagram corresponds exactly to a rule in PSG(One). That is, for each

there must be a rule X → Y + Z.

2. See footnote 2 on p. 52. If you prefer to find the *have* of the perfect construction in the lexicon, how would you go about it?

2.2 Information in the Lexicon

Limiting ourselves to PSG(One) exactly as indicated, and to a lexicon consisting of the seventeen words given in the lexical rules, we can generate exactly 51,840 different deep structures. You may begin to appreciate the power of a PS grammar and the considerable difficulties attendant in keeping track of all its ramifications.

If the PS grammar is to participate properly in the syntactic component, it must be sure to provide only "good" deep structures and to avoid the production of deep structures that would lead to sentences that any native speaker would reject. The sentence derived in the previous section, for example, *A boy will be going the stone*, is patently ungrammatical. Something is wrong with PSG(One) if it allows us to derive such a deep structure.

One thing that can be done to patch it up is to alter the form of the rules, and this *will* be done over the course of the rest of the text. At this point, however, we will limit repair work to considerations of the lexicon, in particular to the incorporation of two types of lexical features: **Grammatical Features** and **Semantic Features**.

2.21 GRAMMATICAL FEATURES

Grammatical features are found in the lexicon, and are properties of words. The first type we have already discussed (p. 52): the feature that indicates the grammatical category of the word. Other features specify grammatical restrictions that are associated with particular words; these features are also frequently called grammatical co-occurrence restrictions.

Consider the sentence, *A boy will be going the stone*; there are various faults we might find with it, but any traditionalist would detect the mistake that *go*, an "intransitive" verb, is here given a direct object, something that cannot happen with intransitives by definition. In our terms, the verb *go* has a grammatical feature restricting the kind of complement that may occur with it. In particular, *go* may occur with a complement of location, but may not occur with either a NP complement or an adjective complement. This restriction may be expressed in the lexical entry for *go* as

go[V],[Comp: Loc]

The verb *see*, on the other hand, can occur with only the NP, and neither of the others, or

see[V],[Comp: NP]

The verb *be*, however, is unrestricted in PSG(One), and would appear in the lexicon as

be[V]

Let us see how these features might operate. In the case of the immediate sequence, ... *go the stone...*, the PS marker (that is, the tree) appears as in Figure 2.8, in which *go* is restricted by its lexical entry to a Loc complement but a NP complement is indicated in the PS marker. Lights flash and the mechanism says, "*Tilt!*".

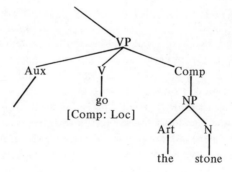

Figure 2.8

By incorporating the indicated grammatical features into *go* and *see*, we immediately reduce the number of permissible deep structures from 51,840 to 33,480.

Just about any fact that we know about a word that relates to its grammatical properties may be represented as a grammatical feature of that word. For example, we know more about the word *water* than the fact that it is a noun; we know also that it is a "mass" noun, or a noncount noun,[1] so that *water* may be

---

[1] So named because water cannot be counted; one cannot say *one water, two waters*, etc.

represented in the lexicon as

water[N],[Noncount]

while *stone*, a countable noun, may be represented as

stone[N],[Count]

We shall add, at various points in the text, to the catalog of grammatical features. It may even begin to appear, sometimes, that there is more grammatical information to be found in the lexicon than there is in any other component. There is, in fact, a school of linguists, generally called lexicalists, that holds that all—or virtually all—grammatical information is in the lexicon.

The total lexicon for PSG(One) now consists of

a[Art]   idea[N],[Count]
be[V]   liquid[Adj]
boy[N],[Count]   school[N],[Count]
can[Mod]   see[V],[Comp: NP]
from[P]   stone[N],[Count]
girl[N],[Count]   the[Art]
go[V],[Comp: Loc]   to[P]
good[Adj]   will[Mod]
happy[Adj]

Exercise 2.21

1. Do the changes as indicated above further reduce the possible number of deep structures that PSG(One) can generate?
2. Indicate lexical entries for the following words. If necessary, invent new features on an *ad hoc* basis, explaining each.
   a. give
   b. three
   c. happily
   d. sand
   e. those

2.22   SEMANTIC FEATURES

Whereas grammatical features indicate the grammatical subclassification of words, semantic features indicate certain semantic properties adjudged to be important. While PSG(One) no longer permits the sentence, *A boy will be going the stone*, it does permit *The idea has seen the stone*. Most people readily agree that this sentence seems grammatical enough (at least more so than the former), but that it is nevertheless anomalous. "Ideas can't see!" would be the normal (and correct) explanation of the anomaly.

The linguist represents this explanation in the lexical entries for both *idea* and *see* in the form of semantic features. *See* would be said to require a subject that has eyes—a human or an animal, or an *Animate* entity, and *idea* would be said to be an *Abstract* entity. Whatever abstractions may be, they are not animate, so *idea* cannot be the subject of *see*. Perhaps the best-known example of a semantically anomalous sentence is Chomsky's *Colorless green ideas sleep furiously* (1957:15), which Chomsky claims to be recognizably grammatical, but which violates a number of selection restrictions: green can't be colorless, ideas can't be green, ideas can't sleep, and no one can sleep furiously.

The designation of semantic features can be best illustrated in nouns. The noun features most commonly discussed are (*Concrete*),[2] (*Living*), (*Animate*), and (*Human*), which are organized as shown in Figure 2.9.

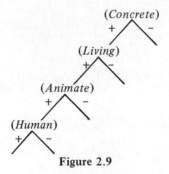

Figure 2.9

This means, first of all, that nouns are either (+*Concrete*) or (−*Concrete*). If they are (+*Concrete*), then they are either (+*Living*) or (−*Living*), and so on. Thus the word *boy* is (+*Concrete*), (+*Living*), (+*Animate*), and (+*Human*). However, it is not necessary to represent all these features in the lexicon; it is sufficient to say that *boy* is (+*Human*), since the nature of the feature relationships is such that if a word is (+*Human*), it must be (+*Animate*), (+*Living*), and so on up the line. This principle has a hook attached to it, however. Let us consider, for example, the word *stone*. Starting at the top, we may quickly establish that *stone* is (+*Concrete*) and (−*Living*). One might be tempted to say that *stone* is also (−*Animate*) and (−*Human*), but in fact these features are irrelevant to stone, since they fall under the (+*Living*) side of the feature tree. Something marked (−*Human*) is assumed to be (+*Animate*) in exactly the same way that something marked (+*Human*) would be, for both (+*Human*) and (−*Human*) derive under (+*Animate*). The feature (*Human*), then, will distinguish between words like *boy* and *dog*, not *boy* and *stone*. To a certain

---

[2] All semantic features will be labeled in italics within parentheses to help distinguish them from the bracketed grammatical features.

extent, the formal system of semantic features does not entirely match our ordinary understanding of the features. In general, it does not matter much, but on occasion care should be taken to avoid confusion. For example, in explaining what is wrong with the phrase *the happy stone*, one should not say that *happy* modifies (+*Animate*) nouns and that *stone* is (-*Human*), for (-*Human*) implies (+*Animate*) in Figure 2.9. The correct explanation is that *happy* modifies (+*Animate*) and therefore (+*Living*) nouns (cf. Figure 2.9), and *stone*, being (-*Living*), does not match up.

We may summarize these observations into two rules:

1. A feature, whether plus or minus, implies "plus-ness" to all features above it.
2. A feature, if minus, implies irrelevancy to all features below it.

The nouns of PSG(One) are now additionally specified:

boy[*N*],[Count],(+*Human*)
girl[*N*],[Count],(+*Human*)
idea[*N*],[Count],(-*Concrete*)
school[*N*],[Count],(-*Living*)
stone[*N*],[Count],(-*Living*)

Exercise 2.22A

Indicate the appropriate features for each of the nouns below:
1. tree
2. water
3. mother
4. music
5. lizard

Another kind of semantic feature is the semantic selection feature, found especially among verbs. We saw before that "ideas can't see"; this may be construed as a semantic property of the verb *see*, that is, in the form, "seeing can't be done by ideas." In other words, *see* is marked as requiring a subject that is itself marked (+*Animate*):

see[V],[Comp: NP],(*subj*: +*Animate*)

Thus the PS marker of *The idea has seen the stone* will include Figure 2.10. Again, the mechanism says "*Tilt!*", but in a softer voice. Because grammatical features are not in contradiction, the sentence is not perceived as being, necessarily, ungrammatical.

In general, most sentences that involve violations of semantic selection restrictions remain simply anomalous: *The stone slept, the idea fell thirty feet*, etc. In many instances, however, the anomaly may clear up, either through reinterpretation of the meaning of the verb or by an alteration of the feature

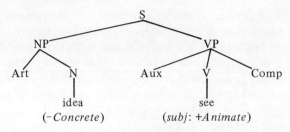

Figure 2.10

assigned to the noun. The process is best characterized as the process of metaphor. When we say things like *the idea fell flat* or *the idea slept*, we are engaged in metaphor, an intrinsically creative process by which lexical characterizations are deliberately altered to suit particular communicative and/or stylistic needs. However, it isn't always easy to determine what phrases involve metaphors and what phrases involve "straightforward" usage. Different individuals will come to different conclusions about any one sentence; our lexicons are not all alike, and differ in particular as to the assignment of semantic features.

If we add the above-discussed semantic features to the words of our lexicon, and include selectional restrictions for *happy* (*subj*: *+Animate*) and *liquid* (*subj*: *−Living*), the lexicon now appears as

a[Art]
be[V]
can[Mod]
from[P]
go[V],[Comp: Loc]
good[Adj]
happy[Adj],*(subj: +Animate)*
idea[N],[Count],*(−Concrete)*
liquid[Adj],*(subj: −Living)*
school[N],[Count],*(−Living)*
see[V],[Comp: NP],*(subj: +Animate)*,*(obj: +Concrete)*
stone[N],[Count],*(−Living)*
the[Art]
to[P]
will[Mod]

and the number of straightforward sentences has been again reduced, from 33,480 to 22,496. Even so, there are still a great many sentences which would be considered peculiar, and which will require further repairs.

Exercise 2.22B

1. What feature(s) might you add to the above system, for example, to disallow a sentence like *the school is liquid*, which PSG(One) permits, even in its latest form?
2. Assign selectional semantic features to *give*.

2.3 What Phrase Structure Rules Mean

Up to now, the PS rules have been discussed and pushed about in terms of how well they work—in terms of their mechanical properties. This is not, however, the criterion that should be brought to bear upon them. Such rules are hypotheses about the way English works, and the only true criterion by which they can be evaluated is whether what they claim about English is true or not and, more particularly, the degree to which they represent what we know about English.

In the next several sections, each rule will be discussed with respect to its claims about English and the light that it throws on English structure. Each such discussion will be followed by a brief review of the general usage of the structure being discussed.

2.31 SENTENCE

Rule 1, S → NP + VP, is a claim that speakers of English basically organize their sentences into two constituents, a noun phrase and a verb phrase or, more generally, into a subject phrase and a predicate phrase. This is no new claim. Implicit in the structuralist's IC analysis of a sentence is precisely the same claim; the first cut lies always between the subject and the predicate, implying that the principal immediate constituents of a sentence are the subject and the predicate. Traditionalists, too, saw things this way. Walsh and Walsh (1972:1) say, "A sentence must have a subject and a predicate," and the Reed-Kellogg diagram indicates the importance of this break by fully cutting the horizontal line at this point.

Hockett (1958:201) (along with a lot of other people) prefers to call the distinction the "topic/comment" relationship, in which the "subject" is the "topic" of a sentence and the "predicate" constitutes a "comment" on it.

DiPietro (1972:57) relates the distinction in turn to a general feature of human biology (presumed to be genetic, or innate), that we use one hand for gripping something (topic) and the other hand for working on it (comment). Thus S → NP + VP derives not from linguistic convenience but from our genes. Who knows?

2.4   Noun Phrase

Rule 2, NP → Art + N, is a claim that noun phrases always consist of an article and a noun. In the course of the discussion following, this rule will be heavily revised.

2.41 NOUN

To begin with, all linguists agree that there are (at least) two kinds of nouns, regular or countable and mass or uncountable. The former literally can be counted—*one boy, two boys*, etc.—while the latter cannot—**one water, *two waters*, etc.—at least not in the ordinary sense.[1] It is convenient to mark nouns as being countable or uncountable through the use of a grammatical feature, [Count], [Noncount], in the lexicon, as indicated previously. One very important syntactic aspect of nouns marked [Count] is that they may be plural whereas [Noncount] nouns must be singular.

Where do "singular" and "plural" come into the noun phrase? The easiest way is to add them to the noun in the NP rule, as:

$$NP \rightarrow Art + N + \#$$
$$\# \rightarrow \begin{Bmatrix} singular \\ plural \end{Bmatrix}$$

It is at this point that we run into a significant difference between deep structure appearances and the form of a finished sentence. The PS rules do not give us any means for putting noun and number together. The deep structure of a plural noun like *boys* is as shown in Figure 2.11. The rule combining *boy* and *pl* is a **Morphophonemic** rule, and properly speaking it falls within the scope of

---

[1] Obviously, *two waters* can mean "two glasses of water," or something to that effect.

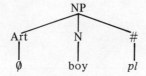

Figure 2.11

the phonological component. Thus even a surface structure, the output of the syntactic component, would preserve the sequence *boy pl*. This state of affairs is potentially confusing and unsatisfactory, and crops up in any number of places in the grammar. It will ultimately happen that we will build morphophonemic rules into the transformational component—illegally—so as to be able to give our surface structures some sort of terminal familiarity. This will be the **MF** rule, to which we will return periodically. It works as shown in Figure 2.12.

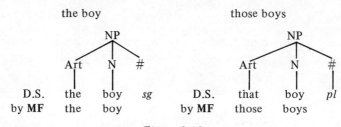

Figure 2.12

A second revision derives from the question: is *John* a noun in the same way that *boy* is? There are a number of reasons to think that perhaps it is not: *John* does not occur with an article, nor does it normally occur with a plural. In writing, *John* always occurs with a capital J, while *boy* is capitalized only at the beginning of a sentence. More important, its semantics are different: *boy* has a dictionary definition and *John* does not. In short, *John* is a name, not a noun. Accordingly, the NP rule is enlarged:

$$NP \rightarrow \left\{ \begin{array}{l} Art + N + \# \\ Name \end{array} \right\}$$

where Name is in turn subject to a rule:

Name → Lex[Name]

and of course names in the lexicon would be appropriately marked—for example, *Bill*[Name].

A third revision results from the discovery that the grammar makes no provision for pronouns. Pronouns are, of course, substitutes for noun phrases and do not occur with articles, so they may be worked into the grammar in a way similar to names:

$$NP \rightarrow \left\{ \begin{array}{l} \text{Art} + \text{N} + \# \\ \text{Name} \\ \text{ProN} \end{array} \right\}$$

ProN $\rightarrow$ Lex[ProN]

However, it is not necessarily the case that all pronouns in a sentence will derive through this rule. Some pronouns—called **Anaphoric** pronouns—are derived transformationally. Consider the sentence, *John told Mary to give it to him*. It is ambiguous, with two possible meanings:

1 a. . . . give it to John.
  b. . . . give it to him (some other person).

Sentences that are ambiguous must have different deep structures; in this case, the difference in the deep structures must indicate how *him* can refer to John on the one hand and someone else on the other (Figure 2.13). The two deep structures are different, with 1a explicitly indicating that *John* is the indirect object. Under normal development, we might expect to derive the sentence **John told Mary to give it to John*, which (as long as we are dealing with only one *John*) is unacceptable. Whenever the same referent appears within the context of a single sentence, one of the referents (usually, but not always, the second) is pronominalized. This is a transformational rule, the **ProN** rule, and it results in the acquisition of an anaphoric pronoun, or a transformationally derived pronoun. Thus, as shown in Figure 2.14, derived structure 1a is now identical to deep structure 1b, and the resulting sentences will be the same.

1 a. . . . give to John    b. . . . give to him (not John)

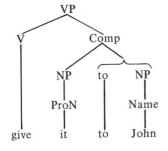
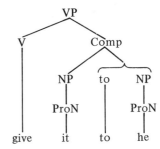

Figure 2.13

However, what about *to he*? In this text, all deep structure (and other abstract) pronouns will be represented by the "subject" form. Properly speaking, they should be represented by something a little more abstract, like "3sm" (for third singular male), but frankly *he* is easier. A version of the **Morphophonemic** rule (**MF**) will obtain final familiar form, as shown in Figure 2.15.

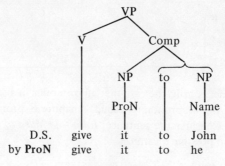

Figure 2.14

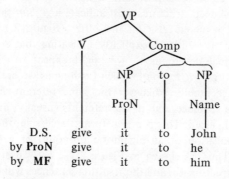

Figure 2.15

There is a very sensible objection to the above concept of the anaphoric pronoun: surely any pronoun is ultimately anaphoric, in so far as it refers back to a known person or thing, which should then be in the deep structure, just like *John* is. After all, the *him* in 1b is really a billion-times ambiguous, for "he" might refer to any of the billion men in the world. In a larger sense, this objection is totally valid. TG grammar, however, relates rules to individual sentences only, and within this very limited context, some pronouns may not be anaphoric.

Exercise 2.41

1. Draw PS trees for each of the following:
   a. John
   b. they
   c. water
   d. the stone
   e. the men
2. Should **ProN** be considered the source of the "expletive" *it* in sentences like *It's raining*?

2.42   ARTICLES

The article in English has always been regarded as a particularly tough nut to crack, from both the linguist's point of view and the English teacher's. The PS rule

Art → {∅, Lex[Art]}

leaves a great deal to be desired.

To begin with, one cannot be entirely sure exactly what is meant by the positive expression of a null article. In structural theory, at least (it isn't entirely clear in TG theory), a null entity is a real entity that happens to be naked of phonological form, and is quite different from the mere absence of something. Thus the claim that there is a null article in *Girls are pretty* is different from claiming that there is no article. However, there seems to be no particular known justification for a null article, and perhaps we would be better off without it. The most usual way of arranging for the absence of an element in a sentence is to make its dominating constituent (the constituent from which it derives) optional, as in the rule fragment

NP → (Art) + N + #

which claims that there are times that there is just no article with the noun. As it will turn out, we will ultimately arrive at a solution that is very similar to this one, only sneakier.

A far more serious matter is the distinction between the "definite" and "indefinite" articles, *the* and *a* (and the rest). One approach is the direct approach, with a rule like the following (cf. Lester, 1971:36):

$$Art \rightarrow \begin{Bmatrix} \text{specified} \\ \text{unspecified} \\ \emptyset \end{Bmatrix}$$

specified → {the, this, . . .}
unspecified → {a, some, . . .}

This is just a modified version of the traditional statement that there are two sorts of articles, definite and indefinite. Neither version is very informative, for neither gives any sort of explanation as to what is going on. Furthermore, it is my contention that the above approach is in fact incorrect and leads to difficulties for the language learner. Without further preamble, the following rules are suggested:

Art → (Quant) + (Det)   (quantity and determiner)
Quant → Lex[Quant] (for example, one, two, . . . , a, some, many, etc.)
Det → Lex[Det] (for example, the, this, that, etc.)

In other words, an article consists of a sequence of an optional quantifier and an optional determiner. If both are realized, a subrule of some sort automatically inserts *of* between the two, as in *one* of *the boys*.

The role of the quantifier is to count the NP and, in particular, to establish whether the NP is singular or plural. There are only two singular quantifiers: *a* and *one*; all others are plural. Thus the NP, *one of the boys*, is syntactically singular because its quantifier is singular, and the NP takes the singular form of the verb—for example, *one of the boys is here*. Quantity is optional, however; when it is not realized, the implied quantity of the NP is universal, or general. Thus an expressed quantity acts to limit the size of the NP.

Since the role of the quantifier is to establish syntactic number, it is necessary to recognize that this role is overridden by the obligatory singularity of [Noncount] nouns. In other words, *some* is a plural quantifier, rendering the NP, *some of the boys*, plural. Because *water* is marked [Noncount], any NP in which it participates must be singular, even if the quantifier is plural otherwise.[2]

The role of the determiner is to establish the fact that the NP involves a known group—known to both the speaker and his audience. Det, too, is optional, and when it is not realized the NP is understood to be unspecified, or indefinite. Thus determiners act to delimit the NP to a particular group.

Since each of the constituents Quant and Det has a limiting function with respect to the NP, Art itself may as well be considered a constituent that serves to restrict NP reference. A completely unrestricted NP would have no article (neither quantity nor determiner) and would be general and indefinite thereby: for example, *girls are funny*. This gives us a minor problem in tree drawing. How best do we represent a constituent whose parts are completely unrealized? One solution would be to represent it as in Figure 2.16. A better way, in my opinion, is to recognize the fact that if a constituent like Art is made up of optional parts, then it is in turn itself effectively optional, whether or not you write parentheses around it. A tree diagram reflecting this notion would appear as in Figure 2.17. It does not really matter how you do it, of course.

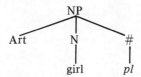

Figure 2.16 Girls.

Figure 2.17 Girls.

[2]Note also that the [Noncount] literally means that no enumerating counter (*one, two, three*, . . .) can be used with such NPs.

The formulation of the article accounts for the form and meaning of the following NPs:

2 a. *Girls are funny.*   No Quant: universal
                               No Det: indefinite
   b. *Two boys went.*   Quant: plural
                               No Det: indefinite
   c. *Those boys laughed.*   No Quant: universal
                               Det: known group
   d. *One of the men fell.*   Quant: singular
                               Det: known group

The first has already been discussed.

The second involves a specific quantifier (*two*), but the NP is "indefinite" since the two boys may be selected from the entire universe of boys.

The third NP has a determiner, *those*, which establishes the boundaries of a particular group—a universe of discourse, as it is sometimes known. The quantifier is universal within those boundaries, meaning "all" of "those boys." When the known group encompasses only one entity (such as *the boy*), the universal quantifier is said to encompass the whole group nonetheless, sort of like "all one boy of him."

In the fourth NP, the determiner *the* establishes the boundaries of a known group, and the quantifier *one* limits the selection from that group of one member, making the NP singular as a whole. Thus one uses the singular form of the verb, as *One of my uncles is bald.* It is an interesting fact (interesting to psycholinguists, at any rate, who debate its significance) that it is not uncommon for people to make a mistake and say *one of my uncles are bald.*

Note, by the way, that the fourth NP is not "definite" as a whole. Despite the determiner, you do not know which man "fell." The function of the determiner is not to make the NP definite, but to isolate a known group. The NP is definite only if no explicit quantifier is also part of the NP.

There is another minor tree-drawing problem that may be disposed of at this point: where and how does *of* appear in the tree? Actually, it doesn't have to appear at all. It could be considered the product of an "output" rule, or a rule which goes into action to "clean up" messy bits of the surface structure after all regular rules have applied. Alternatively, *of* could be inserted by a transformational rule, triggered by the presence of both a quantifier and a determiner. Third, the PS rule can be rewritten in such a way that *of* is there to begin with, but optionally, such that the optionality of *of* is tied to the optionality of either of the other two parts of Art. My personal favorite is somewhat unethical: *of* gets there magically, and I therefore don't have to worry about such questions. My tree diagrams take the appearance of Figure 2.18, in which *of* doesn't "come from" anywhere. You are welcome to use a more rigorous solution.

There are two restrictions on articles that have both Quant and Det. The first is that the Det must establish a group consisting of more entities than are

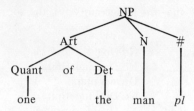

Figure 2.18 One of the men.

mentioned by the quantifier (except when the quantifier is universal, such as *all*). Thus 3a, 3b, and 3c are ungrammatical, while 3d is not.

3 a. *One of the girl
   b. *Four of the three girls[3]
   c. *Three of the three girls
   d. Two of the three girls

The second restriction is on the use of *a* as the quantifier in such articles. *A* may occur only when there is no determiner, which means that it will always occur in "indefinite" noun phrases.

One important aspect of this formulation of the article is the implication that it has with respect to the way in which articles are usually presented in the English classroom.[4] Generally, *a* and *the* are presented as if they were pretty much the same thing (that is, "articles"), differing only with respect to the dimension of "definiteness." This is, I believe, potentially misleading; *a* and *the* are really quite unrelated to each other, and share only the fact that both participate in the same general system of rules, the article rules, along with many other words.

The final aspect of this discussion of the article introduces an element of recursiveness. Most analyses regard the possessive pronouns (*my, his, their,* etc.) as determiners rather than adjectives, mostly because adjectives can occur with determiners (for example, *the red book*) whereas possessives cannot (for example, *the my book*). If possessive pronouns are determiners, then possessive names and nouns should also be determiners (for example, *John's, the boy's*), which can be generalized to the possessive form of any NP. Such possessives can actually be quite complex, as has been pointed out by Gleason (1965:165) with the examples:

4 a. the very old man's beard
   b. that man in the store's pencil

---

[3] There is a great deal of potential confusion of the two numbers that may occur in such noun phrases. The number just before the noun (after *the*) is, in effect, an adjective, and has no syntactic function.

[4] For a more thorough discussion of this point, see Whitman (1974).

c. that friend there's car
d. a friend of mine's house

(Lest anyone point out that 4b, 4c, and 4d are ungrammatical because the possessive form is not attached to the possessing noun, let me quickly remind you of such phrases as *the Queen of England's crown* and many others of that ilk, and say that it just isn't that easy.)

We can account for such phrases pretty easily, by expanding the PS rule

Det → {NP + 's, Lex[Det]}

The recursivity derives from the fact that the NP may consist of an article, a determiner, and a NP in turn, as in Figure 2.19. The structure of this NP makes it clear that a book is being discussed, that the book is defined as being possessed by a father, who is the father of a boy, and that we just know, I guess, who the boy is.

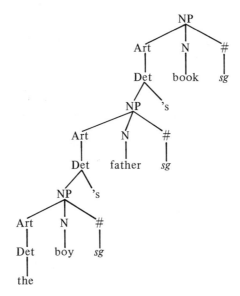

Figure 2.19 The boy's father's book.

Exercise 2.42

Draw trees for the following NPs:

1. a friend
2. that dog
3. these women
4. one of the girls
5. my brother's book
6. my brother's friend's book
7. one of my brother's friend's books
8. some of your blood

2.43 WHAT MOTIVATES DET?

While Det has been described, we have not gone into the question of when and why speakers involve a determiner in their noun phrases. In other words, under what circumstances should a noun phrase be "definite"? This appears to involve a complicated presupposition on the part of the speaker as to what his audience knows about the noun.

Primarily, if the speaker may assume that his audience knows what noun he is talking about, then he can use the definite article. When he says "the dog," he is saying, in effect, "the dog (you know what dog I'm talking about)." If the speaker is wrong in this assumption, dialogues like the following can result:

> The dog came to our house again today.
> What dog?
> The dog I told you about the other day.
> Oh, yeah.

Moreover, there are times when he must make this assumption and use the determiner, for not to do so would result in confusion. A common instance of this might be when the noun has just been referred to:

> A girl is reading over there.
> I see her.
> A girl is sitting in a red chair.
> I only see one girl—do you mean the same one?

Such cases would be instances of "previous mention," in a rule that goes roughly as follows:

> The first time you use a noun, use an indefinite article; thereafter use a definite article.

The rule is drastically oversimplified, however, for the noun involved need not be lexically identical each time. It would be extremely difficult to express the rule properly, but a better approximation might be:

> The first time an "unknown" entity is referred to, no determiner should be used. Thereafter, the entity and all its component and related parts may be taken as known.

In other words, mentioning the noun itself is irrelevant; it is mention of the entity that establishes its "known-ness." In the dialogue,

> Mary is a friend of mine.
> Mm?
> Yes, the girl has a lot of sense.

the use of the determiner can only be explained by the fact that "the girl" refers to Mary, whose existence has just been established. That component parts and related parts are also established is something that may be very confusing to the learner. Once you refer to "a house," you may then refer to "the kitchen," "the driveway," and even "the surrounding countryside."

Prior mention need not occur in the speech of the speaker, of course, just so long as it has occurred somewhere:

I went to a play last night—*Bitter Beds*.
So did I! The cast was terrific, wasn't it?

There are a considerable number of nouns that need no prior mention, for they are virtually unique and are almost always referred to with a determiner: *the moon, the sun, the sky, the President*, and so on.

Far and away the most common use of the determiner involves neither prior mention nor uniqueness. The noun occurs in a self-defining noun phrase, containing a modifier which indicates "which" noun it is that is being referred to. While this may sometimes occur with simple adjectives (usually stressed—for example, *the réd book is mine*) more commonly a self-defining noun phrase will involve a modifier following the noun:

5 a. the man whom I saw yesterday
  b. the salt taken from Siberian caves
  c. the lady from California

That there is still a contextual element in play is without question; there must be many hundreds of ladies from California, so it is assumed that for immediate purposes the designation, *the lady from California*, is sufficient to isolate one individual lady for the particular speaker and audience.

The use of *the* with names is notoriously problematic. About the only simple rule that really works is the rule that says that plural names always take *the* (*the Smiths, the Philippines, the Ozarks*, etc.). Otherwise, the foreign learner is simply stuck with the problem of a confusing set of contrasts:

Use *the* with oceans and seas (*the Atlantic Ocean, the Red Sea*) but not with
  lakes (*Red Lake, Lake Superior*)
  with buildings (*the Ford Building*) but not with institutions (*Ford Hospital*)
  with tollways (*the New Jersey Turnpike*) but not streets (*Main Street, Delaware Avenue*)
  with rivers (*the Mississippi River*) but not streams (*Bear Creek, Trail Brook*)

and so on. The enterprising student may observe that most of these contrasts involve *the* with large and important (and well-known?) entities as opposed to smaller (and less well-known) ones, but it is very difficult to claim this fully, for surely everyone knows Lake Superior.

2.44 GENERIC USES OF THE ARTICLE

A noun phrase that contains neither *Quant* nor Det is universal and indefinite, which is to say (to some extent) *generic*. *Rats* means "all rats." This is sometimes called the generic plural; linguists and teachers alike have always had a problem in trying to account for the equivalent generic singulars:

6 a. Rats are unpleasant animals.
   b. A rat is an unpleasant animal.
   c. The rat is an unpleasant animal.

The difficulty probably stems from feeling that all three mean the same thing. In fact, each means something just a little bit different.

If *rats* means "all rats," then *a rat* means "a sample rat" or "a representative rat" (take a rat, any rat, and it'll be unpleasant), on the assumption that most rats are pretty much alike in this respect and any one rat will be pretty representative. This suggests relatively little variation, and represents a stronger type of generalization than the generic plural. Weak generalizations seldom involve the generic *a*.

6 d. Girls are funny.
   e. ?A girl is funny.

Generic *the*, on the other hand, represents the ideal or archetypical entity; *the rat* is an abstract median rat. If the noun is itself somewhat abstract in character, *the* appears preferred:

6 f. The human male is characterized by. . .
   g. ?A human male is characterized by. . .

If the noun is necessarily abstract, *the* is definitely called for:

6 h. The American family consists of 4.38 persons.
   i. ?An American family consists of 4.38 persons.
   j. ??American families consist of 4.38 persons.

Whether or not the above claims are true, the PS rules governing the article do not account for them. It is not entirely clear whether this is or is not a weakness in the theory. What is called "usage" is generally not accounted for in any sort of linguistic theory—and when some aspect of usage is finally accounted for within the theory, it usually ceases to be considered as usage, and becomes a structural matter instead.

Summary of the NP

The PS rules governing the NP are

$$NP \rightarrow \begin{Bmatrix} Art + N + \# \\ ProN \\ Name \end{Bmatrix}$$

Art → (Quant) + (Det)
Quant → Lex[Quant]   (for example, a, one, two, some, many, . . .)
Det → {NP + 's, Lex[Det]}   (for example, the, this, that, . . .)

N → Lex[N]   (for example, boy, stone, . . .)

$\# \rightarrow \left\{ \begin{matrix} singular \\ plural \end{matrix} \right\}$

Name → Lex[Name]   (for example, John, Mary, . . .)

ProN → Lex[ProN]   (for example, I, you, he, . . .)

Exercise 2.44

1. Examine two or three pages of running text, isolating all instances of *the*. What is the most common type of *the*? How many categories of *the* do you find?

2. What can you say about the lack of any article in the following sentences:
   a. The jaguar's favorite food is *wild pig*.
   b. *Stone* is the best building material.
   c. Her dress was made of *palm-leaf fiber*.

2.5 The Verb Phrase (Aux)

VP → Aux + V + Comp

Or, the verb phrase consists of an auxiliary, a main verb, and a complement. We shall first deal with the auxiliary, and then with verbs and their complements together.

2.51 THE AUXILIARY

Aux → Ten + (Mod) + (Perf) + (Prog)

The auxiliary consists of an obligatory tense element, followed by optional modal, perfect, and progressive structures, with eight possible combinations in all. The order given in the rule cannot be changed; you may say 1a, but not 1b, 1c, or 1d:

1 a. He may have been doing it.   (Mod + Perf + Prog)
  b. *He has may be doing it.   (Perf + Mod + Prog)
  c. *He may be having done it.   (Mod + Prog + Perf)
  d. *He is may have done it.   (Prog + Mod + Perf)

2.52 TENSE

$$\text{Ten} \rightarrow \left\{ \begin{array}{l} present \\ past \end{array} \right\}$$

This rule claims that there are two tenses in English, contrasting with the three tenses that most people think exist (present, past, and future), and certainly with the six tenses discussed by Walsh and Walsh (1972:30): present, past, future, present perfect, past perfect, and future perfect. But if the present and past are the only tenses in English, what happened to the future tense?

The term "tense" has come to have a specialized use in linguistics. For a verb to have a "future tense," it must do more than refer to a future time: there must be a special form of the verb for this purpose. French provides a good illustration. French has two basic ways of indicating futurity, (a) with a verb ending and (b) with an infinitive following the verb *aller* ("to go"). You can translate *I will speak* as:

2 a. Je parlerai
   b. Je vais parler

In so far as futurity is indicated by a special form of the verb in 2a, it is proper to speak of 2a as representing a future "tense" in French. In 2b, on the other hand, a recognizably present-tense form of *aller* is involved and *parler* is just the infinitive form, so that 2b would be spoken of as representing a future "construction" rather than a future "tense." In fact, the construction would be said to be in the present tense in so far as present forms of *aller* are used.

Returning to English, there are four common ways to express futurity:

3 a. He will arrive tomorrow.
   b. He's going to arrive tomorrow.
   c. He's arriving tomorrow.
   d. He arrives tomorrow.

In none of the four is there a special form of the verb *arrive* by which futurity is denoted. What is more, in 3b, 3c, and 3d a recognizably present tense form (*is, arrives*) is involved, with 3d being identical to the simple present tense. The syntax of the modal *will* is identical to the syntax of the other modals, *must, can*, etc. (well almost), so that it would be incorrect to say that *will*, by itself, represents a future tense form (of the verb *will*) unless you are willing to say the same of all the auxiliaries. This line of argument will be taken up again when considering the modals in more detail.

The notion that "future" tenses are really "present" tenses may be less disturbing if you adopt the labels "past" and "nonpast" for the two tenses, where "nonpast" obviously is broad enough to cover both present and future.

Exercise 2.52

Consider the four types of future expression given above. What differences in meaning or connotation can you suggest for them?

Tense appears first in the auxiliary. As you know, tense is always associated with the first-appearing verb in the verbal string, the remaining verbs being participles or uninflected. Since tense is always expressed as a verb ending, it would be nice if the rule could be expressed in such a way as to have tense following the verb to which it will be bonded; but there are severe mechanical problems in writing such a rule in so far as there are a great many different auxiliaries and verb forms that may wind up being first. It could be done, of course, and would look something like this:

$$VP \rightarrow \begin{Bmatrix} V + Ten + Comp \\ Aux + V + Comp \end{Bmatrix}$$

$$Aux \rightarrow \begin{Bmatrix} Mod + Ten + (Perf) + Prog) \\ Perf + Ten + (Prog) \\ Prog + Ten \end{Bmatrix}$$

With the rule as given in PSG(One), however, tense is undeniably out of position, since it precedes the verb to which it will become bonded. In order to get tense into position, a switching rule is required, called the **Flip-flop** rule (or **FF**), a transformational rule (not a PS rule) having the form

FF   Ten + verbal ⇒ verbal-Ten[1]

For example, see Figure 2.20.

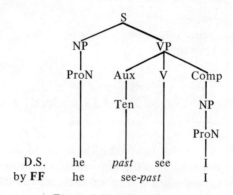

D.S.   he   *past*   see   I
by **FF**   he   see-*past*   I

Figure 2.20   He saw me.

As was mentioned previously, a **Morphophonemic** rule (**MF**) must be applied to attain appropriate surface form for plural nouns; another **MF** rule selects appropriate pronoun form. A third **MF** rule will convert sequences like *see-past* to the more familiar *saw*. All **MF** operations are treated as if they occurred simultaneously, as in the resolution of the surface structure obtained above:

by **FF**   he   see-*past*   I
by **MF**   he   saw   me

Another example is shown in Figure 2.21.

[1] Transformational rules are given with a double-barred arrow (⇒) to distinguish them from PS rule arrows.

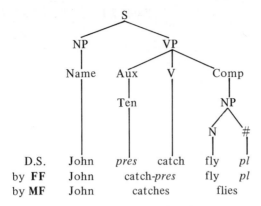

Figure 2.21 John catches flies.

Agreement between the -s ending on the verb and the third person subject is something that we will not go into in the course of this text. The transformational rules that are required are quite complex, and ultimately tell you nothing that you don't already know—that is, that third-person singular present-tense forms of the verb end with -s. We will pretend (wrongly, I assure you) that the -s ending can be handled as if it were just another one of the morphological bits and pieces dealt with by means of the **MF** rule.

2.53 MODALS

In the English verb system, the modal is probably the most peculiar entity we have, and its treatment varies widely from analysis to analysis. Generally speaking, there are two more or less unrelated problems: the relationship between tense and modals, and the meanings of the models.

The modal auxiliaries include *will, may, can, would, shall, ought to, might, could, must,* and *should*. They are especially characterized by not having an -s ending with a third-person singular subject and by being followed by verbs that have no inflectional ending.

Traditionally, the modals were divided up into two groups (this tradition carrying on into many contemporary TG analyses), the "present" and "past" modals (Table 2.1). While there is an excellent historical justification for this analysis, it presents a number of problems in terms of modern English. The principal problem is that the so-called past modals cannot be used in past-time sentences, but can be used in future-time sentences, a contradiction of their label. In other words, 4a and 4b are ungrammatical, while 4c and 4d are grammatical.

Table 2.1

pres	past
will	would
may	might
shall	should
can	could
must	—
—	ought to

4 a. *He might do it yesterday.
  b. *He should do it yesterday.
  c. He might do it tomorrow.
  d. He should do it tomorrow.

In fact, only *could* may be said to occur in the past (but also the future), as in:

4 e. He could do it yesterday.
  f. He could do it tomorrow.

On the other hand, in circumstances where a past tense is normally required by "tense-agreement" rules, the so-called present modals seem to be somewhat unacceptable (opinions vary).

4 g. He said that he did it.
  h. ?He said that he does it.
  i. He said that he might do it.
  j. ?He said that he may do it.
  k. He said that he could do it.
  l. ?He said that he can do it.

In the face of conflicting evidence, no really satisfying solution is probable. The two major schools of thought are the one given above, where modals divide up into present and past forms, and its major alternative, in which all modals are treated alike, and do not differentiate according to tense.

Alternative A

Mod: {will, may, shall, can, must}
  by **FF**   *pres* + will ⟹ will-*pres*
  by **MF**   will
  by **FF**   *past* + will ⟹ will-*past*
  by **MF**   would

Alternative B

Mod: {will, would, may, might, can, could, shall, should, must, ought to}
  by **FF**   *pres* + will ⟹ will-*pres*
  by **MF**   will

by **FF**	*past* + will ⇒ will-*past*
by **MF**	will
by **FF**	*pres* + would ⇒ would-*pres*
by **MF**	would
by **FF**	*past* + would ⇒ would-*past*
by **MF**	would

In other words, it doesn't matter what the tense is; *will* is *will* and *would* is *would*.

Both alternatives have advantages relative to each other, but both founder on the same ground of the relationship the modal has with tense. A third alternative has the advantage of doing away with that problem, and at the same time returning the missing future tense to English, after a fashion. Alternative C involves the revision of the Aux rule:

Alternative C

$$\text{Aux} \rightarrow \left\{ \begin{array}{l} \text{Mod} \\ \text{Ten} \end{array} \right\} + (\text{Perf}) + (\text{Prog})$$

This rule claims that the verb will either be inflected for tense or it will involve a modal, but not both. Modals are an alternative to tense, so they are not themselves inflected for tense. Tense accounts for past and present time; the modal system is usually future.

In those cases where the time reference of a sentence is past (for example, if the sentence includes a time word such as *yesterday*), the time reference cannot be resolved through the use of a past tense, since modals do not occur with tense. Instead, the past time is resolved through the use of the perfect construction, as in *he may have done it yesterday*. (Note that it is only with a modal that a perfect construction can co-occur with explicit past time; otherwise it is ungrammatical, as in **he has done it yesterday*.)

For all that may be said in favor of it, however, even alternative C has its point of failure: it cannot account for the fact that *could* is very obviously inflected for past tense in sentences like *I could run a mile in eight minutes flat when I was a kid*. Nevertheless, we shall opt to use alternative C throughout the remainder of the text.

The second major problem with modals is that they have various meanings associated with them. This is nothing new; according to Traugott (1972:197ff), changes in the meanings of the modals have been going on since the days of Old English, new meanings being added to the old ones.

Somewhere around 1968 (I cannot determine who should be held responsible), a primary distinction was established between **Epistemic** and **Root** meanings for the modals. The epistemic meaning generally has a probabilistic and future flavor to it, while the root meaning has a more explicit semantic content (Table 2.2). Sample sentences are given below Table 2.2.

Table 2.2

Modal	Epistemic	Root
will	definite future	habit, obstinacy (in negatives)
shall	definite future	opinion (in questions)
would	conditional future	past habit; obstinacy
should	probable future	advisability
can	_ᵃ	ability, capacity, permission
could	_ᵃ	past or conditional ability
may	possible future	permission
might	possible future	—
must	logical conclusion	necessity

ᵃAccording to Traugott, epistemic meanings never developed for *can* and *could*.

will:	Epis	John will be here in five minutes.
	Root	Boys will be boys. He just won't help me!
shall:	Epis	I shall not ask again.
	Root	Shall we go?
would:	Epis	I would go if he asked me to.
	Root	Boys would be boys, those days.
should:	Epis	John should be there by now.
	Root	You really should read that book.
can:	Epis	
	Root	He can draw deep structure trees.
could:	Epis	
	Root	He could do that yesterday.
may:	Epis	He may be here by five.
	Root	Yes, you may go out.
might:	Epis	He might be able to help you.
	Root	
must:	Epis	He must be somewhere around here.
	Root	You must be able to draw trees to pass this course.

There have been various attempts to ascribe syntactic regularity to the epistemic/root distinction, but these have been so flawed with exceptions that they must be regarded with suspicion. For example, it has been claimed that when the modal co-occurs with the perfect, it is epistemic in meaning. This is by-and-large true,

5 a. He will have done it.
   b. He would have done it.
   c. He may have done it.
   d. He might have done it.
   e. He must have done it.

but unfortunately not always true,

   f. He should have done it.

g. He could have done it.

h. You must have written all the papers if you want an A.

Granting that there are two meanings, how are they to be represented in our grammar? In so far as a sentence like *He may go out* is ambiguous, it must have two different deep structures. A number of suggestions have been made, most of them tediously complicated (a few almost humorously so), but for our purposes we shall just place the burden on the lexicon. Just as there are two homonyms, *bill* (a birdy growth, a growth in your mailbox), so are there two homonymous modals, *may*:

may[Mod],(*Epis*)
may[Mod],(*Root*)

which have nothing to do with each other beyond the fact of their homonymy.

Exercise 2.53

1. Draw trees for the following sentences:
   a. John may arrive tomorrow. (Attach *tomorrow* to VP)
   b. Mary must have left yesterday.
   c. Those boys should be in school.
   d. My cousin must read this book.
   e. I could do it yesterday.
2. Why is *have to* not considered a modal?

2.54 PERFECT

Perf → have + -en

The perfect construction consists of the auxiliary verb *have* and the past participial ending *-en* (as noted before, *-en* is the linguist's convention for representing this ending; in reality, there are quite a few past participial endings). A deep structure in which the perfect has been "activated" will appear with the *-en* immediately preceding the verb to which it will become affixed, that is, the verb immediately following *have* (Figure 2.22).

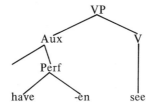

Figure 2.22 . . . have seen . . .

In order to place the ending after the verb, a second version of the **Flip-flop** rule is required, by FF_2 -en verbal $\Rightarrow$ verbal-en

and an appropriate part of the **Morphophonemic** rule will assign the right-looking form to it.

D.S.	. . .have -en see. . .
by **FF**	have see-en
by **MF**	have seen

If there is no modal preceding the perfect, then tense precedes the perfect and we may talk about present perfects and past perfects (Figure 2.23).

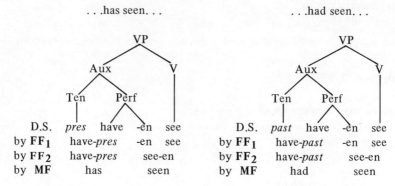

	. . .has seen. . .			. . .had seen. . .	
D.S.	*pres* have -en see		D.S.	*past* have -en see	
by FF_1	have-*pres* -en see		by FF_1	have-*past* -en see	
by FF_2	have-*pres* see-en		by FF_2	have-*past* see-en	
by **MF**	has seen		by **MF**	had seen	

Figure 2.23

In general, the perfect construction is not notoriously a source of learner problems, but it provides its share, mostly because so few other languages have a direct analog of the perfect. The French *passé composé* is superficially the same, *avoir* ('have') plus a past participle, but its use is more generally past, and it is most commonly translated into the English simple past.

The major hurdle for the learner of English may be summarized in the question: what's "present" about the present perfect? The usual answer is that the event is still "relevant" to the present, which just begs the question. A more concrete answer is that the event began in the past and is still true in the present, such that in sentences like *He has been here since Friday*, it is understood that he is still here now. It is customary to compare the present perfect with the simple past in sentences where this is the key difference, as in

6 a. He has been here for three days (and is still here).
   b. He was here for three days (some time ago).

However, this explanation does not account for cases where the event does not continue to the present and may be, in fact, somewhere in the remote past.

6 c. He has written to his mother.
   d. I have visited Paris.

In 6c and 6d, he cannot now be writing, and I can tell you that I am not now in Paris. With respect to time, the best that one can say is that the time is rather indefinite. It is not correct to say that the event may have occurred any time "up to the present," for in many cases it is very clear that the event either could not have occurred very recently (such as 6d above, if you know me), and in fact may have occurred eons ago. This use of the perfect might be called the "experiencial" perfect, for it reports experience rather than events. The question, *Have you ever...?*, means *Is it in your experience that you...?* The experiencial perfect has one rather unexpected restriction, however, that traps the unwary foreigner: in order to report the event as experience with the perfect, the event must still be possible. Thus, for example, 7a below is still possible (at the time of going to press) and therefore grammatical, while 7b is not.

7 a. Have you ever met President Ford?
  b. *Have you ever met President Kennedy?

In the case of 6b, the experience must be reported with the simple past, as in 6c,

7 c. Did you ever meet President Kennedy?

When someone says

7 d. I have written to my mother.

you may not know when he wrote, but you may fairly conclude that his mother is still alive.

Our grammar does not account for the grammaticality of 7a and the ungrammaticality of 7b above. It generates both without favor. The difference in meaning and usage involves presuppositions and, as was indicated at the outset, presuppositions do not play a role in the operations of syntax or even of competence; they are part of the larger performance model of which competence (and syntax) are also parts.

2.55 PROGRESSIVE

Prog → be + -ing

The progressive construction consists of the verbal *be* plus the present participle ending *-ing*. Like *-en* of the perfect, *-ing* precedes the verbal to which it will ultimately become attached, requiring a third version of the **Flip-flop** rule,

by **FF₃**   -ing + verbal ⇒ verbal-ing

(Figure 2.24).

Treatment of the progressive construction usually bogs down in discussions of which verbs can occur with the progressive and which cannot. Perhaps the most

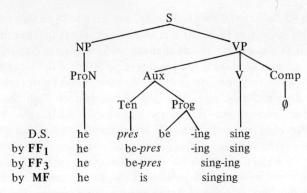

		Ten	Prog		
D.S.	he	*pres* be	-ing	sing	
by **FF**₁	he	be-*pres*	-ing	sing	
by **FF**₃	he	be-*pres*	sing-ing		
by **MF**	he	is	singing		

Figure 2.24 He is singing.

lucid discussion can be found in Lakoff (1966),[2] in which the claim is made that **Stative** verbs cannot occur in the progressive and that **Nonstative** verbs can. The problem remains, however, that we have no clear way of knowing which verbs are stative and which are not. Lakoff (1966:12) says that "in an overwhelming number of cases, **Stative** verbs. . .have the semantic property, **Nonactivity**, and **Nonstative** verbs. . .have the semantic property **Activity**." What is "activity"?

At the least, when someone deliberately, voluntarily, or knowingly engages in doing something, this is an activity. Compare, for example, sentences 8a and 8b:

8 a. I smell something sweet.
 b. I'm smelling the flower.

Sentence 8a involves an event that is largely involuntary: my nose happens to work properly and sweetness is in the air, so I cannot help but smell it. Sentence 8b, on the other hand, means something like "sniffing at" or placing the nose near and deliberately inhaling. Most of the senses are considered involuntary (or inactive, or stative), and many regard 8b as being rather unstylish or even ungrammatical. Some of the sense verbs have an active equivalent (Table 2.3); others, like *taste* and *feel*, can be used both ways.

Table 2.3

Stative	Active
see	look at
hear	listen to
smell	sniff at

The test of voluntariness does not give clear answers for verbs like *believe* and *understand* (the "mental" verbs). Since these verbs do not occur with the progressive, we assert that they are stative or inactive, despite the fact that some

---

[2] Other important references would be King (1970) and Scovel (1970).

voluntation is implied in sentences like *I do not choose to believe you*. Perhaps it is best simply to assert that "activity" must be external and observable to qualify.

The principle of voluntation makes sense only if the subject of the predicate is human (or animate) and is the agent, or causer, of the event. In sentence 9a,

9 a. I hear some music.

it may be argued that *I*, the subject, am not the agent of the event so much as an experiencer of it, equivalent to saying "hearing music is happening to me." However, the same relationship applies in sentence 9b,

9 b. I am bleeding.

that is, that *I* am the experiencer, not the causer of the bleeding. If 9b is not voluntative, how is it that it occurs with the progressive?

The difference between 9a and 9b lies in the fact of a change resulting in me in 9b (I have less blood than before) but not in 9a. In other words, if the event is not voluntative but creates a change in the state of the experiencer, the event is classed as an active event. A great many verbs in what used to be called the "middle voice"[3] occur in this category, frequently with inanimate subjects whose states are clearly changed:

10 a. The cup is cracking.
  b. The door is closing.
  c. The tree is bending.

Then, finally, there is a class of predicates that represent properties of their subjects; these are all stative, since their subjects neither cause the property nor are changed by it.

11 a. I weigh 160 pounds.
  b. The book costs $4.50.
  c. My cat is yellow.

As a special courtesy, the verb *have* (when it means "possess") is placed in this class.

12 a. I have three pencils.
  b. I'm having them over for dinner. (voluntative)

A summary of all this is given in Table 2.4.

Establishing (after a fashion) what verbs *may* occur in the progressive does not tell you when you want to use the progressive. In general, the progressive is most commonly used to establish events occurring "now"; however, this "now" may range from the fraction of time in which the speech occurs to a time span as broad as a century.

---

[3] "Halfway" between the active and passive voices—for example, *I broke the glass* (active); *The glass broke* (middle); *The glass was broken* (passive).

Table 2.4

	Active
Voluntary (subject is agent)	*break* (you're breaking my arm) *smell* (I'm smelling the stew) *jump, look at, hit*
Involuntary (subject is changed)	*break* (my arm is breaking) *bleed, die*
	Stative
Involuntary (subject is unchanged)	*smell* (I smell something nice) *see, hear*
Mental	*believe, understand*
Property of subject	*have* (I have a ball) *weigh, cost*

13 a. It's biting me at this moment!
   b. I'm taking French this year.
   c. More wars are taking place this century than ever before.

Notice that 13c does not require that a war be in progress at the time of speech; while the progressive will usually imply that the event is ongoing at the time of speech, if the event may be considered recurring or cyclical, then it need not be happening at the moment. In fact, one cannot be asleep when saying *I'm sleeping better these days*.

The past progressive is not usually considered a great problem, but it is characteristically misused by European learners (especially those from the Romance-speaking countries), who confuse it with their "imperfect" tense, a tense which expresses characteristic events in the past. In English, the past progressive is pretty well limited to cases in which an event is ongoing at a specific time in the past, whether explicit or understood. Very frequently, the time is itself set through the agency of a subordinate clause beginning with *when* or *while* (for example, *I was reading when the doorbell rang*). The difficulty is not easily resolved by practice with *when* clauses, however, since some *when* clauses do not adequately limit the time, but instead establish a duration in which characteristic action took place (for example, *I was reading a lot when I was young*).

Unfortunately, the past progressive is used to express characteristic events in the past, but only in very particular cases, almost always with a *by then* phrase (for example, *I was walking by the time I was six months old*).

2.56 THE FLIP-FLOP RULE

There have been three **Flip-flop** rules discussed in this chapter; these can be generalized into one rule, as in Lester (1971:71):

All three flip-flop rules attach the verb endings to the following verb. By establishing one symbol to stand for all three verb endings, we can collapse the three rules into one. The symbol used for this purpose is *Af*, which stands for *affix*. We can now write the flip-flop rule this way:

Let Af = Tense, *-en*, or *-ing*
Af⌢Verb ⇒ Verb⌢Af

In other words, the generalized **Flip-flop** rule is a composite of **FF₁**, **FF₂**, and **FF₃**. Since there seems to be no necessary ordering among the three **FF** rules, they may, for convenience, be thought of as occurring simultaneously. As soon as you have understood the separate **Flip-flop** rules, there is no reason why you cannot generalize them into one. The answer to sentence 1a in Exercise 2.56 treats the three rules separately, but in all other sentences the generalized **FF** rule is used.

The **FF** rule(s) is the last rule in the transformational component governing the derivation of individual sentences. It is followed either by appropriate phonological rules (in our treatment, the **Morphophonemic** rule, **MF**) or by a rule that incorporates the sentence into a larger sentence (taken up in Part 3). In other words, no other transformational rule may follow the **FF** rule.

Exercise 2.56

1. Draw trees for the following sentences:
   a. John has been seeing Mary. (How is *see* marked?)
   b. The dog was eating meat.
   c. He may have been telling a lie.
   d. He is interesting. (Be reasonable, now.)
   e. The stew smells funny.
   f. The man had been there.
2. Where might you introduce a *since. . .* or a *for. . .* phrase?
   a. I have lived here since 1948.
   b. That woman has been sitting there for three hours.
3. In sentence 1e above, how might you arrange things so that you can generate 1e and *I smell the stew*, but not *The stew smells the stew*. (That is, what features might be required?)

2.6 The Verb Phrase (V + Comp)

The second part of the phrase structure rule for verb phrases,

VP → Aux + *V* + *Comp*

raises an issue of considerable subtlety: what is a complement? Walsh and Walsh (1939:26) defines complements in the following way:

> A verb which requires a substantive [that is, a noun] or an adjective to complete its meaning is sometimes called incomplete, and the substantive or adjective added is called a *complement*.

Compare Lester's (1971:83) definition:

> A complement is anything following the main verb that is necessary to make the sentence grammatical in the intended sense.

The most important difference lies in the fact that while Walsh and Walsh limited complements to direct objects and adjectives, Lester opens the class of complements to include "anything" as long as it meets the stated requirements. Lester's definition also implies that complements may include complex sequences of words or phrases rather than simply a single NP or Adj.

Lester's definition leads to a simple test for complementhood. Given, for example, a verb followed by three phrases, X, Y, and Z, each phrase may be tested for complementhood in the following way:

1. Delete one phrase.
2. If the result is ungrammatical, then that phrase is part of the complement of V.
3. If the result is grammatical, but the meaning of the verb changes, then that phrase is part of the complement of V.

4. If the meaning of the verb does not change, then the phrase is not part of the complement of V.

Whichever of the phrases or combination of the phrases meets the above test will make up the total complement of the verb. For example, consider the sentence

I put *the box in the closet.*

The verb *put* is followed by two phrases, and we may test each phrase separately:

Deleting *the box* gives *I put in the closet*, which is ungrammatical, so *the box* is part of the complement of *put*.

Deleting *in the closet* gives *I put the box*, also ungrammatical, so *in the closet* is part of the complement of *put* as well, and the complement of *put* includes both phrases, *the box in the closest*. On the other hand, consider the sentence

I fried *an egg on the sidewalk.*

Deleting *an egg* gives *I fried on the sidewalk.* If this is grammatical, the meaning must be considered a metaphoric expression for being awfully hot, and not literally "frying." This constitutes a change in meaning, so *an egg* is part of the complement of *fry*.

Deleting *on the sidewalk* gives *I fried an egg*, which is grammatical and preserves the meaning of "fry." Thus *on the sidewalk* is not part of the complement of *fry*.

In other words, one cannot determine whether a verb has a complement just by looking at the structure of the sentence. Phrases which are part of the complement of one verb may not be part of the complement of another verb. Complements must be assessed, in fact, verb by verb.

There are two techniques for handling verb-complement relationships in the phrase structure. One technique is to classify the verbs according to the type of complement they take, making this classification part of the PS rule for the verb phrase. Such a system would appear something like

$$VP \rightarrow Aux + \begin{Bmatrix} V_1 + \emptyset \\ V_2 + NP \\ V_3 + NP + Loc \\ V_4 + NP + to\ NP \\ etc. \end{Bmatrix}$$

and in the lexicon the individual verb would be marked as being a member of a particular class of verbs. Since this system would engender a very cumbersome VP rule—there being a very large number of distinct complements—a modified form is frequently adopted, which is a carry-over from traditional days:

$$VP \rightarrow Aux + \begin{Bmatrix} V_{tr} + Comp_{tr} \\ V_{intr} + Comp_{intr} \\ Copula + Comp_{cop} \end{Bmatrix}$$

that is, where verbs are divided into three classes, transitive verbs, intransitive verbs, and copulas. Traditionally, transitive verbs were verbs that "took" a direct object. In TG terms, a transitive complement would include at least a NP directly after the verb. Any additions to such complements would have to be indicated in the lexical entry for the verb. Thus, for example, *put* would have the entry

$\text{put}[V_{tr}], [\text{Comp: } + \text{Loc}]$

indicating that a locative phrase would be added to the NP complement signaled by the transitive classification.

The other major technique for handling verb-complement relationships is not to classify verbs at all in the PS rule, but to load all the information concerning complement selection into the lexicon. This has the advantage of simplifying the PS rule to the original

$\text{VP} \rightarrow \text{Aux} + \text{V} + \text{Comp}$

without (as it turns out) really overcomplicating the lexical entry. *Put* comes out

$\text{put}[V], [\text{Comp: } \text{NP} + \text{Loc}]$

The latter technique, however, should not be used by people who are accustomed to thinking in terms of "transitive" and "intransitive" verbs. As long as the teacher's beliefs of English structure are not actually incompatible with TG formulations, he should stick to what he is most familiar with. For the remainder of this text, however, the latter technique will be used.

Regrettably, there are many cases where the test for complementhood does not give us clear results—or at any rate the results that we intuitively desire.

One such case involves, for example, the verb *read*, as in *I am reading a book*. If we delete *a book*, we get *I am reading*, which is unquestionably grammatical, and almost certainly unchanged with respect to the meaning of "read." This would seem to indicate that *a book* is not part of the complement of *read*, a conclusion that must give us some pause in our labors. Consulting Walsh and Walsh (1939:26), we find:

Note: When a verb that is generally transitive [that is, takes a direct object] is used without an object, some call it *absolute transitive* instead of intransitive.

An absolute transitive verb, then, is one that can take a deletable complement. This compromises the deletion test, and we must either account for it somehow or give up the notion of complements altogether.

The character of what Walsh and Walsh call "absolute transitive" verbs is such that all direct objects of a verb must share a specific characteristic implied by the verb. The verb *read*, for example, implies the printed word, and any explicit direct object must provide a locus for the printed word—a book, a gum wrapper, etc. The function of the direct object in such cases is to "narrow" in on the specific locus or form of the object in instances where greater detail is desired or necessary. Such direct objects are very nearly not complements in the spirit of the Walsh and Walsh or the Lester definitions—they are not necessary to "complete" the meaning of the verb so much as to give local specification to it. The relationship between *read* and *book* is hardly any different from that between *sit* and *chair*, since the noun in both cases just gives specific form to properties implied by the verb. The grammar of the relationship is different, of course, for *book* is a direct object to *read* and *chair* will be found in a prepositional phrase after *sit*. If the former is a complement, then is not also the latter? I see no way of differentiating between the two, and thus inevitably come upon the agonizing issue of exactly where you draw the line. If we accept the deletable prepositional phrase in sentence 1a below as a complement, then surely we must consider accepting that in 1b as a complement also.

> 1 a. I sat *in the chair*.
>   b. I fried an egg *on the sidewalk*.

There is no real resolution to this problem. The individual teacher must make his own arbitrary decisions as to what kinds of deletable complements (if any) he will accept. The line in this text will be drawn at the noun phrase. Deletable direct objects will be considered complements, but no other sort of deletable phrase will be considered a complement. I wish to emphasize that this is an arbitrary decision, motivated by personal background and convenience, and indefensible in terms of linguistic theory.

If the problem of deletable complements can be resolved by an arbitrary decision, the following problem cannot. Consider *he went to the store*. Is *to the store* complementary to *go*? Deleting *to the store* gives the grammatical sentence *he went*, but it may be claimed that the meaning of the verb *go* has really changed, that one would use different synonyms in place of *go*.

> 2 a. He went to the store.
>   b. He went.

Substituting *betook himself* for *went*:

> 2 c. He betook himself to the store.
>   d. ?He betook himself.

Substituting *departed* for *went*:

> 2 e. ?He departed for the store.
>   f. He departed.

The question marks on 2d and 2e are intended to query the adequacy of their synonymity with 2b and 2a, respectively, not their grammaticality. The test seems to indicate that *go* in 2a implies a change in location, while in 2b it implies a departure. That there is a meaningful relationship between the two is unquestionable; the question is whether the difference between the two is sufficient to claim that *to the store* qualifies for complementhood. Here again, the teacher must decide for himself. However, because the issue of sufficiency of meaning difference really does involve a true continuum, it is not likely that any individual will be able to express explicitly the point at which he draws the line. I, myself, as represented in this text, resolve the question verb by verb, as represented by verbs discussed in succeeding parts of this text. Thus, for example, I consider *to the store* the complement of *go* in 3a, but not of *walk* in 3b. (I do not require, nor even expect individual readers to share in all these decisions.)

> 3 a. I went to the store.
>   b. I walked to the store.

In my lexicon, the two verbs appear as follows:

    go:[V],[Comp: Loc]
    walk:[V],[Comp: ∅]

Does it matter? It may. For example, if the organization of an English text is going to reflect grammatical principles at all, it is most likely going to be organized according to grammatical classifications. Traditionally, this meant that transitive verbs would be introduced in one location and intransitives in another. If one is going to be more "modern" about it, surely one major distinction will be between verbs that take complements and verbs that do not, and it would do no one any good if the text included a lesson on "fuzzy" verbs the author could not decide about.

With the above dissatisfactions being understood, the more common complements of English include the following:

1. Comp → ∅ or no complement, as with *ring* (*the bell rang*), *go*,[1] *walk*;
2. Comp → (NP), the "absolute transitive," as with *read, write, eat*;
3. Comp → NP, a direct object, as with *hit, fry, see*;
4. Comp → Loc, as with *go*;[1]
5. Comp → Adj, as with *be, smell, seem*;
6. Comp → NP + to NP (+*Animate*), that is, taking a direct and an indirect object, the latter being animate, as with *give, send*;
7. Comp → NP + Loc, or a direct object and a location, as with *put, keep*;
8. Comp → NP + NP, or a direct object and a "predicate objective" (or "objective complement") (cf. Walsh and Walsh, 1972:16), as with *name, choose, appoint*.

There are a great many others as well. Each verb would be listed in the lexicon, with the complement type that it takes indicated as a syntactic feature.[1]

The last of the complement types, NP + NP, as in *We elected him president*, should not be confused with the structurally similar *I gave him an apple*. A moment's reflection should convince you that in the latter *him* represents an indirect object, and that the sentence is a paraphrase of *I gave an apple to him*.

---

[1] Some verbs would be listed twice. For example, the verb *go* might have two entries, with different indicated features for complements, along with different indicated synonyms, etc.

What we have is a rearranging transformation that converts complements of the NP_1 + to NP_2 type to the NP_2 NP_1 order; this transformation may be called the **Object switch (OS)** rule. For an example, see Figure 2.25.

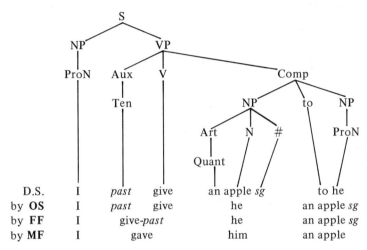

D.S.	I	*past*	give	an apple *sg*	to he
by **OS**	I	*past*	give	he	an apple *sg*
by **FF**	I	give-*past*		he	an apple *sg*
by **MF**	I	gave		him	an apple

Figure 2.25 I gave him an apple.

The question can be raised as to why we claim that NP_1 + to NP_2 is the "deep structure" order, and that the NP_2 NP_1 order is transformationally derived from it, rather than the other way around. In other words, why not begin with NP_2 + NP_1 as the deep structure expression, deriving NP_1 to NP_2 transformationally? There are two reasons:

1. When the direct object (NP_1) is a pronoun, the NP_2 NP_1 order is awkward (as far as I am concerned, ungrammatical):

*I gave John it.
*I gave the boy it.

while the NP_1 to NP_2 order is fine:

I gave it to John.
I gave it to the boy.

No corresponding pronominalization of the indirect object obtains preference for either order:

I gave him the ball.
I gave the ball to him.

2. There are some verbs, such as *explain*, which regularly take NP_1 to NP_2 complements, but not NP_2 NP_1:

I explained the answer to John.
*I explained John the answer.

(There is only one verb, *ask*, and then only with the direct object *question*, which observes the opposite preference:

    I asked him a question.
    *I asked a question to him.)

It is apparent that there are a number of restrictions on NP_2 NP_1, and, in general, few restrictions on NP_1 to NP_2. In such circumstances, the less restricted formulation will be claimed to be the deep structure form.

Exercise 2.6

Draw deep structure trees for and derive the following sentences:
1. Mary sent her mother a letter.
2. I put the ball in the closet.
3. They named Masters chief.
4. He looks strange.
5. I kept it under a handkerchief.

2.7   Adverbial Phrases

If a phrase following a verb is determined not to be part of the complement of that verb, then what is it? It most commonly will be adjudged an Adverbial Phrase (AP), attached either to the verb phrase or, in some cases, to the sentence node itself, as indicated in Figure 2.26. Calling these adverb phrases VAP and SAP, respectively, we shall briefly examine them, beginning with the latter.

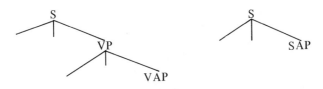

Figure 2.26

2.71 SENTENCE ADVERBS

Sentence adverbs are accounted for by adding an optional element (SAP) to the sentence rule:

$$S \rightarrow NP + VP + (SAP)$$

The most commonly met sentence adverb is the one which expresses some comment by the speaker on the events related in his sentence. For example,

1 a. Happily, the Dodgers lost.
   b. The Dodgers lost happily.

Sentence 1a is a common enough sentence, in which, by use of the SAP *happily*, the speaker makes it clear that he is happy at the event of the Dodgers' losing. Sentence 1b, on the other hand, would probably be considered somewhat anomalous, unless circumstances can be imagined in which the Dodgers would be happy at losing. Thus 1b does not involve a SAP, but a VAP.

SAPs have the characteristic of being quite movable, although usually separated from the sentence by commas or pauses (to indicate, presumably, that the SAP is not an integral part of the sentence). Thus,

1 a. Happily, the Dodgers lost.
   c The Dodgers, happily, lost.
   d. The Dodgers lost, happily.

In consequence, the deep structure SAP may be located anywhere.

2.72 VERB PHRASE ADVERB PHRASES

Most other adverbial phrases fall under the heading of VAPs, and a VP may string together quite a few. The major headings are Manner, Time, and Location adverbs, normally in that order:

He woke up groggily at three o'clock in the toolshed.
     (Manner)   (Time)   (Location)

The VP rule may be expressed as

VP → Aux + V + Comp + (VAP)
VAP → (Manner) + (Time) + (Loc)

Manner adverbs are usually single-word adverbs, and include almost all the adverbs ending in *-ly*.

There are several single-word Time adverbs: *yesterday, then, now*, etc., but most temporal VAPs are prepositional phrases.

With but a few exceptions (*here, there*, etc.), locational VAPs are prepositional phrases.

Both Time and Loc VAPs may have nested adverbial structures, usually in the order of increasing specificity (*downtown at the library, yesterday at three o'clock*). Both are, consequently, recursive in nature. In fact, adverbs are, in general, a great deal more complicated than their rather subordinate position in English syntax gives them a right to be. In order to expose and understand their syntactic structure fully, more time and place would be required than is desirable, at least in a text of this sort. Readers interested in tackling adverbs in greater detail should probably begin by reading Kuroda (1970) and Lakoff (1965).

For the above reason, this text will adopt henceforth the practice of denoting the deep structures of all adverb phrases by the use of the triangle that TG grammarians use to short circuit some of the burdensome work that fully detailed trees would require of them. For example, rather than writing out the fully detailed tree for *her daughter's husband*, especially if his point does not concern that structure, the linguist is free to draw it as in Figure 2.27.

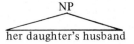

NP

her daughter's husband

Figure 2.27

You are cordially invited to follow suit with any phrase in addition to the adverb phrase, but only after you have learned to draw out the proper tree without hesitation.

Some of the sharper-witted among you may have noticed the curious absence of Frequency (Freq) adverbs from the list above. This absence results from a peculiar difficulty that they provide the grammarian. Frequency adverbs find themselves most commonly before the verb, but after any auxiliary. This suggests that they should appear, in the deep structure of the sentence, between the Aux and the V. This, however, will not work for the simple reason that the **Flip-flop** rule cannot cause tense to leap over intervening elements to get to the verb, as would be required in the example in Figure 2.28. At this point, we

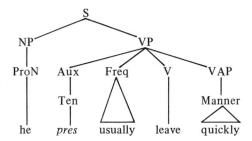

Figure 2.28 He usually leaves quickly.

would like to apply the **FF** rule but find that what follows tense is an element (*usually*) that cannot "take" tense. In Section 3.12, we shall see what happens in such cases; suffice it to say for the moment that tense cannot attach to the verb. Thus Frequency cannot occupy that particular position in the deep structure. Wherever else we put it, we will be obliged to move it into preverbal position by means of a transformational rule, a classic "fudge" rule if there ever was one. However, the adverbs generally are highly mobile, and may be found just about anywhere in a sentence, so adverb-moving transformations are going to be required in any case.

Freq, then, may be "built into" the VAP rule,

VAP → (Freq) + (Manner) + (Time) + (Loc)

or it may be introduced in the VP rule (see Exercise 3 at the end of this section),

VP → (Freq) + Aux + V + Comp + (VAP)

Exercise 2.7

1. Which of the prepositional phrases in the sentences below are adverbs, and which are part of the complement? Draw trees accordingly and derive.
   a. He placed the book under the chair.
   b. He's digging with a shovel.
   c. He bought a house for his mother.
   d. He handed the cat to me.
   e. He usually hid the bottle in the desk.
2. Draw trees for and derive the following sentences.
   a. Unfortunately, he got drunk.
   b. We leave tomorrow at three o'clock.
   c. He jumped awkwardly over the log.
3. Consider the two rules suggested above for introducing Freq into sentences. Discuss their merits.

2.8 Two-Word Verbs

There is, finally, a special type of verb construction, variously called "two-word verbs" and "compound verbs," that is a ready source of foreign learner confusion. Most of the problem comes from the idiomaticity of these phrases, or the fact that their composite meanings often have little or nothing to do with the lexical meanings of the verb and preposition. For example, the meaning of *bring up* (as in *they brought up their children well*) has no discernible relationship to the meanings of either *bring* or *up*. This suggests that each two-word verb deserves its own lexical entry, separate from the one for the verb alone.

The idiomaticity of these phrases makes them a natural source for new combinations, with the result that many two-word verbs have a slangy or mod sense to them, as exemplified by the expression (current in the 1960s) "Tune in, turn on, drop out." This has resulted in a two-way tug of war in many cases, between foreign students, who have—for some reason—a fascination for American slang and idiom, and the more traditional teacher, who deplores such phrases, preferring to teach the dictum, "never use two words when one will do," by which two-word verbs are generally disposed of.

The problem is complicated by a peculiarity of two-word verb syntax: some of the phrases are "separable," others are not. A separable two-word verb is one whose preposition may move to a position after the complement: for example, *call up*.

1 a. I called up the girl.
   b. I called the girl up.

If the complement is a pronoun, the separation must occur:

1 c. I called her up.
   d. *I called up her.

The problem is further complicated by the fact that separability is arbitrary and totally unpredictable. The verb *call on*, for example, is nonseparable, whether or not a pronoun is the complement.

1 e. I called on the girl.
   f. I called on her.
   g. *I called the girl on.
   h. *I called her on.

Verbs that are accompanied by two prepositions are normally nonseparable— *put up with, stand up to*, etc.—although their meanings are no less unpredictable. *Put up with* doesn't even have a meaningful relationship to *put up*! There being no way to bring such verbs cohesively to the learner, probably the best that can be done is to recommend that he obtain a dictionary of two-word verbs for home study. One possibility would be Crowell's (1957) *A Glossary of Phrases with Prepositions*.

The transformational structure of two-word verbs offers no particular difficulties. For example, see Figure 2.29. The only care, as usual, is that you must be sure that your deep structure actually does involve a two-word verb. *I called up the stairs*, for example, does not. The movement of the preposition can be discussed in terms of a **Preposition Switch (PS)** rule, which can operate only on two-word verbs that are marked [Separable].

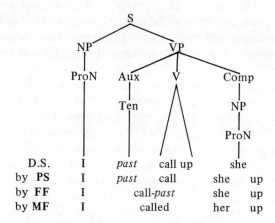

D.S.	I	*past* call up	she	
by **PS**	I	*past* call	she	up
by **FF**	I	call-*past*	she	up
by **MF**	I	called	her	up

Figure 2.29 I called her up.

Exercise 2.8

Draw trees for and derive the following sentences:
1. He turned the radio on.
2. I made off with it.
3. She took off her gloves.
4. We called for her the next day.

2.9 Summary: Phrase Structure Grammar (Two)

1 S → NP + VP + (SAP)   (in fact, SAP may occur anywhere)

2 NP → $\left\{\begin{array}{l} \text{Art + N + \#} \\ \text{Name} \\ \text{ProN} \end{array}\right\}$

3 Art → (Quant) + (Det)

4 Det → $\left\{\begin{array}{l} \text{NP + 's} \\ \text{Lex[Det]} \end{array}\right\}$

5 VP → Aux + V + Comp + (VAP)

6 Aux → $\left\{\begin{array}{l} \text{Mod} \\ \text{Ten} \end{array}\right\}$ + (Perf) + (Prog)

7 Comp → $\left\{\begin{array}{l} \text{(NP)} \\ \text{NP} \\ \text{NP + to NP} \\ \text{NP + Loc} \\ \text{NP + NP} \\ \emptyset \\ \text{Loc} \\ \text{Adj} \\ \text{etc.} \end{array}\right\}$

8 VAP → (Freq) + (Manner) + (Time) + (Loc)

9 Loc → $\left\{\begin{array}{l} \text{L-Adv} \\ \text{PP} \end{array}\right\}$ (that is, a prepositional phrase)

10 PP → P + NP

11 Ten → {*present, past*}

12 # → {*singular, plural*}

13 Perf → have + -en

14 Prog → be + -ing

15 N → Lex[N]
16 V → Lex[V]
17 Adj → Lex[Adj]
18 Quant → Lex[Quant]
19 Mod → Lex[Mod]
20 Name → Lex[Name]
21 ProN → Lex[ProN]
22 P → Lex[P]

Several transformational rules were discussed:

1. The **Flip-Flop** rule (**FF**), which attaches a verb affix to the verb following the affix. This rule cannot apply if the word following the affix cannot "take" the affix.
2. The **Morphophonemic** rule (**MF**), which is not really appropriate to the rules of syntax, but which otherwise converts surface strings into more-or-less recognizable form. **MF** accounts for all final word forms in one fell swoop.
3. The **Object Switch** rule (**OS**), which converts an NP$_1$ + to NP$_2$ type of complement to NP$_2$ NP$_1$ form, so that the indirect object precedes the direct object.
4. The **Preposition Switch** (**PS**) rule, which moves the preposition of a separable two-word verb to a position after the object.

Exercise 2.9

1. Draw deep structure trees for and derive:
   a. Two of his brother's friends stomped him.
   b. He must have gone there yesterday.
   c. He's been feeling better since Monday.
   d. He keeps dingbats in the cellar.
   e. He's very interesting. (Whence *very*?)
   f. She may be studying in the library.
   g. Horribly, he ran a dog down with his car.

2. Are sentences 2a and 2b paraphrases? How do you know?

   2 a. I gave Mary a book.
      b. I gave a book to Mary

3. Consider the verb *answer*; what is "odd" about it? What kinds of problems do you think foreign learners might have with it?
4. Your students have made the following mistakes. First, determine exactly what the mistake consists of. Then explain the mistake to the student, but without using trees or terminology that he does not understand. You may assume that he at least understands the words "noun," "verb," and so on. Your explanation should, of course, be consistent with your analysis of the mistake.

a. I gave it Mary.
b. I saw cow for the first time.
c. Some of friends visited me.
d. I'm having worked here since two.
e. One of the boys are here.

References: Part 2

Chomsky, Noam. 1957. *Syntactic Structures*. The Hague: Mouton.

Chomsky, Noam. 1965. *Aspects of the Theory of Syntax*. Cambridge, Mass.: M.I.T. Press.

Crowell, Thomas. 1957. *A Glossary of Phrases with Prepositions*. Englewood Cliffs, N.J.: Prentice-Hall.

DiPietro, Robert. 1972. *Language Structures in Contrast*. Rowley, Mass.: Newbury House.

Gleason, H. A. 1965. *Linguistics and English Grammar*. New York: Holt, Rinehart & Winston.

Hockett, Charles. 1958. *A Course in Modern Linguistics*. New York: Macmillan.

Jacobs, R., and P. Rosenbaum. 1967. *Grammar 1, Grammar 2, Grammar 3, Grammar 4*. Boston: Ginn.

King, Harold. 1970. "Action and aspect in English verb expressions." *Language Learning*, XX.

Kuroda, S.-Y. 1970. "Some Remarks on English Manner Adverbials," R. Jakobson and S. Kawamoto, eds., *Studies in General and Oriental Linguistics*. Tokyo: TEC Co., Ltd.

Lakoff, George. 1965. "On the Nature of Syntactic Irregularity," The Computation Laboratory, Harvard University, Report No. NSF-16.

Lakoff, George. 1966. "Stative verbs and adjectives in English" (mimeo.).

Lester, Mark. 1971. *Introductory Transformational Grammar of English*. New York: Hold, Rinehart & Winston.

Scovel, Thomas. 1970. "Getting tense in English: A linguistics for our time," *TESOL Quarterly*, V/4.

Traugott, Elizabeth C. 1972. *The History of English Syntax*. New York: Holt, Rinehart & Winston.

Walsh, J. M., and A. K. Walsh. 1939, 1972 (6th ed.). *Plain English Handbook*. New York: McCormick-Mathers.

Whitman, R. L. 1974. "Teaching article in English." *TESOL Quarterly*, VIII/3.

3

TRANSFORMATIONS

3.0   Introduction

The transformational component serves to relate deep and surface structures. A transformation is not supposed to change meanings; meanings are, after a fashion, embodied by the deep structures generated by the phrase structure component. It will develop that this restriction will require us to alter and refine yet again our phrase structure grammar.

In relating deep and surface structures, transformations do the following things: they may shift elements around into a new order, they may add elements, they may delete elements, and they may do a combination of these three. For example, the **Object switch** rule involves both a rearrangement of the order of the two noun phrases and a deletion of the preposition *to*. The kinds of transformations that will be discussed in the first chapters of this part are those which apply to "simple" deep structures—those generated by the PS grammar as we know it this far, more or less. The transformations discussed thus far—the **OS** rule, the **Preposition switch** rule, **FF**, and **MF**—all belong in this category. In succeeding chapters of this part, the transformations will involve more complex deep structures, those having embedded or conjoined sentences.

Before continuing, one thing should be made perfectly clear: as implied in our discussion in Part 1 of the role of the transformational component, all deep structures must "go through" the transformational cycle. With many sentences, however, the only operations involved in this part of the derivation are the **FF** and **MF** rules (this is especially true of most simple active sentences, sometimes leading the unwary to conclude that deep structures are themselves statements).

3.1 Two New Constituents

Questions and negatives are obviously different in nature from statements and positives. The issue is whether this difference means that there is a difference in meaning such that different deep structures are required. Many linguists (Lester, 1971, Chomsky, 1965, and others) feel that they do not, but that questions and negatives are grammatical paraphrases of each other and of their equivalent statements. Other linguists (Jacobs and Rosenbaum, 1967, and others) feel that there is an important difference in meaning and that the deep structures should differ accordingly. In this text we will follow the latter view and thus depart (even if in a minor way) from the Standard Theory.

Jacobs and Rosenbaum (1967:57) suggest that the first phrase structure rule should be

S → (Question) + (Negative) + NP + VP

such that the deep structure of questions will include the constituent *Question* and that of negative sentences will include *Negative*. In all cases, the NP + VP part will remain unchanged; the only difference between this formulation and the Standard (Chomskyan) Theory formulation lies in the presence and function of these two constituents.

The constituent *Question* represents your knowledge that your sentence is going to be a question. In addition to representing this knowledge, it serves as an explicit deep structure source or motivation for the "question" transformation. As much as possible, we want to account for why transformational events occur in the history of a sentence. One way of accounting for them is to posit "triggers" for them—bits of the deep structure that automatically call them into play. In some cases, the trigger may be an explicit constituent like *Question*, representing some aspect of the speaker's knowledge. In other cases, the trigger may be the presence of a certain word or class of words in the deep structure string (such as any of the *wh-* words, as we shall see). The trigger may be found in the syntactic features of a word; the feature [Separable] in the verb *call up*, for example, motivates the optional **PS** transformation (cf. pp. 101-102). The **FF** transformation may be said to be triggered by the determination that there's nothing else left to do, and is, so to speak, the exit sign for the transformational cycle as it applies to any one sentence (remembering that **MF** doesn't really belong in the transformational component). There are, nevertheless, a few operations that appear to be entirely unmotivated, that strike unpredictably like lightning. The **OS** rule is one of these. No one can begin to explain why English feels it necessary to maintain both *John gave the apple to Mary* and *John gave Mary the apple*, but maintain it she does, with such ramifications elsewhere in the grammar that the rule cannot just be ignored. There are, happily, not very many of these wholly unmotivated transformations.

3.11 SIMPLE QUESTIONS

The presence of *Question* in the deep structure triggers a number of transformational operations in the syntactic and phonological components of the grammar. Syntactically speaking, the operation can be summarized as the **Question switch (QS)** rule, which inverts the subject and the first verbal element of a sentence. In formal terms,

QS: NP Tense (v) $\Rightarrow$ Tense (v) NP

where v is defined to be the *first* verbal auxiliary following the tense, or the verb *be*. The parentheses around v in the rule means that if there is a v, both tense and the v will invert with the noun phrase; otherwise only Tense will invert with the NP. (If v is a modal auxiliary, of course, then there is no tense.)

A few examples should give you a better idea of how **QS** works. For your convenience, v has been underlined in each of the deep structures.

1 a.   John <u>can</u> go
     by **QS**   can John go
   b.   John <u>must</u> have -en go
     by **QS**   must John have -en go
   c.   John *past* <u>have</u> -en be -ing go
     by **QS**   *past* have John -en be -ing go
   d.   John *pres* <u>be</u> happy
     by **QS**   *pres* be John happy
   e.   John *past* go
     by **QS**   *past* John go

Note especially that in 1c, v included only *have*, and not *-en*, even though *have -en* is derived together through the Perf rule. In terms of the definition of v, *-en* has no status, and is thus left behind. There is an enormously practical reason for leaving *-en* behind; look what happens if it isn't:

D.S.   John *past* have -en be -ing go
by QS   *past* have -en John be -ing go
by FF   have-*past* -en John be go-ing
by MF   had   -en John be going

In other words, *-en* has to be left where it was, next to *be*, so that it can combine with *be* in the course of the FF rule. As has been stated before, the FF rule cannot make affixes jump over intervening words to "get to" their verbs.

3.12 WHERE DOES <u>DO</u> COME FROM?

What happens when an affix winds up out of touch with a verb through natural causes? When an affix (tense in particular) is followed by an element that cannot absorb it, the FF rule is necessarily aborted. This serves as a trigger for the *Do* insertion (DI) rule, which calmly inserts *do* into a position after the lonely tense, so that the FF rule will thenceforth work. In formal terms:

DI   Tense X ⇒ Tense do X

where X is any element that cannot "take" tense. Because the DI rule is triggered by an inability to apply the FF rule, it always immediately precedes FF in the transformational cycle.

Let us look back at example 1c above

D.S.   John   *past* go
by QS   *past*   John go
by FF   !@#%&$!
by DI   *past* do John go
by FF   do-*past* John go
by MF   did   John go

A complete example may suffice to demonstrate simple questions (see Figure 3.1). You will notice, I am sure, that in this deep structure I have begun to make

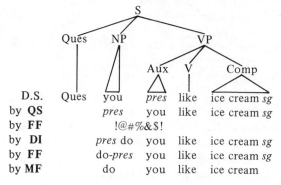

Figure 3.1 Do you like ice cream?

liberal use of the triangular shortcut. You may also wonder what happened to *Ques*. In effect, *Ques* was "used up" by the application of the **QS** rule. This cuteness is principally a device to remind you of the relationship between the constituent and the operation.

Exercise 3.12

1. Draw deep structure trees for and derive the sentences below:
   a. Is he helping you?
   b. Has John given the book to Mary?
   c. Were the girls at school?
   d. Did you fix my bicycle?
   e. Will you read it to me?
2. How would you account for the distinction between the use of *have* in British and American dialects?
   a. (Amer.) Do you have a match?
   b. (Brit.) Have you a match?

3.13   WHO, WHAT, WHERE, WHEN, WHY, HOW

There is, of course, another type of question, the *wh-* question, representing all questions beginning with *who, what, which, how, where, when,* or *why*. Such questions also have the *Question* constituent in their deep structures, triggering the same **QS** rule as before. If this represents the question aspect of *wh-* questions, what is the function of the *wh-* word?

Regular questions ask about the truth of the proposition of the sentence (that is, the NP VP part). The question, *Did John see Mary?*, asks, in effect, "Is it true that John saw Mary?" With *wh-* questions, on the other hand, the truth of the proposition is taken for granted, and the question involves, instead, a search for particular information about the proposition. In other words, when you ask *Who did John see?*, you take it for granted that John saw someone and are requesting the identity of that someone.

It is not easy to find a completely satisfactory means for representing this demand for particular information in the deep structure. For better or worse, we will adopt the following logic: almost any constituent in the sentence may be unknown and queried. The speaker knows which constituent he is seeking information about and generates a *wh-* form directly under that constituent. We could, if we wanted, represent this more abstractly, by having a *?* represent the unknown. There would then be a transformational rule converting *?* to *wh-* at some appropriate moment. As long as you know what *wh-* represents in the grammar, however, there seems to be very little lost in adopting the convenience of generating *wh-* directly.

Let us say that you know John saw someone, and wish to determine the identity of that someone (Figure 3.2). This requires that *who* be listed in the lexicon with the syntactic feature [ProN]. The *wh-* words appear in the lexicon with the markings:

who [ProN] (+*Human*)
what [ProN] (not +*Human*)
what [Det]
which [Det]
where [Loc]
when [Time]
why [Cause]
how [Manner]
how many[1] [Quant]

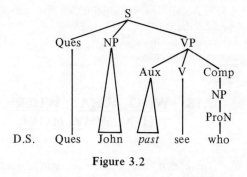

Figure 3.2

All these possibilities can be seen in the tree in Figure 3.3.

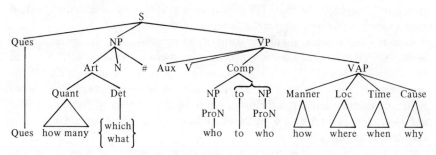

Figure 3.3

---

[1] The *how* in *how many* deserves additional comment. It appears to be the same *how* that occurs with adjectives like *how old*, etc., which is itself quantificational in nature, prompting as it does numerical answers (such as "five years old"). This is quite different from the Manner *how*. It may be that quantificational *how* should be derived under the constituent Intensifier, which is responsible for adverbs like *very*, etc.

The *Question* constituent continues to do its thing, triggering the **QS** rule. The presence of a *wh-* word triggers a self-moving operation by which the *wh-* word is moved to the front of the sentence. This operation is called the *Wh*-**fronting** (**WF**) rule. For example, see Figure 3.4.

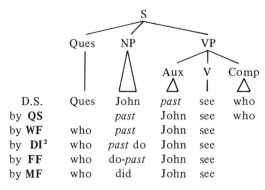

				Aux	V	Comp
D.S.	Ques	John	*past*	see	who	
by **QS**			*past*	John	see	who
by **WF**	who		*past*	John	see	
by **DI**[2]	who		*past* do	John	see	
by **FF**	who		do-*past*	John	see	
by **MF**	who		did	John	see	

Figure 3.4 Who did John see?

In most cases it doesn't seem to matter whether you do **QS** before **WF** or vice versa, but in one case it does: when the *wh-* form lies in subject position. We shall do the example shown in Figure 3.5 twice, with **QS** first then with **WF** first, to see what happens. In this example, with **WF** preceding **QS**, we get the wrong surface structure. With **QS** preceding **WF**, on the other hand, we have a peculiar situation where the two rules cancel each other out. What kind of rule system is that?

Speaking as a linguist, it is preferable to have all questions undergo the same operations, and those are the breaks if some operations tend to undo what others have done.

Speaking as an English teacher, on the other hand, I can see that it might needlessly confuse an English learner to insist that both operations are really there, cancelling each other out.

Recognizing the difficulties attendant on attempting to deal with both the *Who did Mary see?* and *Who saw Mary?* types of *wh-* question, Lado and Fries (1957) (followed, perforce, by Krohn, 1971) decided to separate them, introducing the former in Lesson IV and the latter in Lesson IX. The purpose of this separation was, presumably, to defer the student's observation of a syntactic nonconformity, thus lessening potential confusion.

It is especially interesting to take a look at Krohn's treatment of the two types. The regular *wh-* question (that is, where *wh-* is in nonsubject position) is treated in a way that reflects transformational assumptions (1971:30):

---

[2] It is assumed as of now that you understand what triggers the DI rule, and that it is therefore no longer necessary to go through the !@#$%! step.

STATEMENT   John likes coffee.
YES/NO QUESTIONS: Does John like coffee?

                                                  Does John like coffee? ⟵(what)
Wh- QUESTIONS: What does John like?

The circle-and-arrow business is Krohn's way of presenting a movement transformation. In Chapter 9, where he discusses the "S pattern" (where the *wh-* word is in subject position), he presents it as follows (p. 94):

STATEMENT   John sees Mary.
YES/NO QUESTION: Does John see Mary?
Wh- QUESTION: Who sees Mary?
   (S Pattern)

The message we get from this is that when the *wh-* word is in subject position, no rules "apply," nothing happens, etc. Well, perhaps this is the only reasonable

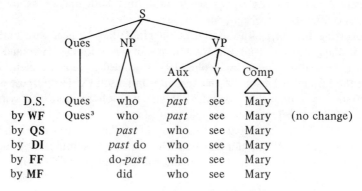

(QS THEN WF)

D.S.	Ques	who	*past*	see	Mary
by **QS**		*past*	who	see	Mary
by **WF**	who	*past*		see	Mary
by **FF**	who	see-*past*		Mary
by **MF**	who	saw		Mary

(WF THEN QS)

D.S.	Ques	who	*past*	see	Mary	
by **WF**	Ques[3]	who	*past*	see	Mary	(no change)
by **QS**		*past*	who	see	Mary	
by **DI**		*past* do	who	see	Mary	
by **FF**		do-*past*	who	see	Mary	
by **MF**		did	who	see	Mary	

Figure 3.5 Who saw Mary?

[3]Constituents like Ques and Neg are not part of the sentence as far as **WF** is concerned.

way to handle it. One might otherwise expect students to attempt *Does who see Mary?* or *Who does see Mary?* in trying to make it hang together.

When the *wh-* word derives under the article, the **WF** rule brings forward not only the *wh-* word, but the entire NP (Figure 3.6).

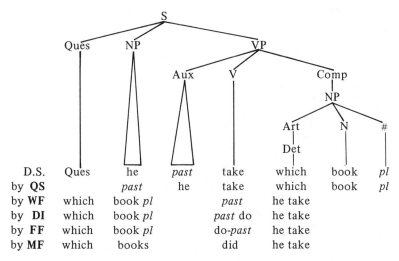

D.S.	Ques	he	*past*	take	which	book	*pl*
by **QS**		*past*	he	take	which	book	*pl*
by **WF**	which	book *pl*		*past*	he take		
by **DI**	which	book *pl*		*past* do	he take		
by **FF**	which	book *pl*		do-*past*	he take		
by **MF**	which	books		did	he take		

Figure 3.6 Which books did he take?

When the *wh-* word is derived within a prepositional phrase, there is apparently an option as to whether the preposition will also be moved to the front or not. Thus both *What did he put the book in?* and *In what did he put the book?* are derived from the same deep structure, differing in their derivations only by the degree to which **WF** is applied to the prepositional phrase

Exercise 3.13

1. Draw deep structure trees for and derive the sentences below:
   a. What did the man give to you?
   b. Who has read the book?
   c. When did he leave?
   d. How many children were here?
   e. Whose friend are you?
2. Consider the nature of the "tag" question (for example, *John left already, didn't he?*). How would you formulate the rule or rules that are involved? For further background, see Langendoen (1970:chap. 2).

3.14 NEGATIVES

The constituent *Negative* triggers the *Not*-insertion (NI) operation, which inserts *not* directly after v (the same v as in the QS rule, p. 111) or, if there isn't any v, directly after tense. Formally:

NI   Tense (v) ⇒ Tense (v) not

For example: (v underlined for your convenience)

2 a.   John <u>will</u> go
   by **NI**   John will not go
   b.   John <u>must</u> have -en go
   by **NI**   John must not have -en go
   c.   John *pres* <u>have</u> -en be -ing go
   by **NI**   John *pres* have not -en be -ing go
   d.   John *pres* <u>be</u> happy
   by **NI**   John *pres* be not happy
   e.   John *past* go
   by **NI**   John *past* not go

Almost exactly the same observations may be made of these examples that were made of the examples of the QS rule. Note in particular that in 2e, *not* comes directly after tense, making it necessary to apply the DI rule.

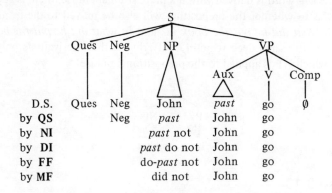

	Ques	Neg	NP	Aux	V	Comp
D.S.	Ques	Neg	John	*past*	go	∅
by QS		Neg	*past*	John	go	
by NI			*past* not	John	go	
by DI			*past* do not	John	go	
by FF			do-*past* not	John	go	
by MF			did not	John	go	

(and with **NI** before **QS**):

	Ques	Neg				
D.S.	Ques	Neg	John	*past*	go	
by NI	Ques		John	*past* not	go	
by QS			*past*	John not	go	
by DI			*past* do	John not	go	
by FF			do-*past*	John not	go	
by MF			did	John not	go	

Figure 3.7   Didn't John go?

2 e.   John *past* go
   by **NI**   John *past* not go
   by **DI**   John *past* do not go
   by **FF**   John do-*past* not go
   by **MF**   John   did   not go

When both *Question* and *Negative* occur in the deep structure of a sentence, **QS** comes first. The example in Figure 3.7 shows why. In the latter derivation, where **NI** preceded **QS**, the resulting sentence, *Did John not go?*, is not itself ungrammatical, but it has a hectoring flavor, a school-masterish style that is quite different from the more usual *Didn't John go?* It might be said that the less usual formulation reflects an emphasis on the negative, and that this emphasis somehow leads the speaker to apply **NI** first.

Negation offers much more to the connoisseur than has been suggested in this text, providing several exquisite syntactic puzzles. See, for example, Klima (1964) and Jackendoff (1969).

Exercise 3.14

Draw deep structure trees for and derive the sentences below.
1. He can't help you.
2. He didn't see them.
3. Won't John be angry?
4. Doesn't Mary look lovely?

3.15 PASSIVE

Let me quote first from Robin Lakoff (1969:129):

Little is known about the exact form of most transformational rules. Among the most mysterious are the favorites of writers of textbooks, like passivization and relativization, about which practically nothing positive is known. . . . Passivization is a rather touchy subject now among most transformational grammarians who are aware of recent thought in the field. It is embarrassing because, until a few years ago, it was one of the best understood rules in the grammar.

Poor old passive; what's wrong with it? While we know exactly what passive sentences look like on the surface, we are somewhat stuck for an adequate explanation of it. We can, of course, make up a rule, and the first formulation [in Chomsky's *Syntactic Structures* (1957:43)] was

Pass NP_1 Aux V NP_2 $\Rightarrow$ NP_2 Aux be -en V by NP_1

This is fine, except for one thing: why? What motivates it? The lack of a trigger for the passive reduces the formulation to a purely *ad hoc* rule that tells you nothing you didn't know already. Moreover, it would be insufficient to establish a constituent *Passive* (like *Question* and *Negative*) as a trigger, for this constituent would itself be *ad hoc*, responding only to the stated need for a triggering device. *Question* represents the speaker's knowledge that he is going to ask a question, and it is reasonably well understood why he would want to. Saying that *Passive* represents the knowledge on the part of the speaker that his sentence will take passive form is insufficient because we don't have any inkling why he should want to do that.

Chomsky (1965:130) suggested a means for motivating the passive, involving what would be (in this grammar) a triggering constituent *Passive* located under a Manner node. *John was seen by Mary* would have had the deep structure in Figure 3.8. One reason Chomsky advanced for deriving *Passive* under Manner was that it had been observed that verbs which could participate in passive constructions were those verbs which could take a manner adverb.[4] Chomsky's suggestion has been abandoned, however, partly because of the oddity of the implied claim that *by Mary* was some kind of adverb of manner, and partly because *by Passive* left no room for a real manner adverb that might legitimately occur.

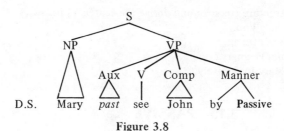

Figure 3.8

There are, moreover, other problems. Most passives, for example, occur without any *by* phrase at all. These are called truncated passives,[5] and their relative commonality is presumably responsible for the fact that the Michigan materials hardly touch on the "full" passive at all. While Krohn (1971:209) mentions the expression of agents in passive sentences in a note to the learner, he includes no exercises for the learner to practice the full passive in. Amazingly, Lado and Fries (1957) don't even go this far; the learner simply never learns about *by* phrases in the passive.

The older TG approach was to claim that the truncated passive was derived from the full passive through an operation that deleted the *by* phrase.

---

[4] Such as *furtively*: one can say *John called Mary furtively*, and *call* can participate in passive constructions, such as *Mary was called*. One cannot say, however, **The book cost \$5 furtively*, nor can *cost* participate in passive constructions: **\$5 was cost by the book*.

[5] Truncated passive: *John was seen*; full passive: *John was seen by Mary*. *Mary* is the agent of the sentence.

D.S.	John *past* see Mary
by **Pass**	Mary *past* be -en see by John
by **Trunc**	Mary *past* be -en see

There are two arguments that serve to throw doubt on this claim, however.

The first is that generative grammarians are hesitant to involve deletion operations unless the deleted material is "understood" or recoverable in the finished sentence. An example of a recoverable deletion might be the subject *you* in imperative sentences. Traditionalists always said that there was an "understood *you*" as the subject of imperatives, and TG grammarians agree. *You* is in the deep structure, and is transformationally deleted on route to the surface. However, you cannot recover *Mary* once you delete her from *John was seen by Mary*. The sentence *John was seen* gives you no more reason to think that the agent is *Mary* than any other person or animal.

The second objection derives from the assumption that sentence complexity is related to transformational complexity, and that a sentence that involves one more operation in its derivation than another sentence is more complex than that other. (This hypothesis is the basis of the Derivational Theory of Complexity, cf. Fodor and Garrett, 1967). The deep structures of sentences 3a and 3b are identical,

3 a. John was seen by Mary.
  b. John was seen.

and the derivations of the two sentences are also identical except that 3b involves a deletion transformation that 3a does not. The derivational theory of complexity would then claim that 3b is thereby more complex than 3a, a conclusion that is properly greeted with considerable suspicion.

3.16 THE PASSIVE OPERATION

Since I cannot suggest a formulation for the passive that reflects, for me, a genuine understanding of the phenomenon, I will instead suggest a practical *ad hoc* formulation. This formulation involves a formal constituent *Passive* and the presence in the deep structure of the passive auxiliary verb structure *be -en*. The Aux rule must be revised:

$$\text{Aux} \rightarrow \begin{Bmatrix} \text{Mod} \\ \text{Ten} \end{Bmatrix} + (\text{Perf}) + (\text{Prog}) + (\text{Passive})$$

and

Passive $\rightarrow$ be + -en

The **Passive** operation itself is:

Pass $NP_1 \ldots$ be -en V $NP_2 \ldots \Rightarrow NP_2 \ldots$ be -en V $\ldots$ (by NP_1)

(the dots represent other things that may be in the deep structure.) The crucial difference between earlier formulations of the passive and the one above lies in the optionality of the expression of the agent *by* phrase. This means that no deletion operation need be involved. The truncated passive is one in which the optional agent was not realized. Relative complexity is no longer a problem in so far as it may be argued that an unrealized option is simpler than a realized option, and thus the truncate simpler than the full passive. An example of the **Passive** operation at work (both options) is given in Figure 3.9. Note that the deep structure of both sentences is the same.

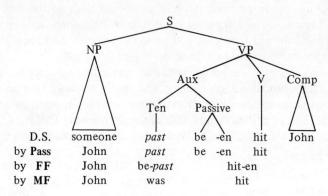

Figure 3.9A John was hit.

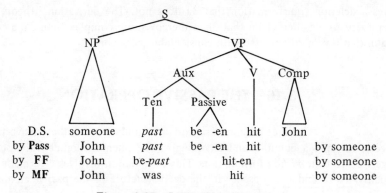

Figure 3.9B John was hit by someone.

It has long been recognized that passives can occur with the indirect object surfacing as the passive subject, as well as the direct object. One can have both *The apple was given to John* and *John was given the apple*. I have known teachers who led their students in drills of the type:

Make the two passives for *Mary gave the apple to John.*
    (Response):   a.   The apple was given to John by Mary.
                 b.   John was given the apple by Mary.

This presupposes that the **Passive** rule can select either of the noun phrases of the complement type NP to NP, but in fact it can't. It is an extremely common foreign student mistake to say things like **John was explained the answer*, which results naturally from the above incorrect presupposition. After all, if 4a leads to 4b, why doesn't 4c lead to 4d?

4 a. Mary gave the apple to John.
  b. John was given the apple.
  c. Mary explained the answer to John.
  d. *John was explained the answer.

The point is that 4a doesn't lead directly to 4b. There is an intervening step, the **Object switch** rule, which establishes the indirect object noun phrase as the NP immediately following the verb, as shown in Figure 3.10. The **Passive** operation does *not* work on direct objects or indirect objects so much as on whatever NP happens to come after the verb. The problem with 4d is that the **OS** rule does not work with verbs like *explain*, so the indirect object (*John*) cannot become the NP following the verb, and therefore cannot be moved to subject position by the **Passive** rule. In other words, **John was explained the answer* is ungrammatical to exactly the same degree and for exactly the same reasons as **They explained John the answer*.

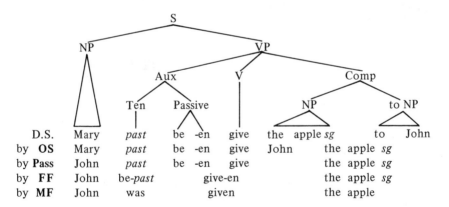

Figure 3.10 John was given the apple.

A deep structure containing both *Passive* and *Question* or *Passive* and *Negative* will process *Passive* first, although this is principally for convenience's sake in terms of formally locating the subject position before you start moving it around (see Figure 3.11).

It ought to be mentioned—no more than that—that there is an odd constraint on the auxiliary: if both Prog and Passive are involved, then neither Modal nor Perfect may intrude. Thus, **He must be being shot* and **He has been being talked about* are both ungrammatical. Who knows why, though?

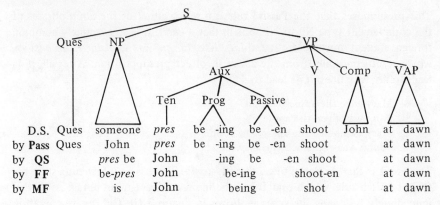

			Ten	Prog	Passive				
D.S.	Ques	someone	*pres*	be -ing	be -en	shoot	John	at	dawn
by **Pass**	Ques	John	*pres*	be -ing	be -en	shoot		at	dawn
by **QS**		*pres* be	John	-ing	be	-en shoot		at	dawn
by **FF**		be-*pres*	John	be-ing		shoot-en		at	dawn
by **MF**		is	John	being		shot		at	dawn

Figure 3.11 Is John being shot at dawn?

Exercise 3.16

Draw trees for and derive the sentences below.
1. She has been given the prize.
2. Wasn't he seen there?
3. Hasn't that been corrected?
4. Shouldn't it be destroyed immediately?
5. The book must have been taken by Peter.

3.17 WHY DO WE BOTHER WITH A PASSIVE, ANYWAY?

An awkward question, and one that may even creep up on you unexpectedly. About the only answer that can be related to demonstrable phenomena is that we use the passive when we wish not to mention the agent of the sentence. We might come to such a desire for a variety of reasons:

1. We don't know very much about the agent. Rather than saying *Someone or something hit John*, we might prefer *John was hit*.

2. We feel that the agent is irrelevant information.

3. We prefer to withhold information about the agent for reasons of security, fear, vindictiveness, or any of a hundred squalid human weaknesses. Rather than "tattle" on a friend, we may prefer to report his deeds in the passive.

4. There is a stylistic dictum (in scholarly writing, at least) that says that writers should avoid "I." Since reported research tends to be about "my" ideas and deeds, there is a heavy use of passives in scientific writing. Rather than say "I then decanted the ipso into the facto," we say "The ipso was then decanted into the facto."

Fine and good, and it can be shown that a huge majority of passive sentences occur without an agent *by* phrase. If it is indeed the purpose of the passive to get rid of the deep structure agent, then one can get some idea as to why the passive takes the form it does. If you wish to get rid of a sentence subject in English, you must replace it with something, for English does have a pressing requirement for a grammatical subject. As it happens, the passive seizes upon the very first free noun phrase that it comes upon, and advances it, willy-nilly, to subject position. In this understanding, the NP after the verb is the helpless victim of a speaker's determination to do away with his original subject.

However, we all know that passives may and do occur with their agent retained. In such cases, we can hardly claim that the purpose of the passive was to get rid of that same agent. The traditional claim is that the purpose of the passive is to "topicalize" or "focus greater attention on" the new subject. It has been suggested that the subject of a sentence has the spotlight, and thus should be considered the most important NP in a sentence. When we wish to focus more attention on a direct or an indirect object, what could be more natural than to place it in subject position? At this point the old subject becomes the helpless victim of the passive, and his likely disappearance of casual import at the most.

A third view takes the position that passives are invoked mostly for stylistic purposes, to relieve the tedium of endless active sentences. In this case, the movement and disappearance of noun phrases is independent of their respective merits entirely.

The teacher, then, is faced with a choice. He can teach the passive from any of the above three points of view, but will probably be unconvincing no matter how he does it. To avoid the issue of explanation entirely (the "cop-out" approach) is probably awfully appealing, under the circumstances, but it works only so long as your students permit it.

That the passive is somewhat unusually rich as a source for speculative treatment may be reflected in the work of Agnes Niyekawa-Howard (1968), who theorizes that (in Japanese, at any rate) the passive is culturally tied to a deeply rooted tendency to avoid personal responsibility for events, which are perceived as having been caused by fate (or whatever) rather than by the individual involved in them. To say, for example, "I broke the glass" is to accept direct responsibility for the event. To a people who think of such things as just "happening," there may be a tendency to report the incident in some other way: "The glass broke," "The glass broke on me," "The glass was broken," etc.

3.18 SUMMARY: BASIC TRANSFORMATIONS

The following phrase structure rules were modified or added:

S → (Question) + (Negative) + NP + VP + (SAP)

Aux → $\left\{ \begin{matrix} \text{Modal} \\ \text{Tense} \end{matrix} \right\}$ + (Perf) + (Prog) + (Passive)

Passive → be + -en

The *wh-* words were added to the lexicon, with the following syntactic features:

who [ProN] (+*Human*)
what [ProN] (not +*Human*)
what [Det]
which [Det]
how many [Quant]
how [Manner]
where [Loc]
when [Time]
why [Cause]

The three new constituents, Question, Negative, and Passive, triggered their respective transformations:

1. Question: the **Question switch (QS)** rule, which interchanged the subject and some part of the auxiliary.

QS   NP Tense (v) $\Rightarrow$ Tense (v) NP

(where v represents the first verbal element in the auxiliary or *be*).

2. Negative: the *Not* **insertion (NI)** rule, which adds *not* into the auxiliary string.

NI   Tense (v) $\Rightarrow$ Tense (v) not

3. Passive: the **Passive (Pass)** rule, which advances the NP after the verb to subject position, demoting the original subject entirely out of the sentence or into a *by* phrase.

Pass NP_1...be -en V NP_2... $\Rightarrow NP_2$...be -en V. . . (by NP_1)

Two other rules were introduced and discussed:

4. The *Do* **insertion (DI)** rule, which applies whenever the **FF** rule is blocked, and which inserts *do* immediately after Tense.

DI   Tense X $\Rightarrow$ Tense do X

(where X is any element that cannot "take" tense).

5. The *Wh*-**fronting (WF)** rule, triggered by the presence of a *wh-* word and moving it to the front of the sentence. When the *wh-* appears anywhere in the article, **WF** will move the entire NP. When the *wh-* appears in a prepositional phrase, **WF** will optionally move the preposition.

Exercise 3.18

1. Draw trees for and derive the sentences below.
   a. Why shouldn't he be forgiven?
   b. Aren't they always being seen there?
   c. Wasn't Mary given those books?
   d. How many men were sent that letter?
   e. Who did they speak to?

2. Another operation which might have been included in this section is the **Imperative**. Assuming that you would use the constituent *Imperative* somewhat like *Question* and *Negative*, how would you fit it into the grammar as developed up to this point? For background, review Bolinger (1967).

3. Attempt to apply the **Passive** transformation to *The slipper fit Cinderella*. Why doesn't it work?

3.2 Sentences Embedded Within Sentences

The recursivity of language was discussed in the first chapter. Until now, we have seen only one aspect of recursivity, in the reintroduction of NP at various points in the phrase structure grammar (first in the S rule, and then recursively in the Comp, PP, and Det rules). The full flower of recursivity will be seen, however, in the reintroduction of sentence nodes within the body of the "parent" sentence, each new S being subject to the full body of phrase structure rules and most—if not all—of the transformational rules as well. These reintroduced S nodes are "embedded" sentences or "lower" sentences.

Lest all this send a chill down your back, let me reassure you that if you have gotten this far you should have no trouble assimilating the linguistic technology of embedding.

There are three archetypes of embedded S:

1. Modifying S, which is introduced by the rule

$$NP \rightarrow NP + S$$

in which the S modifies the NP before it;

2. Nominalized S, which is introduced by the rule

$$NP \rightarrow S$$

in which case the sentence acts as a noun phrase in the main sentence;

3. Conjoined S, which is introduced by the rule

$$S \rightarrow S + S$$

where the two sentences may be independent clauses, or one may be dependent on the other.

3.21 MODIFICATION

According to the Standard Theory, all instances of NP modification derive from sentences embedded after the modified NP. The same general idea accounts for all the NPs below,

1 a. The man who never was. . .
   b. The lady from Chicago. . .
   c. The frozen pizza. . .
   d. The red balloon. . .

without fear or favor. We shall develop a somewhat different assessment of modification as it applies to adjectives, but only after the Standard Theory approach has been discussed.

3.22 RELATIVE CLAUSES

We all know what relative clauses are. However, those of us who were raised on a diet of traditional grammar were taught that there were two kinds of relative clauses: "restricted" and "unrestricted," differing in whether they were written without commas or with, respectively.

Restricted: The man who is smiling is my brother.
Unrestricted: The man, who is smiling, is my brother.

The former provides essential information for the identification of the man being discussed. Without the relative clause, the audience could not be sure which man is my brother. The latter, unrestricted relative clause, on the other hand, provides extra and inessential information. The audience already knows which man is being discussed, and the clause is thrown in like the thirteenth doughnut in a baker's dozen. As will be pointed out later, the unrestricted relative clause is not really a modifier at all, but derives from a conjoined subordinate sentence. Therefore, in this section our comments refer to the restricted relative clause alone.

The deep structure of our example is shown in Figure 3.12. This deep

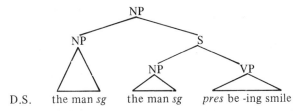

Figure 3.12   The man who is smiling. . . .

structure illustrates one essential aspect of all modifiers: the modifying sentence must contain somewhere within itself the NP that the sentence is modifying.

The first operation, triggered by the fact of the repeated NP (they don't have to be right next to each other as in the example in Figure 3.12), involves the replacement of the second NP with an appropriate relative pronoun. This is **Whir**, or **Wh- replacement**.

	D.S.	the man *sg*	the man *sg*	*pres* be -ing smile
	by **Whir**	the man *sg*	who	*pres* be -ing smile

Whir will replace the NP with one of three *wh-* words: *who* if the NP is (+*Human*), *which* otherwise, or *that*, which can be used for any NP.[1]

I hasten to add *whom* to the list of relatives that **Whir** will generate. Poor old *whom*, she's been greatly neglected in recent years, much to the chagrin—if not outrage—of the more traditionally minded English teacher. The argument is (and has been since early structuralist days) that nobody ever says "whom" except in formal circumstances, so why teach it in a class of spoken English? Krohn (1971:181) may be typical:

> *Whom* can be used in Pattern O only. [Pattern O = when *who* is not the subject.] *Whom* is used in formal writing and speeches.

Krohn never illustrates the use of *whom* in a sentence. What has happened to *whom* is not so much a case of deliberate corruption as a case of benign neglect.

The second major operation is the movement of the relative word to the front of its sentence, or to a position directly after the NP it modifies. This is the **Wh-movement (Whim) rule**.[2] For example, see Figure 3.13. The modified NP itself takes part in a sentence, of course (Figure 3.14).

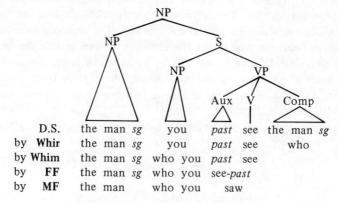

	D.S.	the man *sg*	you	*past* see the man *sg*
	by **Whir**	the man *sg*	you	*past* see who
	by **Whim**	the man *sg*	who you	*past* see
	by **FF**	the man *sg*	who you	see-*past*
	by **MF**	the man	who you	saw

Figure 3.13 The man who you saw. . . .

[1] Some linguists prefer to handle *that* as a sort of degeneration of *who* and *which*. In our terms, they would say that **Whir** introduces *who* and *which*, either of which may be replaced by *that* by a second transformational rule.

[2] There are considerable similarities between **WF** and **Whim**. It will turn out, however, that there are reasons to keep them distinct from each other.

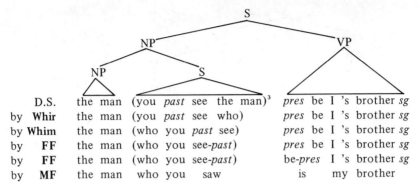

D.S.	the man	(you *past* see the man)[3]	*pres* be I 's brother *sg*
by **Whir**	the man	(you *past* see who)	*pres* be I 's brother *sg*
by **Whim**	the man	(who you *past* see)	*pres* be I 's brother *sg*
by **FF**	the man	(who you see-*past*)	*pres* be I 's brother *sg*
by **FF**	the man	(who you see-*past*)	be-*pres* I 's brother *sg*
by **MF**	the man	who you saw	is my brother

Figure 3.14 The man who you saw is my brother.

Two **Flip-flops**? Right. A **FF** rule is applied to an individual sentence. As a rule of thumb, there will usually be as many instances of **FF** as there are sentence nodes. Note in particular that I completed all operations on the lower sentence before I moved on to the higher sentence. This is another general procedural rule: begin at the lowest level, completing all operations before moving up to the next higher level.

A more complex example, shown in Figure 3.15, can illustrate the procedure. At this point it might be useful to review a rule of thumb about testing the correctness of deep structures of complex sentences. The nouns and verbs of a D.S. must, when read in sequence from left to right, agree in sense with the meaning of the sentence being analyzed. Thus, in assessing the adequacy of the D.S. in Figure 3.15, we would read *the cow bit the man, someone saw the man*, which agrees with the sense of the sentence in question.

If the rule says that all operations on the lower sentence must be completed before moving on to the next, why is there no **MF** operation for the lower sentence in Figure 3.15? As a matter of fact, if you want to apply **MF** at that point you may. In the example above, I was simply taking the opportunity to remind you that **MF** is not, strictly speaking, a proper transformational rule, and thus is not subject to rules about procedures.

Why did the application of **Passive** in the main sentence move both the NP and its modifying sentence? The real answer, of course, is that it had to in order to get to the right answer. The TG answer is that the relative clause is actually part of the NP that is moved.

How, finally, do we account for relative clauses which don't have a relative pronoun? Everyone knows that nonsubject relative pronouns can be deleted, and

---

[3] The parentheses are for convenience, to keep track of the boundaries of the lower modifying sentence.

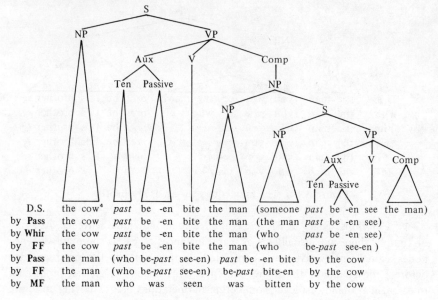

D.S.	the cow[4]	*past*	be -en	bite	the man	(someone *past* be -en see the man)		
by **Pass**	the cow	*past*	be -en	bite	the man	(the man *past* be -en see)		
by **Whir**	the cow	*past*	be -en	bite	the man	(who *past* be -en see)		
by **FF**	the cow	*past*	be -en	bite	the man	(who be-*past* see-en)		
by **Pass**	the man	(who be-*past*	see-en)	*past* be -en bite	by the cow			
by **FF**	the man	(who be-*past*	see-en)	be-*past* bite-en	by the cow			
by **MF**	the man	who	was	seen	was	bitten	by the cow	

Figure 3.15　The man that was seen was bitten by the cow.

deletions are part and parcel of TG grammar. So we have an optional **Wh-deletion (Whiddle)** rule (Figure 3.16). (Note that the relative pronoun so deleted is "recoverable"; cf. Section 3.15.)

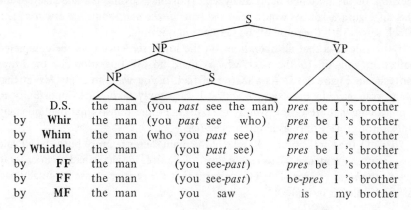

D.S.	the man	(you *past* see the man)	*pres* be I 's brother
by **Whir**	the man	(you *past* see who)	*pres* be I 's brother
by **Whim**	the man	(who you *past* see)	*pres* be I 's brother
by **Whiddle**	the man	(you *past* see)	*pres* be I 's brother
by **FF**	the man	(you see-*past*)	*pres* be I 's brother
by **FF**	the man	(you see-*past*)	be-*pres* I 's brother
by **MF**	the man	you saw	is my brother

Figure 3.16　The man you saw is my brother.

As with the **WF** rule, if the *wh-* word lies within the article, the entire NP is moved by **Whim**; if the *wh-* word lies within a prepositional phrase, the preposition may or may not be moved (Figure 3.17).

---

[4]In the interests of space, most *sg* notations will henceforth be left out of the deep structure.

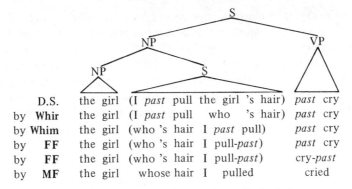

D.S.	the girl	(I	*past*	pull	the girl	's hair)		*past*	cry
by **Whir**	the girl	(I	*past*	pull	who	's hair)		*past*	cry
by **Whim**	the girl	(who	's hair	I	*past*	pull)		*past*	cry
by **FF**	the girl	(who	's hair	I	pull-*past*)			*past*	cry
by **FF**	the girl	(who	's hair	I	pull-*past*)			cry-*past*	
by **MF**	the girl		whose hair	I	pulled			cried	

Figure 3.17   The girl whose hair I pulled cried.

Exercise 3.22

1. Draw trees for and derive the sentences below.
    a. The dog that bit me was examined.
    b. The student who didn't pass the exam failed.
    c. The girl I bought the ring for returned it.
    d. Wasn't the girl who didn't come your sister?
    e. The girl who was given an F didn't graduate.
2. Show how the sentence, *Someone examined the dog that I was bitten by,* demonstrates that the **Passive** must come before **Whim.**
3. There are several alternatives to the given **Whiddle** formulation for getting rid of the relative pronoun. Some of them are even more efficient. See if you can come up with one.

3.23   WHIZ

In this section, the major rule introduced is the **Wh-** and *is* deletion (**Whiz**) rule, a massive deletion rule that optionally eliminates the sequence *wh-* Tense *be* from the relative clause. In all of the following post-NP modifiers, for instance, you can insert "who is" after *the man* without changing the meaning.

2 a. The man smiling is my brother.
    b. The man from Chicago is a cousin of mine.
    c. The man to be shot at dawn is my sister's husband.
    d. The man seated over there is Uncle Joseph.
    e. The man being investigated by the police is my no-good son.

Each of the examples, then, underwent **Whiz** at some point. No one has the remotest explanation for **Whiz**; why it happens in English at all is just one of those oddities that bedevil the English teacher.

From the examples above, it may also be seen that **Whiz** makes no distinction between the various sources of *be*, operating happily on copula, progressive, and passive *be*'s alike.

Nor does it matter to **Whiz** what the tense is. You can insert the adjective "late" before brother, cousin, etc., without altering the grammaticality of the sentences. Thus each of the examples above is actually ambiguous with respect to tense, although the pressure of the present tense in the main sentence makes the ambiguity difficult to perceive in some cases. An example might make this clearer—see Figure 3.18.

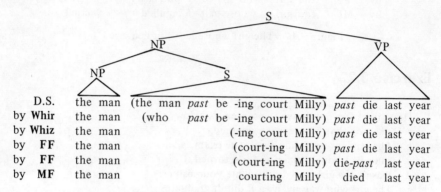

D.S.	the man	(the man	*past*	be	-ing	court	Milly)	*past* die	last year
by **Whir**	the man	(who	*past*	be	-ing	court	Milly)	*past* die	last year
by **Whiz**	the man				(-ing	court	Milly)	*past* die	last year
by **FF**	the man				(court-ing		Milly)	*past* die	last year
by **FF**	the man				(court-ing		Milly)	die-*past*	last year
by **MF**	the man				courting		Milly	died	last year

Figure 3.18 The man courting Milly died last year.

Whiz accounts for virtually every post-noun phrasal modifier. The only such modifier that it does not generate is the modifier that begins with *of*:

A friend of my uncle's
The top of the table
To the left of the tree
A discussion of the topic
A man of faith
The University of Hawaii
A meeting of minds
A touch of madness
    etc.

Most of these discernibly do not come from sentences with *be*. We cannot say, for example, **A friend is of my uncle's*, or **The top is of the table*, etc., which suggests rather strongly that these phrases do not come to us via **Whir** and **Whiz**. There has never been a really plausible accounting for the *NP of NP* construction, at least not in terms of a transformational derivation of the NP-plus-modifier sort.

The problem is that there is just no consistent semantic relationship that holds between the two NPs in *NP of NP*. Our ability to interpret the proper relationship depends almost entirely on our knowledge of the kinds of relationships that may obtain between them. Interpretations of specific cases thus turn out to be just a wee bit *ad hoc*, as do equivalent suggestions for deep structure sources. Probably the most accurate statement that can be made is that *of* is a generalized linking device for pairs of NPs that have some sort of relationship to each other.

Exercise 3.23

1. Draw trees for and derive the sentences below.
   a. The lady walking her dog is not a lady.
   b. The boy at the door is a Boy Scout.
   c. The theory proposed by Chomsky was revolutionary.
2. Discuss the meaning of each of the following phrases, as if to a foreign student.
   a. the pocket of my jacket
   b. his box of crackers
   c. a suggestion of some importance
   d. the destruction of the temple
   e. a teacher of Spanish extraction (not a dentist, thank you)

3.24   ADJECTIVES: STANDARD THEORY

Modifiers before the noun are mostly adjectives and participles. Because I cannot bring myself to believe in the Standard Theory approach to adjectives, I shall follow the Chomskyan adjective with an alternative formulation.

The Standard Theory maintains that adjectives, like any other modifier, begin life in sentences after the noun. A general rule states that whenever **Whiz** leaves a single word after the noun, that word should be moved about to a position before the noun. I call this rule the **Unicorn** rule, after a bit of folk knowledge, to wit: if an animal has a single horn on its nose, the horn is moved up to its forehead. Now it is true that the rule does not seem to apply to one-horned rhinoceroses, but then **Unicorn** has its exceptions, too, for example, *the man smiling is my brother* and *that man there is my father*.

At any rate, Figure 3.19 shows how it works. Note that **Unicorn** places the modifier directly before the noun, not before the NP.

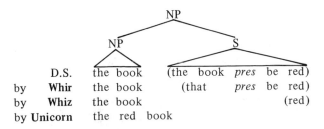

Figure 3.19   The red book....

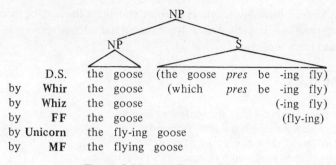

		D.S.	the	goose	(the	goose	*pres*	be	-ing	fly)
by	Whir		the	goose	(which		*pres*	be	-ing	fly)
by	Whiz		the	goose					(-ing	fly)
by	FF		the	goose					(fly-ing)	
by	Unicorn		the	fly-ing	goose					
by	MF		the	flying	goose					

Figure 3.20 The flying goose....

With a participle, see Figure 3.20. Oh, dear. **Unicorn** comes after **FF** (otherwise we run afoul of the requirement that **Unicorn** works on single words only). Come to think of it, however, maybe this is as it should be. **Unicorn**, after all, really has nothing to do with the structure of the lower S, but functions instead to integrate the lower S into the higher sentence. We shall find other operations of this nature and they, too, will come after **FF**.

It frequently happens that a noun may be modified by two adjectives. This can be accounted for by adding another S to the NP rule, gaining

NP → NP + (S) + (S)

(see Figure 3.21). As a matter of fact, there can be theoretically any number of Ss after the NP. Moreover, there is no need to deal with each of the Ss in the same way. One might be an adjective, and another a relative clause (Figure 3.22).

		D.S.	the	book	(the	book	*pres*	be	big)	(the	book	*pres*	be	red)
by	Whir		the	book	(that		*pres*	be	big)	(the	book	*pres*	be	red)
by	Whiz		the	book				(big)		(the	book	*pres*	be	red)
by	Unicorn		the	big	book					(the	book	*pres*	be	red)
by	Whir		the	big	book					(which		*pres*	be	red)
by	Whiz		the	big	book								(red)	
by	Unicorn		the	big	red	book								

Figure 3.21 The big red book....

		D.S.	the	book	(the	book	*pres*	be	big)	(the	book	*pres*	be	on	the	table)
by	Whir		the	book	(which		*pres*	be	big)	(the	book	*pres*	be	on	the	table)
by	Whiz		the	book				(big)		(the	book	*pres*	be	on	the	table)
by	Unicorn		the	big	book					(the	book	*pres*	be	on	the	table)
by	Whir		the	big	book					(that		*pres*	be	on	the	table)
by	FF		the	big	book					(that		be-*pres*		on	the	table)
by	MF		the	big	book					that		is		on	the	table

Figure 3.22 The big book that is on the table....

You will probably have noticed that conditions were ripe for an application of **Whiz** in the second modifier, too, which would have led to *the big book on the table*. **Whiz**, however, is optional.

3.25 ADJECTIVES: NONSTANDARD THEORY

Not everyone likes the Standard Theory of adjective derivations. Many of the objections are personal and intuitive. For example, the Standard Theory requires that the two sentences

3 a. The man smiling is Chomsky.
  b. The smiling man is Chomsky.

be paraphrases, and many people feel that they are not, somehow, the same.

Another objection involves the derivational theory of complexity (see the discussion on the passive, p. 000), which suggests that the relative clause form of a modifier is far simpler than any other form (since other forms inevitably involve more rules), so that 3c is thereby simpler than 3d.

3 c. the book that is red . . .
  d. the red book . . .

The one greatest objection is strictly subjective, and that is that no matter how well it works out mechanically, it is very difficult to believe that adjectives *really* start out life in sentences following the noun.

In the Nonstandard Theory of adjectives, they begin life in the deep structure in front of the nouns they modify. In other words, the relevant phrase structure rule would be

NP → Art + (Adj) + (Adj) . . . (Adj) + N + #

where enough room is left for as many adjectives as we might possibly want (seldom more than two, in practice). Who could possibly object to this formulation?

TG grammarians rejected the formulation very early on, on the basis of the fact that they felt that participles had to be related to verbs in sentences (either progressive or passive). They claimed that one had to account for the *smiling man* and *the frozen fish* as deriving from deep structures which also underlay *the man is smiling* and *(someone) froze the fish*. Specifically, they said that 4a and 4b were paraphrases, as were 4c and 4d:

4 a. the smiling man . . .
  b. the man who is smiling . . .
  c. the frozen fish . . .
  d. the fish that someone froze . . .

The Nonstandard Theory denies the paraphrasehood of the above pairs (we can't have our cake and eat it too). There is, of course, an obvious relationship between the *smiling* of 4a and the verb *smile* of 4b. The Nonstandard Theory claims that the relationship is not transformational, however, but lexical. The participle *smiling* would be listed in the lexicon as being an adjective, but also as having been derived from the verb *smile*. Thus, while 4a and 4b are very similar in their meanings because of the lexical relationships involved, they are not paraphrases in the TG sense. The Nonstandard deep structure of *the frozen fish*, then, is as shown in Figure 3.23.

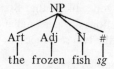

Figure 3.23

If participles can be adjectives, this means that a sentence like *The fish was frozen* is really ambiguous, having the two deep structures shown in Figure 3.24. The difference in meaning would presumably relate to the difference between a stative adjective and an active verbal process, or the difference between the state of being frozen and the process of being frozen.

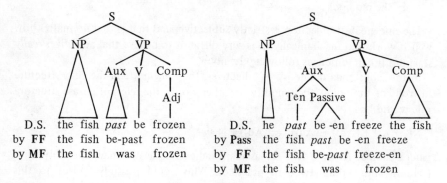

Figure 3.24

What's sauce for the goose is sauce for the gander, unfortunately, so it should equally turn out that *The man is smiling* is ambiguous. As yet, I have been unable to convince anyone even to consider the possibility. So be it. The Standard Theory is unreasonable, and the Nonstandard Theory has bugs.

In such circumstances, there is a perfectly natural reaction on the part of a great many English teachers, summarized in the phrase, "a plague on both your houses." This is a pity, for it is the English teacher who provides the majority of the insights and observations that underlie advances in English linguistics. It is a sometime joke that linguistics should be considered a branch of language teaching, but there is much to be said for the idea.

3.26 ADJECTIVE ORDERING

One of the most interesting phenomena of English is the fact of adjective ordering before nouns. Other languages don't seem to have such ordering, so there is no reason to think that it is "natural," yet we all manage to come to agreement about it without any training and with hardly any inkling that there is, in fact, an order to adjectives.

If we include everything in the NP before the noun, we have articles, adjectives, and nouns, in that order.

Art   Adj   Noun

My father's new terry-cloth robe

The field of adjectives is itself divided into several ordered classes: numbers, comparatives, subjective, objective, and derived adjectives, in that order.

There are two kinds of numbers, ordinal (*first, second*, etc.) and cardinal (*one, two*, etc.), in that order—for example:

5 a. the first two books on the right
   b. ?the two first books on the right

Comparative adjectives include the "comparative" (*-er*) and "superlative" (*-est*) forms of adjectives.

Subjective adjectives are those for which there are no specific standards, such as *pretty, odd*, and *incredible*.

Objective adjectives are associated with standards. There are, moreover, two kinds of objective adjectives, those with numeric standards and those without. The numeric standards include all of the measuring adjectives—*tall, young, hot*, etc.—and the nonnumeric adjectives include adjectives of texture, shape, and color. While there is no specific order among subjective adjectives, there is a definite order holding among both numeric and nonnumeric adjectives.

Numeric: Value (*cheap*), Size (*wide*), Age (*old*), Temperature (*cold*).
Nonnumeric: Texture (*rough*), Shape (*round*), Color (*red*).

Derived adjectives are those which are derived in the lexicon from other parts of speech, verbs and nouns (in that order). Adjectives derived from verbs include the participles; those derived from nouns include words like *Egyptian* and *colonial*.

The nouns that serve to modify nouns are themselves divided into two ordered classes, material nouns (*rubber, cotton, . . .*) and function nouns (*a grammar book, a fishing pole*, etc.).

Pre-noun ordering is summarized in Table 3.1.

How might adjective ordering be represented in the grammar? In the Nonstandard Theory, the different adjectives in the string of adjectives represented by (Adj) + · · · + (Adj) might represent the different classes on the chart. In other words, the rule might actually look something like this:

NP → Art + (Ordinal) + (Cardinal) + (Comparative) + (Subjective) + (Value) + ··· + (Function) + N + #

Writing it out this way is so cumbersome, however, that we will forget it forthwith.

Table 3.1 Adjective Ordering[a]

			Article	
Quantity				a, one, some, many, . . .
Determiner				the, this, the man's, . . .
			Adjective	
Number	{ Ordinal			first, second, last, . . .
	Cardinal			one, two, many, . . .
Comparative				bigger, biggest, . . .
Subjective				pretty, odd, nice, . . .
		Numeric	{ Value	cheap
			Size	tall, heavy, wide, . . .
			Age	young, new, . . .
			Temperature	hot
Objective	{		{ Texture	rough, furry, . . .
		Nonnumeric	Shape	round, square, . . .
			Color	red, dark, . . .
Derived	{ Verb +		{ -ing	floating
			-en	frozen
	Noun + -al, -an			colonial, Egyptian, . . .
			Noun	
Material				rubber, stone, cotton, . . .
Function				grammar, fishing, . . .

[a]It goes without saying that the order given is no more than the "usual" order. A number of things may intervene to alter the word order of modifiers. For example, while age generally precedes color, most speakers will say *a dark young man* rather than the expected *a young dark man*. What appears to be the cause of this reordering is a sort of natural "bond" between certain adjectives and certain nouns that overrides customary ordering.

Exercise 3.26

1. Draw trees for and derive (using either theory):
   a. the clever fox that ate the stupid chicken. . .
   b. the ripe red apple on the tree. . .
   c. one of the two trees. . .
2. Why is *a floating fishing pole* acceptable, while *a fishing floating pole* is not?

3.27 NOUN-NOUN: A BRIEF DIGRESSION

One feature of Krohn's presentation of modifiers (1971:41) is his inclusion of both adjective and noun modifiers in the same framework, with the attendant implication that they are in essence the same thing (Figure 3.25).

sg	The store is new.	It is a *new* store.
pl	The stores are new.	They are new stores.
sg	The store sells books.	It is a *book* store.
pl	The stores sell books.	They are book stores.

Comments

1. The modifier of a noun can be either an adjective or a noun.
2. Such modifiers are placed before the noun.
3. Modifiers that precede plural nouns have the same form as those that precede singular nouns.

Figure 3.25

However, suggestions as to deep structure sentencial sources for noun-noun structures are even less plausible than suggestions about the sources of *NP of NP* structures, for approximately the same reason: the interpretation of noun-noun phrases depends on what is possible together with what we know about the world. As Katz and Fodor suggest (1964:489), it shouldn't have to be the linguistic theory that explains why we know that "horse shoes" are shoes for horses and "alligator shoes" are shoes made out of alligator hide rather than the other way around. There are innumerable relationships that may obtain between two nouns, any of which could possibly be involved in the correct interpretation of a specific noun-noun phrase. Shoes happen to make a good example:

horse shoes: shoes for horses
alligator shoes: shoes made out of alligator leather
bowling shoes: shoes for bowling in
tennis shoes: soft shoes, such as are used for tennis
snow shoes: shoes for walking on snow
dress shoes: shoes to go with formal dress
high-heel shoes: shoes with high heels
saddle shoes: shoes with a "saddle" of contrasting color
Murphy shoes: shoes designed by an orthopedist named Murphy

with undoubtedly many more. It is easy enough to coin new ones, such as nurse shoes, mud shoes, and soul shoes (cf. soul food). The idiomaticity of compounds makes it likely that the only place they can be dealt with adequately is in the lexicon, with each compound having its own entry.

3.28   SUMMARY OF MODIFICATION

This summary will include both the Standard and Non-standard Theory approaches, where appropriate.

In the Phrase Structure component, only the NP rule is altered, expanded to:

$$
\text{Standard} \qquad\qquad\qquad\qquad \text{Nonstandard}
$$

$$
NP \rightarrow \left\{ \begin{array}{l} NP + (S) + \cdots + (S) \\ Art + N + \# \\ Name \\ ProN \end{array} \right\} \qquad NP \rightarrow \left\{ \begin{array}{l} NP + (S) + \cdots + (S) \\ Art + (Adj) \cdots (Adj) + N + \#' \\ Name \\ ProN \end{array} \right\}
$$

The following transformational operations were introduced:

1. **Whir:** the replacement of the NP in the modifier with an appropriate *wh-* word;

2. **Whim:** the movement of the *wh-* word to the front of the modifying sentence;

3. **Whiddle:** the optional deletion of the *wh-* word if it originated in nonsubject position;

4. **Whiz:** the optional deletion of *wh-* Tense *be.*

5. **Unicorn:** (*Standard Theory only*) the movement of a single word left after the operation of **Whiz** to a position directly before the noun.

Unicorn is not found in the Nonstandard Theory because adjectives and participles (which are what **Unicorn** operates on) are generated before the noun in the phrase structure.

3.3 Nominalized Sentences

3.30 INTRODUCTION

The other major type of embedded sentence is the nominalized sentence, or the sentence which acts, as a whole, as a noun phrase within a higher sentence. Such sentences act usually as either subjects or objects of higher verbs. There are three major kinds of nominalized sentences: relative nominals, which will be the subject of this section, and gerunds and infinitives, which will be the subject of the next section.

Some examples of typical relative nominal sentences (RNSs) follow.

In subject position:
>*That he came to the party* amazed us.
>*Why he came to the party* amazed us.
>*What he did yesterday* amazed us.

In object position:
>I didn't know *that he had come to your party.*
>I didn't know *why he said that.*
>I didn't know *if he was there.*

The test of the fact that the sentence is a nominalization involves simply replacing the RNS with *something*, and seeing if the resulting sentence is still grammatical:

>Something amazed us.
>I didn't know anything.

3.31 RELATIVE NOMINAL SENTENCES

In most respects, the relative nominal sentence (RNS) is pretty straightforwardly "sentence-like." However, before we can discuss its syntactic properties, it is necessary to recognize that there are at least two types of RNS. Compare the following:

1 a. Do you know that John is here?
   b. Do you know if John is here?

In 1a the speaker presupposes that "John is here," while in 1b he does not. In 1a, then, the RNS is presented as a fact, and in 1b the RNS is an implied question. We can distinguish between the two by giving them slightly different phrase structure sources.

$$NP \rightarrow \begin{Bmatrix} that + S \\ if \ + S \end{Bmatrix} \begin{matrix} (\text{"factive" RNS}) \\ (\text{"questive" RNS}) \end{matrix}$$

Thus 1a and 1b have very nearly identical deep structures, differing only in the *that/if* distinction (Figure 3.26).

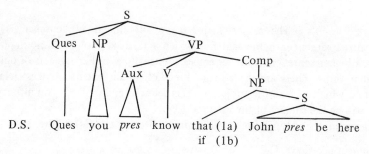

Figure 3.26

Wh- type RNSs can also be questive in nature, and thus derive under the *if + S* rule. Since there is a *wh-* word, it must be **Wh**imed, and as a special aspect of this operation *if* is eliminated. For example, see Figure 3.27.

Most English teachers are quite familiar with the foreign student mistake of the sort **I don't know who is he* and **I don't remember what did he do*, and so on, in which the RNS is given question word order. Transformationally speaking, the mistake lies in performing the **QS** operation in the lower sentence without a Ques constituent to motivate it. In ordinary terms, the RNS simply isn't a question, even though it may imply one.

The very sharp-eyed among you may have noticed a possible inconsistency with an earlier rule, the **Wh- fronting (WF)** rule (see p. 115). The WF rule is triggered by the presence of both Ques and *wh-* in the deep structure, conditions met in the last example, and moves the *wh-* to the front of the sentence—which

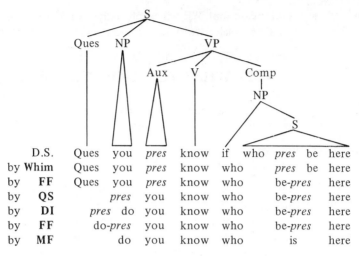

Figure 3.27   Do you know who is here?

it did not do in the last example. It cannot be claimed that **WF** won't work when the *wh-* word is in a lower sentence, for under certain circumstances it will operate perfectly happily (Figure 3.28).

What is the difference between the example in Figure 3.28 and the example in Figure 3.27? The secret lies in realizing that the RNS in Figure 3.27 involved the questive *if* + *S*, while the RNS in Figure 3.28 involved the factive *that* + *S*.[1]

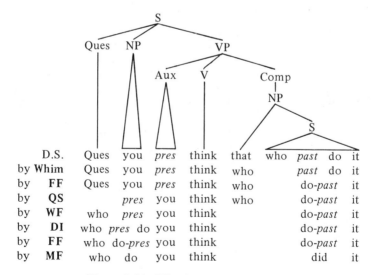

Figure 3.28   Who do you think did it?

[1] *Think* cannot be followed by the questive RNS, as can be seen in the ungrammaticality of sentences like *I don't think if he can come.*

Whim applies in either case, but **WF** will apply only to *wh-* words in factive RNSs. Why should **WF** be so selective? I do not know.

3.32   WHAT YOU DON'T KNOW . . .

There is another type of relative construction that looks very much like a *wh-* RNS. Compare, for instance,

2 a. I don't know what he gave me.
   b. I drank what he gave me.

Sentence 2a is another RNS of a type discussed previously. Sentence 2b, on the other hand, involves a special type of relative clause that can be paraphrased by the expression *that which*, as in *I drank that which he gave me*. The deep structure of 2b appears in Figure 3.29. By and large, it is not too difficult to tell the two apart. Application of the *that which* test—in which *what* is replaced by *that which*—is usually definitive. As it turns out, most cases of a *what* clause serving as a sentence subject are instances of *that which* relative clauses (for example, *What you don't know can't hurt you.*).

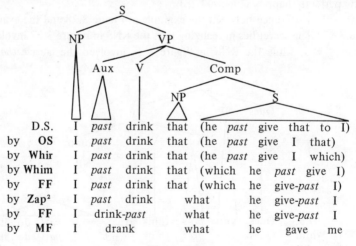

D.S.	I	*past*	drink	that	(he	*past*	give	that to	I)
by **OS**	I	*past*	drink	that	(he	*past*	give	I	that)
by **Whir**	I	*past*	drink	that	(he	*past*	give	I	which)
by **Whim**	I	*past*	drink	that	(which	he	*past*	give	I)
by **FF**	I	*past*	drink	that	(which	he	give-*past*		I)
by **Zap**[2]	I	*past*	drink	what		he	give-*past*		I
by **FF**	I	drink-*past*		what		he	give-*past*		I
by **MF**	I	drank		what		he	gave		me

Figure 3.29

Exercise 3.32

1. Draw trees for and derive the sentences below.
    a. Did he tell you that Mary wouldn't go?
    b. John didn't know who was caught.
    c. Where do you think they will go?

---

[2] **Zap** will usually represent the name of an operation that has not been assigned a name in the course of the text.

2. Suggest a treatment for the class of RNSs represented by
   I demand that he be here by noon!

3. Suggest a treatment for RNSs preceded by *the fact, the claim,* etc.—for example, *The fact that John did it amazed us.* Account for the ambiguity of *The fact that John remembered bothered Bill.*

4. Explain to a foreign student why his sentence, **I don't know whom you saw,* is ungrammatical.

3.4   Gerunds and Infinitives

I will introduce this section with a confession: it took me years to be convinced that gerund and infinitive phrases might indeed be derived from underlying embedded sentences, and that a sentence like *I wanted to do it* actually had two sentence nodes in it rather than one. I am, therefore, very sympathetic to those of you who find this entire subsequent section difficult to believe. I do ask you, however, to suspend disbelief for the moment, so that you may more easily understand the discussion. At a more leisurely moment, I would certainly recommend that you take a month or two to work out the alternative—that gerunds and infinitives are gerunds and infinitives in deep structure—to see what kinds of problems this ultimately leads you to.

3.41   GI PHRASE STRUCTURE

To begin with, gerunds and infinitives (GIs) are set apart by having a specialized phrase structure grammar initiated by a somewhat different sentence node, S′. S′ is the sentence node for "tenseless" sentences, although more than just tenselessness is involved. Consider, for instance,

1 a. Flying is fun.
  b. To fly is fun.

Assuming that *flying* and *to fly* derive from an underlying embedded sentence, the tense of that sentence is somewhat vague, and in fact may be said to relate to any time. This is what is meant by tenselessness. There is, in addition, another vagueness: who is doing the flying? The subject of the verb *fly* is (in these examples) immaterial, for it may be any person: such underlying sentences may be subjectless as well as tenseless.

The phrase structure grammar that underlies GI phrases is, then:

NP → S'
S' → (NP) + VP'
VP' → (Aux') + V + (Comp)
Aux' → (Perfect) + (Progressive) + (Passive)

Note that in addition to lacking tense, Aux' also lacks modals.

A great many GI phrases involve no more than a lone verb in the deep structure, since all other elements of S' are optional. Both *Flying is fun* and *To fly is fun* are said to come from the same deep structure, shown in Figure 3.30.

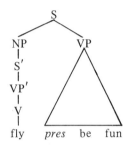

Figure 3.30

An underlying sentence derived under S' will undergo either the **Gerund** or the **Infinitive** rule, which converts the verb into a gerund or infinitive, respectively. Thus,

D.S.   fly *pres* be fun   D.S.   fly *pres* be fun
by **Ger**   flying *pres* be fun   by **Inf**   to fly *pres* be fun

A more fully fleshed S' may be invoked, with complements and adverbials, as in *flying planes on weekends is fun*, which has the deep structure in Figure 3.31.

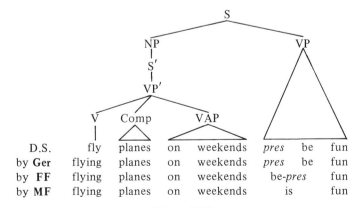

	V	Comp			VAP				
D.S.	fly	planes	on	weekends	*pres*	be	fun
by **Ger**	flying	planes	on	weekends	*pres*	be	fun
by **FF**	flying	planes	on	weekends	be-*pres*	fun
by **MF**	flying	planes	on	weekends	is	fun

Figure 3.31

GI phrases may have subjects, in which case they are subject to portions of the **Gerund** and **Infinitive** rules. The **Gerund** rule gives the subject NP possessive form, and the **Infinitive** rule makes the subject NP the object of the preposition *for*. For example, if the above S′ had the subject NP *John*,

D.S.	John fly planes on weekends *pres* be fun
by **Ger**	John's flying planes on weekends *pres* be fun

and

D.S.	John fly planes on weekends *pres* be fun
by **Inf**	for John to fly planes on weekends *pres* be fun

We may as well mention a rather awful suspicion at this point, that perhaps gerunds and infinitives do not actually come from the same deep structures. Evidence for this suspicion derives from realizing that from deep structure 2a,

2 a. D.S.   you fly *pres* be terrible

we can derive both 2b and 2c,

2 b. (after **Ger**) your flying is terrible.
   c. (after **Inf**) for you to fly is terrible.

Since transformational operations are not supposed to change meaning, 2b and 2c should mean the same thing. But they don't: 2b means that the *manner* of "your flying" is terrible, and 2c means that the *fact* of "your flying" is terrible. This suggests that **Gerund** and **Infinitive** are probably motivated by specific features of the deep structure; the problem, however, is one of considerable complexity and is, as yet, unresolved.

Before going on to the next topic, it should be pointed out that you now have sufficient information to explain how *Flying planes can be dangerous* is ambiguous (see p. 37).

3.42   EXTRAPOSITION

A curious operation may be introduced at this point, **Extraposition (Extra)**, whose results have caused more than one English teacher grief. In general, if the subject of a sentence is a nominalized sentence—whether RNS or S′—and the predicate complement is one of a limited class of adjectives, such as *clear* or *hard*, then the entire nominal may suddenly up and move around to a position after the adjective, leaving an *it* in its wake to hold down the subject position. For example, see Figure 3.32.

Extraposition occurs in other circumstances as well, but somewhat unpredictably (although always with the verb *be*):

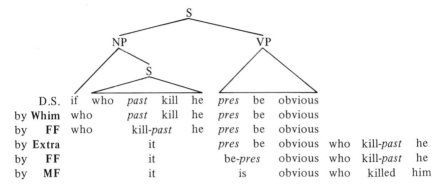

Figure 3.32   It is obvious who killed him.

3 a. It was just my bad luck that they caught me.
   b. It was suggested that he leave.
   c. It was a pleasure to meet you again
   d. It was nice of you to call.
   e. It was John who did it.

This last is sure to cause some minor controversy, for many linguists regard it as the product of an operation called *It*-extraction, which takes an NP from a sentence, moves it to the front of the sentence in the form, *It was NP*, leaving the rest of the sentence as a relative clause on the NP. Figures 3.33A and 3.33B show how the sentence is derived through each system. The same number of rules is involved in both derivations, and if the former deep structure is "simpler" than the latter, this is made up for by the fact that **It-extraction** must introduce a number of words and terms that **Extraposition** does not. On balance, both derivations are reasonable and in their own way well motivated. Why, then, do I apparently prefer **Extraposition?** Simply because I already have **Extraposition**. Other things being equal, a new operation should be considered only when the present inventory of operations will not do the trick adequately.

More curious even than **Extraposition** is an operation that is highly restricted to a very few adjectives (*easy, hard, awkward, pleasant*, and the like), and which

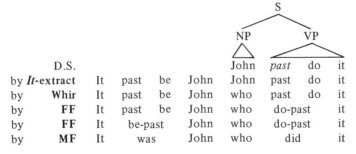

Figure 3.33A   Via *It*-extraction.

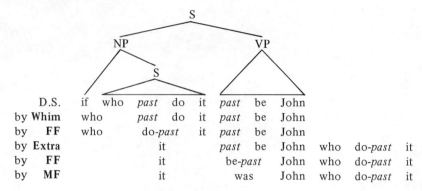

D.S.	if	who	*past*	do	it	*past*	be	John			
by **Whim**		who	*past*	do	it	*past*	be	John			
by **FF**		who		do-*past*	it	*past*	be	John			
by **Extra**					it	*past*	be	John	who	do-*past*	it
by **FF**					it		be-*past*	John	who	do-*past*	it
by **MF**					it		was	John	who	do-*past*	it

Figure 3.33B Via **Extraposition**.

extraposes the verb leaving the complement NP behind as the surface subject. This is **Extraposition-plus (Extra+)**. For example, see Figure 3.34. We might equally have gone through **Extraposition** to obtain *It is hard to understand women*, or even just left it at **Infinitive**, getting *To understand women is hard*. Both **Extraposition** and **Extraposition-plus** are optional operations, having no discernible motivating triggers.

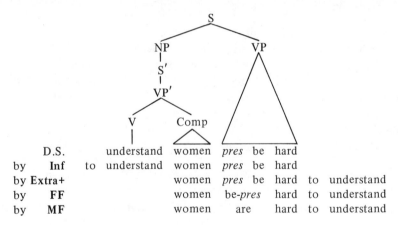

D.S.		understand	women	*pres*	be	hard	
by **Inf**	to	understand	women	*pres*	be	hard	
by **Extra+**			women	*pres*	be	hard	to	understand
by **FF**			women	be-*pres*	hard	to	understand
by **MF**			women	are	hard	to	understand

Figure 3.34 Women are hard to understand.

The *it* that is "left behind" by **Extraposition** is so left, of course, because English requires a subject in its surface sentences. In earlier days, *it* was called an "expletive," and it was acknowledged that *it* had no more than a subject-filling function in such sentences. Expletive *it*, however, is not necessarily accounted for by extraposing operations, for it is found as well in a host of relatively simple sentences like *It is raining*. It might therefore be fruitful to consider that there is an independent (of **Extraposition**) *it*-supplying rule called **Expletive (Exp)** that will supply an *it* to a sentence that either does not have a subject or has just lost it. In other words, *It is raining* (Figure 3.35) would be subjectless in

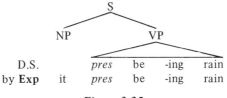

Figure 3.35

deep structure (as it is in meaning), and the example given in Figure 3.33B would be revised to that in Figure 3.36.

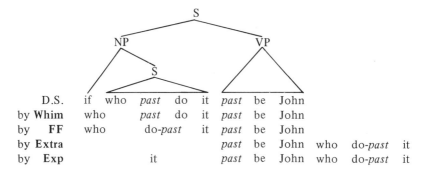

Figure 3.36

Exercise 3.42

1. Draw trees for and derive the following sentences:
   a. For you to lie to me is what hurts most!
   b. His arguing won't help him.
   c. It won't matter what he does.
   d. The pin may be difficult to find.
   e. It is his desire to be recognized.
2. Another "expletive" is *there*, in *There are two chairs in the room.* How might you account for *there* and also allow for the fact that this sentence may be paraphrased by *Two chairs are in the room*?

3.43   COMPLEMENT GIs

GIs, of course, may act as complement NPs as well as subject NPs, but with one major difference. Whereas the subject GI frequently lacks a deep structure subject of its own, the complement GI always has a subject, even though this subject is frequently not expressed in the surface sentence. For example, if we consider the sentence, *I want to go*, it is clear that the subject of *go* is *I*—more or less along the line of *I want that I will go*. This second *I* is "understood," which is to say it is present in the deep structure, which appears as in Figure 3.37. What happens to the second *I*? It is deleted automatically after a **Subject-matching (SM)** operation has established that it is identical with the next higher subject, that is, in this case, the subject of *want*. If it had not been identical, it would have been preserved. Thereafter, the **Infinitive** operation is invoked, and the derivation proceeds smoothly.

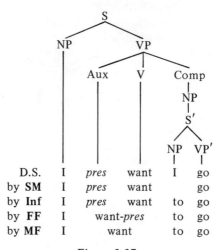

D.S.	I	*pres*	want	I	go
by **SM**	I	*pres*	want		go
by **Inf**	I	*pres*	want	to	go
by **FF**	I	want-*pres*		to	go
by **MF**	I	want		to	go

Figure 3.37

Complement GIs may be stacked up on top of each other. Each has its own S', and unraveling the sentence begins at the bottom, as usual (Figure 3.38).

How do we know that the subject of *admit* should be ultimately expressed in object form—that is, as *him* rather than as *he*? This is accounted for within the scope of the **Subject-matching** rule if we make a slight addendum to what happens if the subjects do not match. The lower subject is not only preserved, but it is simultaneously "raised" from its position as subject of the lower verb to a new position as object of the higher verb. This is what is known as **Subject-raising**. Diagrammatically, there is a change from Figure 3.39(a) to Figure 3.39(b). The real importance of this operation will not become apparent in this text, but at least it serves to indicate why the pronoun is in object rather than subject form.

Both gerunds and infinitives may involve a number of internal operations, such as negation and passivisation. For example, see Figure 3.40.

In the event that S' contains an interrogative *wh-*, it is **Whim**ed and then **WF**ed to the front of the sentence, as in Figure 3.41.

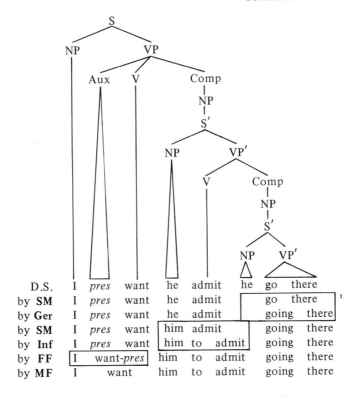

D.S.	I	*pres*	want	he	admit		he	go	there	
by **SM**	I	*pres*	want	he	admit			go	there	¹
by **Ger**	I	*pres*	want	he	admit			going	there	
by **SM**	I	*pres*	want	him	admit			going	there	
by **Inf**	I	*pres*	want	him	to	admit		going	there	
by **FF**	I	want-*pres*		him	to	admit		going	there	
by **MF**	I		want	him	to	admit		going	there	

Figure 3.38   I want him to admit going there.

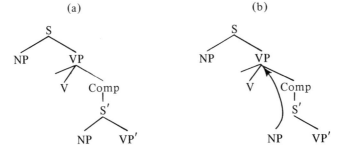

Figure 3.39

---

¹ The boxes indicate that portion of the structure which is being "processed," starting with the bottom-most sentence, of course.

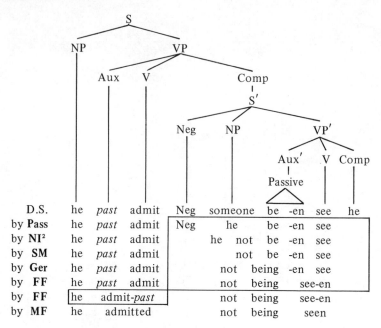

	NP	Aux	V	Neg	NP	Aux'	V	Comp
D.S.	he	*past*	admit	Neg	someone	be	-en	see he
by **Pass**	he	*past*	admit	Neg	he	be	-en	see
by **NI²**	he	*past*	admit		he not	be	-en	see
by **SM**	he	*past*	admit		not	be	-en	see
by **Ger**	he	*past*	admit		not	being	-en	see
by **FF**	he	*past*	admit		not	being	see-en	
by **FF**	he	admit-*past*			not	being	see-en	
by **MF**	he	admitted			not	being	seen	

Figure 3.40 He admitted not being seen.

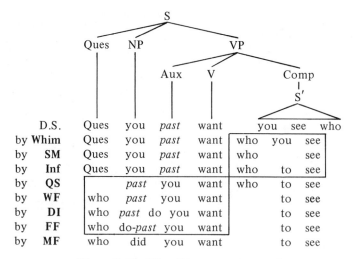

	Ques	NP	Aux	V	Comp	S'
D.S.	Ques	you	*past*	want		you see who
by **Whim**	Ques	you	*past*	want	who	you see
by **SM**	Ques	you	*past*	want	who	see
by **Inf**	Ques	you	*past*	want	who	to see
by **QS**		*past*	you	want	who	to see
by **WF**	who	*past*	you	want		to see
by **DI**	who	*past* do you	want			to see
by **FF**	who	do-*past* you	want			to see
by **MF**	who	did	you	want		to see

Figure 3.41 Who did you want to see?

---

² Note that *not* is inserted here before *be* rather than after. This is a fudging alteration in the NI mechanism when applied to tenseless sentences.

Exercise 3.43

1. Draw trees for and derive the sentences below.
   a. John asked me to consider allowing him to do it.
   b. She hated not being told who did it.
   c. Who do you think will be told to go?
   d. What would you like me to admit having done?
2. Certain verbs appear to require a reflexive form of the pronoun, as *I told myself to shape up* and *I caught myself ogling Ralph's wife*, rather than deleting the subject after **Subject-matching**. Discuss.
3. Some verbs followed by gerunds involve the gerund subject in possessive form (as per the **Gerund** rule, p. 150) rather than the object form (as per **SM**). Some can even do it both ways—for example, *We heard him playing* and *we heard his playing*. Discuss.

3.44 GERUND OR INFINITIVE?

Hypotheses as to the deep structure sources of gerunds and infinitives do not, unfortunately, give any aid to the embattled teacher who is trying to help his students distinguish between verbs that take gerund complements and those that take infinitives. The tendency has always been to present lists of verbs that take gerunds, infinitives, and both, telling the student that he will have to memorize the lists. In so far as a great many verbs are involved (perhaps as many as 200), this is a demand of no small proportions.[3]

Kiparsky and Kiparsky (1970) suggest that there is a major semantic consideration involved in distinguishing gerunds from infinitives, which they call "factivity." The Kiparskys claim that, in general, when a speaker presupposes the truth of the complement sentence (presupposes that it expresses a fact), then the complement is realized as a gerund, and otherwise as an infinitive. One can see this best when considering the pair,

   4 a. He remembered doing it.
     b. He remembered to do it.

In 4a what he remembered was the fact that he had done it, and it would be odd to contradict the presumption of the fact, as:

   4 c. ?He remembered doing it, but I don't know if he did.

In 4b, on the other hand, he didn't remember a fact so much as an obligation, and it is possible that he didn't carry through:

   4 d. He remembered to do it, but then forgot again.

[3] Only slightly simplified by pointing out that after a preposition one must use a gerund, whatever else may be involved—for example, *he demanded to do it* but *he insisted on doing it*.

The notion of factivity is not, as you may imagine, an easy one to communicate, especially when you are dealing with people whose English is a little faint.

A rule of thumb that may help is a sort of temporal logic: facts are events that have occurred, and thus are of the past. Events in the future are speculations, not facts.

You are dealing with two verbs, a main verb (MV) and a complement verb (CV), and in most cases you can make an assessment of the temporal relationship between them. If the CV is past relative to the MV, then a gerund is called for:

5 I remember (now) doing that (yesterday).

If the CV is future relative to the MV, then an infinitive is used:

6 I remembered (yesterday) to do that (today).

Even if the gross times of the MV and the CV are the same, as in

7 I will remember (tomorrow) to do that (tomorrow).

it is nevertheless true that at the relevant time the two events are sequenced: first you remember, then you do it. The temporal relationships are a property of the main verb; a considerable majority of verbs are accounted for by considering the temporal relationship they impose on their complements. *Remember* is unusual in that it may relate to both past and future complements.

A special case of temporal relationships is involved in what can be called the "boundary" verbs—*begin*, *continue*, and *stop*. The CV to *stop* is always past (relative to stopping, of course), and therefore in the gerund.[4] The verb *continue* may look in both directions for its CV, for it implies both past and future time; its CV may thus be in either gerund or infinitive. *Begin* looks to the future, thus taking an infinitive. However, it may also take a gerund, an undeniable exception to our expectations.

There are some verbs whose complements are recognizably simultaneous or nonsequenced. They may still be discussed in terms of "factivity," however, since the nonfactive verbs are so obviously nonfactive: *seem, appear, claim*, etc., as in

8 a. He seems to be a sailor.
   b. He claims to be a sailor.

which quite frankly throw some doubt on the proposition that he is, in fact, a sailor. There is no contradiction at all in saying

8 c. He appears to be a sailor but he isn't one.

Factive simultaneous verbs, on the other hand, tend to be verbs of the senses: *see, feel, hear*, etc., as in

---

[4] *Stop* may be followed, however, by an infinitive-of-purpose (cf. Section 3.45).

9 a. I saw him feeding the fish.
   b. I heard him creeping about.

in which there seems to be no doubt in the speaker's mind that he is reporting facts. If there were doubt, the verb would have been different:

10 a. He appeared to be feeding the fish.
   b. It sounded like he was creeping about.

Regrettably, the "emotive" verbs—*like, love, hate, prefer*, etc.—fit no category, taking both gerunds and infinitives. The temporal relationships between these verbs and their CVs are usually indeterminate, but even when they are known, it doesn't seem to influence selection. For example, you can say *I hate doing this to you* before, during, or after the fact, and you can equally say *I hate to do this to you* in all circumstances.

Another problem involves assessing the temporal relationships (or factivity) of events that don't occur, or following verbs that deny events. Most of these (*avoid, deny, delay*, etc.) take gerund CVs, but some (such as *forget*) take infinitives.

3.45 GI RESIDUALS

There are still a great meny aspects of the infinitive and gerund that deserve discussion, both because they are linguistically interesting and because they represent serious problems for the foreign student. We can, however, do no more than briefly mention a few.

A. Adjective Plus Infinitive

Quite a few predicate adjectives may "take" infinitive complements of their own, for example, *John is eager to please*, which involves a deep structure like the one in Figure 3.42, in which the S' *John please* is a sort of direct complement to the adjective *eager*. You will recall, of course, that this

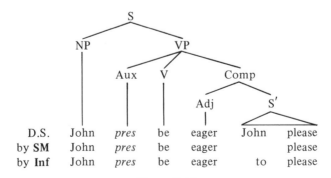

Figure 3.42

sentence is one of a quasi-ambiguous pair (see p. 39), of which the other was *John is easy to please*, whose deep structure and derivation are totally different, as in Figure 3.43.

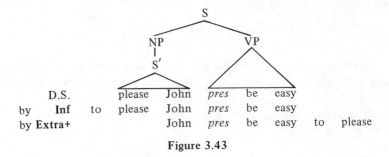

Figure 3.43

B. Noun Plus Infinitive

There are occasions when nouns are followed by infinitives:

11 a. He's a hard man to know.
    b. John's an easy guy to please.

The key to understanding the syntax of these structures lies in realizing that they contain adjectives from the same class of adjectives that are involved in **Extra+** (*hard*, *easy*, etc.). The underlying structure of such sentences is that of NP and modifying sentence (Figure 3.44). **Zap** is an operation that is somewhat

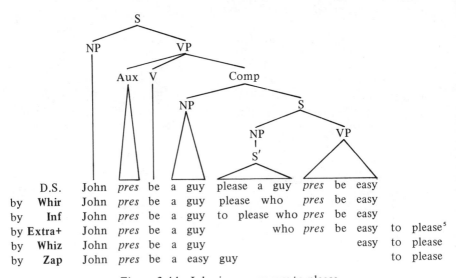

Figure 3.44   John is an easy guy to please.

---

[5] As would lead to *John is a guy who is easy to please*.

related to **Unicorn** (see p. 135) with a crucial difference. Where the adjective moved by **Unicorn** had to modify the noun it was moving around, the same is not true of **Zap**: *easy* does not modify *guy*. **Zap** is, under the circumstances, a wholly *ad hoc*, unmotivated rule, whose existence is supported only by the above interpretation of what is happening below the surface of this rather small class of sentences.

C.   Infinitive-of-Purpose

Most verbs can be followed by an infinitive which expresses a purpose for the verb—*I came to fix the drains*, *he reads to improve himself*, and so on. In so far as the semantic relationship is consistently one of purpose, we might as well assign the underlying S′ to the same node under which the term *why* is generated (see p. 114), Cause, itself found under VAP. Thus, *I came to fix the drains* has the structure in Figure 3.45.

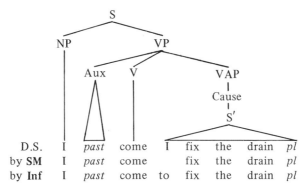

Figure 3.45

This suggests that the infinitive operates, in this instance, as an adverbial phrase closely related to the question word *why*. The closeness may be perceived in the fairly common use of an infinitive to answer *why* questions.

D.   Too Hot to Drink

Although at first glance the structure *too Adj to verb* looks very much like some earlier adjective-infinitive structures, it turns out to offer unique problems. If we consider the sentence, *The lamb is too hot to eat*, we can recognize that it is ambiguous, but that in both readings *hot* actually modifies the word *lamb*, so that the two deep structures differ only in their organizations of the S′ complementary to the adjective (Figure 3.46). The new thing offered here is that *lamb* must be deleted whether it is subject or object in the S′. SM might account for the deletion in Figure 3.46(b), but not in Figure 3.46(a). We have, then, a new general rule: if the S′ complementary to a predicate adjective contains the NP which is the subject of the adjective, it is deleted.

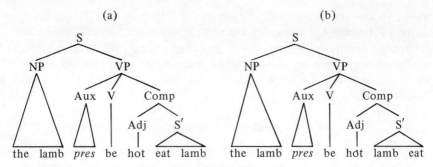

Figure 3.46

In neither of the above structures was it indicated where *too* comes from. The entire structure is intimately connected with *too*; many adjectives that can take a S′ complement with *too* cannot without it:

12   a.   The tea is too bitter to drink.
      b.   *The tea is bitter to drink.

It may be that we can best represent this dependency in something like the form:

$$
\begin{array}{c}
\text{Comp} \\
| \\
\text{too} - \text{Adj} \\
\overset{\displaystyle\overbrace{}}{\text{too} \quad\quad \text{Adj} \quad\quad \text{S}'}
\end{array}
$$

The PS rule would probably indicate that S′ is optional,

too-Adj → too + Adj + (S′)

allowing for the frequent occurrence of *too* + Adj without any explicit complementary sentence.

E.   The Reduced Infinitive

      A few verbs—*make, let, have,* and the "sense" verbs *see, feel,* etc.—take a complement of the form *NP V Comp*, where the verb has no affixes at all or is in the "plain" form, sometimes called the "plain infinitive" or the "reduced infinitive." One may treat these as having derived from S′ as before, but undergoing neither **Gerund** nor **Infinitive** (Figure 3.47). These structures are not usually considered problems for foreign learners, but do present a common difficulty when contrasted in meaning to the gerund complement, as in:

13   a.   I saw him cross the street.
      b.   I saw him crossing the street.

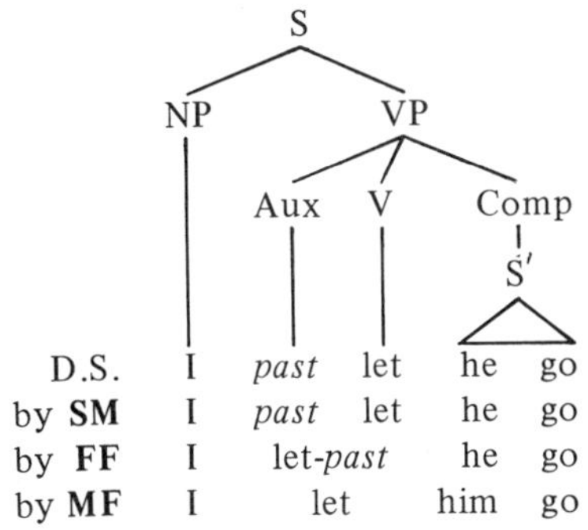

Figure 3.47 I let him go.

The explanation usually given is that when you say 13a you imply that you saw the crossing from beginning to end (or from one side to the other, in this case), whereas when you say 13b you imply that you saw a part of the whole event, or somewhere in the middle. This explanation is not always entirely satisfactory, but it is truer than not and has the virtue of being the only explanation around.

3.46 SUMMARY OF NOMINALIZED SENTENCES

A. Relative Nominal Sentences (RNSs)

There are two principal types of RNS:

the "factive" RNS, from NP → that + S
the "questive" RNS, from NP → if + S

The "questive" RNS includes RNSs with *wh-* words. In this case, when **Whim** applies, the movement of *wh-* to the front of the RNS erases (so to speak) *if*. In some cases, a *wh-* word may arise in a "factive" RNS (but only if the overall sentence is a question); in this case, too, **Whim** will involve the erasure of *that*.

Care should be taken to avoid confusing a "questive" RNS with *what* (for example, *I don't know what he gave me*) and the *what* form of a *that which* relative clause (for example, *I drank what he gave me*).

B. Gerunds and Infinitives (GIs)

GI phrase structure involves a specialized set of PS rules:

$NP \rightarrow S'$
$S' \rightarrow (NP) + VP'$
$VP' \rightarrow (Aux') + V + (Comp)$
$Aux' \rightarrow (Perfect) + (Progressive) + (Passive)$

Sentences under a S' node have applied to them either the **Gerund** or the **Infinitive** operations (except for a small class of verbs—*let, make*, etc.—which involve no equivalent operation)

Gerund   (NP) + V . . . ⇒ (NPs) + V-ing . . .
Infinitive   (NP) + V . . . ⇒ (for NP) + to V . . .

When S' derives under the complement of a higher verb, the first operation is that of **Subject-matching**. If the lower and next higher subjects are identical, the subject of the lower S' is deleted or reflexivized (depending on the higher verb). If the two subjects are different, the lower subject is preserved in object form (cf. **Subject-raising**).

C.   Expletive <u>it</u>

Whenever a sentence which otherwise would require a subject is lacking a subject, **Expletive** supplies *it*.

D.   Extraposition and Extraposition-plus

These two rules move the subject nominalized sentence (or part of it) to a position after the predicate. **Extraposition** works in conjunction with **Expletive** as it involves the complete removal of the erstwhile subject.

E.   Various and Sundry

Too hot to eat structures derive from the PS rules:

Comp → too-Adj
too-Adj → too + Adj + (S')

A general deletion rule applies to instances of S' derived under this rule, which deletes a NP if it is identical to the subject of the predicate adjective.

3.47 FIFTY VERBS AND THEIR COMPLEMENTS

The categorization of verbs according to the type of complement sentence they may take is an exercise of dubious value. In Table 3.2, fifty verbs are given with the type of complement sentences that may follow them, including the following, in order: *if* S (*I asked if he could come*), *that* S (*I admitted that he had given me some candy*), *that* tenseless S (*I demand that he be shot*), Inf (*He appeared to laugh*), *self* Inf (*I allowed myself to smile*), *him* Inf (*I allowed him to go*), reduced Inf (*I let him go*), Ger (*He admits going*), *self* Ger (*He caught himself staring*), *him* Ger (*I felt him squirming*), *his* Ger (*He admitted my returning the candy*). Few verbs are alike; among the fifty verbs there would be thirty-five "categories," ranging from *let*, which occurs with only one type of complement sentence, to *feel*, which may occur with seven.

Table 3.2

	if S	that S	that tS[a]	Inf	self Inf	him Inf	red Inf[b]	Ger	self Ger	him Ger	his Ger
admit		X						X			X
allow					X	X					X
appear		it		X							
ask	X		X	X	X	X					
avoid								X			X
begin				X				X			
believe		X									
catch									X	X	
cause					X	X					X
claim		X		X							
continue				X				X			X
demand			X	X							
deny		X						X			X
expect		X		X	X	X					X
feel		X			be	be	X		X	X	X
find		X			be	be			X	X	
finish								X			X
force					X	X					
forget	X	X		X				X			X
hate				X				X			X
hear	X	X					X		X	X	X
hope		X		X							
insist		X	X								
keep								X	X	X	
know	X	X			be	be					X
let							X				
love		X				X		X		X	X
make							X				
order			X		X	X					
permit					X	X					X
prefer			X	X		X		X		X	X
promise		X		X							
recall	X	X						X	X	X	X
refuse				X							
regret		X						X			X
remember	X	X		X				X	X	X	X
remind					X	X					

Table 3.2 (continued)

	if S	that S	that tS[a]	Inf	self Inf	him Inf	red Inf[b]	Ger	self Ger	him Ger	his Ger
say	X	X		X							
see	X	X					X		X	X	X
seem		it		X							
show		X			be	be			X	X	X
start				X				X	X	X	X
stop								X	X	X	X
teach		X			X	X					
think		X			be	be					
tell	X	X			X	X					
try				X				X			
want				X	X	X					
wish		X		X		X					
wonder	X										

[a]tS = tenseless S
[b]red Inf = reduced Inf

Exercise 3.47

1. Consider the following sentences with *have*, and show their underlying structure.
   a. I'll have him paint the barn.
   b. I have to sell my Jaguar.
   c. Will you have something to eat?
2. Draw trees for and derive the following sentences.
   a. I've been anxious to meet you.
   b. It's too hot to drink coffee.
   c. That dress is too small for you to wear.
   d. I heard myself say something.
3. Now that you know which verbs take the infinitive and which take the gerund, how can you build this information into the grammar? (*Hint:* in the lexicon.)

3.5   Conjoined Sentences

While an embedded sentence is one that has been recursively introduced somewhere within the body of another sentence, conjoined sentences are sentences joined to one another at the very top, through a rewrite rule that looks something like

$$S \to S + X + S \quad \text{or}$$

(tree: S dominating S, X, S)

where X is the class of clause connectors.

There are many different kinds of conjoined sentences, but we shall be able to deal with only a few in the next several sections.

3.51   And

If we consider the simplest of all conjoined sentence types, sentences connected by the conjunction *and*, we find a certain amount of debate and confusion. There is no confusion at all over such obvious cases as *John kissed Mary and Peter drank beer*, which has the deep structure in Figure 3.48. However, it used to be claimed that virtually any instance of the connector *and*

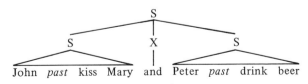

Figure 3.48

reflected a deep structure of this type, with subsequent transformational condensation. For example, the sentence *John and Bill left early* was said to derive from the structure in Figure 3.49.

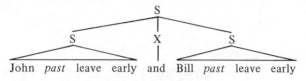

Figure 3.49

However, it has been noted that there are systematic ambiguities with such sentences that throw doubt upon this assumption of their genesis. In the sentence, *John and Bill left early*, for example, there are two possible interpretations: that they left together and that they left independently of each other. The sentence, *John and Bill left early*, seems to favor the former interpretation, while *John left early and Bill left early* appears to favor the latter. This suggests that the two are not really paraphrases, and that another deep structure should be found for *John and Bill left early*.

The best alternative is to suggest that constituents within a sentence may be coordinated directly, through a general rule of the form

$$Z \rightarrow Z + \text{and} + Z$$

where Z may be any constituent, such as NP, VP, V, etc. The application of this rule implies a certain amount of "togetherness" as it were, although this is not a necessity.

Thus the sentence, *John and Bill kissed Mary and Helen*, may be said to derive from the deep structure in Figure 3.50, in which a total of four kisses are accounted for. However, if we add *respectively*, obtaining *John and Bill kissed Mary and Helen, respectively*, only two kisses are involved, and the above deep structure is thereby unsatisfactory. In fact, this sentence is a paraphrase of *John kissed Mary and Bill kissed Helen*; the sentence with *respectively* probably has

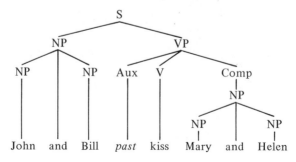

Figure 3.50

the deep structure shown in Figure 3.51. The condensation to *John and Bill* and *Mary and Helen* is accomplished by what has been called the **Respectively** transformation.

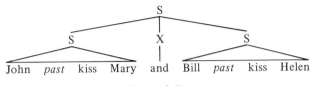

Figure 3.51

Another type of sentence that derives from *and* conjunction is the . . . *and so did John* type, along with its cousin, . . .*and John did too*. The deep structure of such conjoined sentences is constrained, however, in the following way: the VP of both sentences must be identical. The deep structure that is realized as *Bill kissed Mary and John kissed Mary* may also be realized as *Bill kissed Mary and so did John* or as *Bill kissed Mary and John did too*.

3.52 COORDINATE RELATIVE CLAUSES

It was mentioned previously (p. 129) that while the so-called restricted relative clause derives from an embedded sentence serving to modify the NP to which it is attached, the so-called unrestricted relative clause is derived from a conjoined sentence. In other words, the deep structures for the sentences 1a and 1b below are quite different (see Figure 3.52).

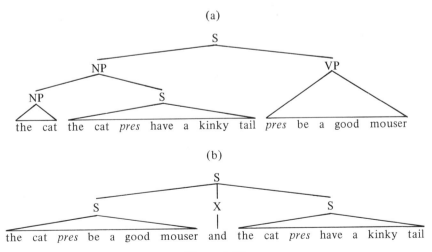

Figure 3.52

1 a. The cat that has a kinky tail is a good mouser.
   b. The cat, which has a kinky tail, is a good mouser.

In circumstances such as those in Figure 3.52b, where you have two conjoined sentences sharing an NP and where one of the sentences is perceived to contain extra or irrelevant information, the irrelevant sentence may be inserted into the other sentence as a parenthetical clause, right after the common NP. Thus you obtain

The cat (the cat has a kinky tail) is a good mouser.

(Dashes may be used in place of the parentheses if so desired.) If the clause is to be preserved as a parenthetic observation, the chances are excellent that *the cat* will be pronominalized to *it* or *she*. Otherwise, recourse to the relative clause rules **Whir** and **Whim** will most likely ensue. Thus the sentences 1c and 1d are considered paraphrases in the TG sense.

1 c. The cat (she has a kinky tail) is a good mouser.
   d. The cat, which has a kinky tail, is a good mouser.

In so far as the two types of relative clause have quite different deep structures, it should not be surprising that learners (whether foreign or English speaking) should have considerable difficulty in achieving an understanding of the difference as long as their teacher approaches both from the point of view of modification. Perhaps the first step is to abandon the term "relative clause" for the conjoined type, so that the two will not be presented with similar terminology. Many texts handle the problem by avoiding mention of the conjoined type, Lado and Fries (1957) being a typical example. Krohn's discussion (1971:185) is, I think, about as good as you can get:

> The relative clauses which have been presented in this lesson are called limiting, restricting or defining relative clauses. There is also a second type, called additive, nonrestrictive, or appositive relative clauses. . .[which] give further information that is not essential to the meaning or identification of the noun phrase; *they are equivalent to separate statements* [emphasis added].

3.53 CLAUSES SHOWING CAUSE

The majority of subordinate clauses involve a cause-and-effect relationship with their main clauses. All derive through the phrase structure rules

X → Cause
Cause ↔ Lex[Cause]

and words like *because* are marked in the lexicon with the feature [Cause]. For the most part, such conjoined sentences have relatively straightforward deep structures. For example, *Tom wobbled home because he had drunk too much* has the form in Figure 3.53. This deep structure also underlies the sentence, *Because he had drunk too much, Tom wobbled home*, in which a clause-moving operation is evidenced. By convention, subordinate clauses follow their main clauses in deep structure.

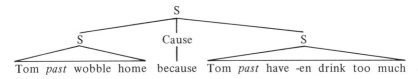

Figure 3.53

There are a few cases in which the structure of the subordinate clause is not so straightforward. For example, *Tom wobbled home on account of having drunk too much* would have the structure in Figure 3.54, in which the subordinate clause consists of a tenseless sentence.

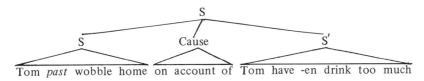

Figure 3.54

3.54 TIME AND PLACE

It is not the case that all subordinate clauses derive from conjoined sentences as above, however. If one considers a sentence like *I left when he arrived*, there is an immediate temptation to assign to it a structure analogous to those above, that is, like the structure in Figure 3.55. However, the function of the subordinate clause is adverbial in the above case, identical to an adverb of time, such as in *I left at two o'clock*. This may be allowed for if we permit sentences to be derived under the adverbial constituent VAP, as

VAP → S

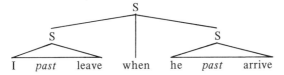

Figure 3.55 Incorrect deep structure for
I left when he arrived.

in which case the sentence would have the structure in Figure 3.56. Note that the embedded sentence itself contains a VAP, realized as a *wh-* word. The fact that, in this example, *when* is an adverb of time defines the whole adverbial sentence as an adverb of time.

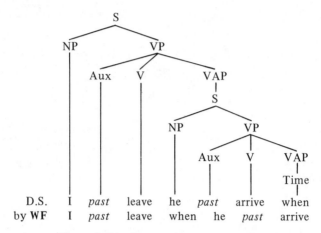

Figure 3.56 Correct deep structure for
I left when he arrived.

3.55 CONDITIONAL CLAUSES

Conditional sentences have such peculiar features that they are almost always treated apart from other sentences containing subordinate clauses. These features provide considerable problems for both the linguist and the foreign learner.

To begin with, the learner frequently perceives what he regards to be a contradiction in the fact that a past tense may be used with future meaning in certain conditional sentences, for example, in *If he came to your party tomorrow, you'd be just as unhappy*. Such discoveries contribute to the learner's feeling that English is a contrary language, a feeling that is better avoided. The manner in which the phenomenon has been accounted for has varied with the linguistic philosophy of the teacher.

The structuralist would agree that the tense of the verb in question was past, but would deny any contradiction. Meaning, after all, played no role in the designation of forms, so that it would be incorrect to think in terms of contradictions between forms and meanings. In effect, the structuralist would chide the learner for having related verb tenses with time.

The traditionalist would have agreed, at least, that there was no contradiction, but he would have denied that a past tense was involved. We find in Jespersen (1933:255):

Originally this use [the contrary-to-fact conditional] was restricted to . . . the preterit subjunctive, and the unreality was denoted by the mood rather than by the tense. But in the course of time the distinction between the forms of the subjunctive and those of the indicative came to be blotted out, and in 99% of cases it is impossible to tell which of the two moods is used.

In other words, instead of a past indicative, the sentence contains a future subjunctive. Admittedly, it *looks* past, but this is only the result of a historical accident, a delinquent merging of forms.

Regrettably, the transformationalist has no light to shed on the issue; there is no TG formulation of the conditional.

A second problem is far more important. Many foreign learners speak languages in which there is no distinction between factual and counterfactual (or true and contrary-to-fact) conditions, and for such students there is an obvious conceptual problem.

With some variations, the standard presentation of the conditional system involves six types of sentences, as follows:

	NONPAST	NONPAST
factual:	If you mail it tomorrow, she'll get it Friday.	
counterfact:	If you mailed it tomorrow, she'd get it Friday.	

	PAST	NONPAST
factual:	If you mailed it yesterday, she'll get it tomorrow.	
counter:	If you'd mailed it yesterday, she'd have gotten it tomorrow.	

	PAST	PAST
factual:	If you mailed it yesterday, it didn't go out.	
counter:	If you'd mailed it yesterday, it wouldn't have gone out.	

When dealing with counterfactual conditions, there is seldom great difficulty in understanding that the condition itself might be known to be untrue, that in *If today were Tuesday* the speaker knows full well that, in fact, today is *not* Tuesday. Similarly, it is not too difficult to recognize circumstances where one can only be uncertain about the truth. In general, factual and counterfactual conditions divide along this line:

Factual: uncertainty as to the fact
Counterfactual: certainty as to the nonfact

For example,

If this is an apple (I am not certain whether it is or not)
If this were an apple (I know that it is not)

The problem lies principally in accounting for nonpast counterfactual conditions that lie in the future, where it is usually difficult to be sure of a nonfact. Theoretically, the difference between future factual and counterfactual conditions is said to be a matter of presumed probability or intention. In point of fact, however, I know of no evidence that shows that English speakers really do use the two consistently, and in some cases the choice may be largely arbitrary. It may be, then, that the careful distinction between *If you mail it tomorrow* and *if you mailed it tomorrow* is an exercise of dubious value, especially when compared to the troubles that it causes.

Exercise 3.5

Draw trees for and derive the following sentences.
1. John kissed his wife and so did Bill. (Pay close attention to just whose wife Bill kissed.)
2. I put the box down where he told me to. (You will have to invent a **Zap** for this one.)
3. This text, which I have slaved over, has come to an end.
4. Since he asked me to, I helped John wash and wax his car.
5. John kissed and kicked his wife and his dog, respectively.

3.6 Summary: Transformational Component

The following additions were made to the PS rules in the course of Part 3:

$$S \rightarrow \left\{ \begin{array}{l} (\text{Ques}) + (\text{Neg}) + \text{NP} + \text{VP} + (\text{SAP}) \\ S + X + S \end{array} \right\}$$

$$X \rightarrow \{ \text{Cause, et al.} \}$$

$$NP \rightarrow \left\{ \begin{array}{l} \text{Art} + (\text{Adj}) + \cdots + (\text{Adj}) + \text{N} + \# + (\text{S}) + \cdots + (\text{S}) \\ \text{if} + \text{S} \\ \text{that} + \text{S} \\ S' \end{array} \right\}$$

$$S' \rightarrow (\text{NP}) + \text{VP}'$$

$$\text{VP}' \rightarrow (\text{Aux}') + \text{V} + (\text{Comp})$$

$$\text{Aux}' \rightarrow (\text{Perf}) + (\text{Prog}) + (\text{Passive})$$

$$\text{Aux} \rightarrow \left\{ \begin{array}{l} \text{Mod} \\ \text{Ten} \end{array} \right\} + (\text{Perf}) + (\text{Prog}) + (\text{Passive})$$

$$\text{Passive} \rightarrow \text{be} + \text{-en}$$

$$\text{Comp} \rightarrow \left\{ \begin{array}{l} \text{Adj} + S' \\ \text{too-Adj} \end{array} \right\}$$

$$\text{too-Adj} \rightarrow \text{too} + \text{Adj} + (S')$$

$$\text{VAP} \rightarrow \text{S}$$

The following transformational operations were discussed:

1. **Question switch (QS)**, motivated by the presence of *Ques*, switches the position of a subject NP and a combination of tense and the first verbal in the auxiliary, or the verb *be*.

2. *Do* **insertion (DI)**, motivated by an inability to perform the **Flip-flop** rule, inserts *do* into position immediately following tense.

3. *Not* **insertion (NI)**, motivated by the presence of *Neg*, inserts *not* into position following the first verbal in the auxiliary, or the verb *be*, or if neither should exist, following tense.

175

4. *Wh-* **fronting (WF)**, motivated by the presence of an interrogative pronoun, moves the *wh-* to the front of its sentence.

5. **Passive (Pass)**, motivated by the presence of the constituent Passive, moves the NP following the verb into subject position and shifts the original subject NP either out of the sentence entirely or into a *by*-agent phrase at the end of the sentence.

6. *Wh-* **replacement (Whir)**, motivated by a repeated NP within a modifying sentence, replaces the repeated NP with an appropriate relative pronoun.

7. *Wh-* **movement (Whim)**, motivated by the presence of a relative pronoun, moves that pronoun to the front of its sentence.

8. *Wh-* **deletion (Whiddle)**, unmotivated, optionally deletes a relative pronoun, so long as it does not represent the surface subject of the modifying sentence.

9. *Wh-*, **Tense, and** *be* **deletion (Whiz)**, unmotivated, optionally deletes the sequence *wh-* Ten *be* from a modifying sentence.

10. **Unicorn**, motivated by the presence of a single modifying term following the modified NP, moves that term to a position before the NP.

11. **Gerund (Ger)**, motivated in part by the feature [*+Fact*], transforms the verb of a S′ into gerund form. If the verb has a subject that is not subject to the **SM** rule, then the NP will be given possessive form.

12. **Infinitive (Inf)**, motivated in part by the feature [*−Fact*], transforms the verb of a S′ into infinitive form. If the verb has a subject NP not otherwise subject to the **SM** rule, then the NP will be made the object of the preposition *for*.

13. **Subject-matching (SM)**, motivated by an embedded S′, compares the subject NP of the S′ with the subject NP of the next higher sentence. If they are identical, the lower NP is deleted. If they are different, the lower NP is preserved in object form.

14. **Extraposition (Extra)**, unmotivated, moves the subject NP to a position following the verb.

15. **Extraposition-plus (Extra+)**, unmotivated, moves all but the object NP of a RNS in subject position to a position following the verb.

16. **Expletive (Exp)**, motivated by the absence of a required subject NP, supplies *it* to fulfill that requirement.

17. **And so did**, motivated by conjoined sentences with identical VPs, replaces the second sentence with *and so* Ten *do* followed by the subject NP of the original second sentence.

Three additional operations were discussed, but not named (that is, **Zaps**):

(a) that transformed the sequence *that which* into *what*;

(b) that deleted an NP from an S′ complementary to a predicate adjective, if the subject of the adjective were identical to the deleted NP;

(c) that inserted a conjoined sentence containing unneeded information about a NP in the first sentence into a parenthetical statement following the NP in the first sentence.

Exercise 3.6

1. Order the following transformations with respect to each other, on the assumption that they are found within the same sentence node: **SM, Gerund, Passive, NI**.
2. What are the limits of the uses of *but*? Consider the following sentences:
   a. John likes tea but Mary likes it.
   b. John likes tea but he dislikes it.
   c. John likes tea but he likes coffee.
   d. John likes tea but Mary dislikes coffee.
3. An operation, called **And so did** (p. 176), has a more complex formulation than is implied, for it is also involved in sentences like *John can ski and so can Mary*. How would you formulate it?
4. Under what circumstances can *unless* mean *if. . .not*?

References: Part 3

Bolinger, Dwight. 1967. "Imperatives in English." *Studies Presented to Roman Jakobson on the Occasion of His Seventieth Birthday*. The Hague: Mouton.

Chomsky, Noam. 1957. *Syntactic Structures*. The Hague: Mouton.

Chomsky, Noam. 1965. *Aspects of the Theory of Syntax*. Cambridge, Mass.: M.I.T. Press.

Fillmore, Charles. 1968. "The case for case." E. Bach and R. Harms, eds., *Universals in Linguistic Theory*. New York: Holt, Rinehart & Winston.

Fodor, Jerry A., and M. Garrett. 1967. "Some syntactic determinants in sentential complexity." *Perceptions and Psychophysics*, 2/7:289–296.

Jackendoff, Ray. 1969. "An interpretive theory of negation." *Foundations of Language*, V.

Jacobs, R., and P. Rosenbaum. 1967. *Grammar 3*. Boston: Ginn.

Jespersen, Otto. 1933. *Essentials of English Grammar*. London: George Allen and Unwin.

Katz, J. J., and J. A. Fodor. 1964. "The structure of a semantic theory." *Language*, 39:170–210. Reprinted in J. A. Fodor and J. J. Katz, eds., *The Structure of Language*. Englewood Cliffs, N.J.: Prentice-Hall.

Kiparsky, Paul, and Carol Kiparsky. 1970. "Fact." M. Bierwisch and R. Heidolph, eds., *Progress in Linguistics*. The Hague: Mouton. Reprinted in Steinberg and Jacobovits, eds. (1971), *Semantics*. Cambridge: Cambridge University Press.

Klima, Edward. 1964. "Negation in English." J. A. Fodor and J. J. Katz, eds., *The Structure of Language*. Englewood Cliffs, N.J.: Prentice-Hall.

Krohn, Robert. 1971. *English Sentence Structure*. Ann Arbor: University of Michigan Press.

Lado, Robert, and C. C. Fries. 1957. *English Sentence Patterns*. Ann Arbor: University of Michigan Press.

Lakoff, Robin. 1969. "Transformational grammar and language teaching," *Language Learning*, XIX/1,2:117-140.

Langendoen, D. T. 1970. *Essentials of English Grammar*. New York: Holt, Rinehart & Winston.

Lester, Mark. 1971. *Introductory Transformational Grammar of English*. New York: Holt, Rinehart & Winston.

Niyekawa-Howard, Agnes. 1968. "A psycholinguistic study of the Worfian hypothesis based on the Japanese passive." Paper presented at the 13th Annual National Conference on Linguistics, New York, March 10 (mimeo.).

APPENDIX

Summary of Rules

PHRASE STRUCTURE GRAMMAR (THREE)[1]

1 S → $\begin{cases} \text{(Ques) + (Neg) + NP + VP + (SAP)} & (61,97,110) \\ \text{S + X + S} & (167) \end{cases}$

2 NP → $\begin{cases} \text{Art + (Adj) + ... + (Adj) + N + \#} & (137) \\ \text{Name} & (64) \\ \text{ProN} & (65) \\ \text{NP + (S) + ... + (S)} & (128,136) \\ \text{if + S} & (144) \\ \text{that + S} & (144) \\ \text{S}' & (148) \end{cases}$

3 Art → (Quant) + (Det)   (67)

4 Det → $\begin{cases} \text{NP + 's} & (71) \\ \text{Lex[Det]} & (67) \end{cases}$

5 VP → Aux + V + Comp + (VAP)   (76,90)

6 Aux → $\begin{cases} \text{Mod} \\ \text{Ten} \end{cases}$ + (Perf) + (Prog) + (Passive)   (76,81,121)

7 Comp → $\begin{cases} \text{(NP)} \\ \text{NP} \\ \text{NP + to NP} \\ \text{NP + Loc} \\ \text{NP + NP} \\ \emptyset \\ \text{Loc} \\ \text{Adj} \\ \text{Adj + S}' & (159) \\ \text{too- Adj} & (162) \end{cases}$ (94)

[1] Page references are given within parentheses after each rule.

8 VAP → $\begin{cases} (\text{Freq}) + (\text{Manner}) + (\text{Time}) + (\text{Loc}) & (98) \\ \text{S} \quad (171) \end{cases}$

9 Loc → $\begin{cases} \text{Locadv} \\ \text{PP} \end{cases}$ (99)

10 PP → P + NP
11 too–Adj → too + Adj + (S′) (162)
12 S′ → (NP) + VP′ (149)
13 VP′ → (Aux′) + V + (Comp)
14 Aux′ → (Perf) + (Prog) + (Passive)
15 X → {Cause, et al.} (167)
16 Ten → {*pres, past*} (76)
17 # → {*singular, plural*} (63)
18 Perf → have + -en (83)
19 Prog → be + -ing (85)
20 Passive → be + -en (119)

Lexical rules, all of the form Z ↔ Lex [Z] , are discussed from p. 53, and exist for all constituents not otherwise accounted for by a PS rule. These include:

Adj	Manner
N	Locadv
Name	P
ProN	Cause
Quant	Mod
V	Time
Freq	

LEXICON

The lexicon consists of entries for words. Each entry contains information about the words, including their grammatical (p. 55) and semantic (p. 57) features.

TRANSFORMATIONAL RULES

In the course of the text, we discussed twenty-six transformational operations, three of which were not named (that is, **Zaps**), not including any operations that were discussed in the answers to the questions. The operations are summarized below, more or less in order of their appearance in the text, and organized into the following sections:

A. Operations that may occur with simple deep structures (that is, deep structures with no embedded or conjoined sentence nodes);
B. Operations that are involved with modifying sentences;
C. Operations that are involved with nominalized sentences;
D. Operations that are involved with conjoined sentences.

A. Simple Sentence Operations

1. **Morphophonemic (MF)** alterations: Changes morphological compounds into surface words, especially verbs with their affixes, nouns, and pronouns. The **MF** rule is not really a proper syntactic rule at all, as it belongs in the phonological component of the grammar. However, without **MF** it is awfully difficult to talk about syntactic derivations, so it has been included (p. 64).

2. **Pronominalization (ProN)** of a repeated NP. Usually, the second instance of the NP is pronominalized, but not always. Such pronouns are called anaphoric pronouns, and are to be distinguished from pronouns generated by a PS rule (p. 65).

3. **Flip-flop (FF)** of a verb and the affix which precedes it. Three separate instances are discussed: tense + verb, -en + verb, and -ing + verb, condensed into one rule (p. 89):

Affix + verbal ⇒ verbal-affix

The **FF** rule is the last rule applied within the context of any particular sentence or embedded sentence.

4. **Object switch (OS)** applies only to the NP + to NP complement structure (that is direct and indirect object structure), inverting the NPs, and getting rid of *to*. More formally,

$NP_1 + to\ NP_2 \Rightarrow NP_2 + NP_1$

No known motivation exists for the **OS** rule. Certain verbs, such as *explain*, are marked as not allowing **OS** (p. 95).

5. **Preposition switch (PS)** applies only to those two-word verbs marked [Separable], switching the position of the preposition and the object NP (p. 102).

6. **Question switch (QS)**, motivated by the presence of the constituent *Ques,* switches the position of the subject NP with that of the tense and a following auxiliary verbal (or the verb *be*). If what follows tense is the main verb, then only tense switches with the NP.

NP + Ten + (v) ⇒ Ten + (v) + NP   (p. 111)

7. **Wh- fronting (WF)**, motivated by the presence of an interrogative pronoun, moves the pronoun to the front of its sentence (p. 115).

8. **Do insertion (DI)**, motivated by an inability to apply **FF** to tense (because tense is followed by some term that connot "take" tense), inserts *do* directly after tense (p. 112).

9. *Not* **insertion (NI),** motivated by the presence of the constituent *Neg* in the deep structure, inserts *not* directly after the same v as mentioned in **QS,** above. If no v exists, then *not* is inserted directly after tense (p. 118).

10. **Passive (Pass),** motivated by the presence of the constituent *Passive* in the deep structure, moves the first NP after the verb into subject position. The deep structure subject is either removed entirely or, in some cases, may be preserved in a *by*-agent phrase at the end of the sentence (p. 121).

B. Modifier Operations

11. *Wh-* **replacement (Whir),** motivated by the presence, in a modifying sentence, of an NP identical to that being modified, replaces the NP with an appropriate relative pronoun (p. 129).

12. *Wh-* **movement (Whim),** motivated by the presence of a relative pronoun, moves that pronoun to the front of its sentence (p. 130).

13. *Wh-* **deletion (Whiddle),** optionally deletes the relative pronoun so long as it does not represent the subject of the modifying sentence (p. 132).

14. *Wh-* **tense, and** *be* **deletion (Whiz),** optionally deletes the sequence *wh-* + Ten + *be* from modifying sentence (p. 133).

15. **Unicorn,** motivated by a single modifying term after a NP, moves the term to a position directly in front of the NP (p. 135).

16. **Zap** optionally transforms the sequence *that* + *which* into the term *what* (p. 146).

C. Nominalization Operations

17. **Gerund (Ger)** transforms a verb into its gerund form, and its subject into possessive form if it is not subject to the **SM** rule. In some cases—for example, when as complement to another verb—the **Gerund** rule is motivated by the feature [+ *Fact*] in the other verb (p. 149).

18. **Infinitive (Inf)** transforms a verb into its infinitive form, and its subject into the object of the preposition *for* if it is not subject to the **SM** rule. In some cases—for example, when as complement to another verb—the **Infinitive** rule is motivated by the feature [−*Fact*] in the other verb (p. 149).

19. **Extraposition (Extra)** optionally moves a nominalized sentence in subject position to a position following the main VP, for example,

to fly planes *pres* be easy
　　　pres be easy to fly planes　　(p. 150).

20. **Extraposition-plus (Extra+)** optionally moves a nominalized sentence in subject position to a position following the main VP, but leaves the object of the nominalized sentence behind, for example,

to fly planes *pres* be easy
　　　planes *pres* be easy to fly　　(p. 152)

21. **Expletive** *it* **supplier (Exp)** supplies *it* as a subject to sentences which either never had a subject or which are missing one as a result of an operation—as, for example, the sentence illustrating extraposition above:

> *pres* be easy to fly planes
> it *pres* be easy to fly planes   (p.152)

22. **Subject-matching (SM)**, motivated by the presence of a subject in a S' complementary to a higher verb, compares that subject NP with the subject NP of the next higher verb. If they are identical, the NP (of the lower S') is deleted; otherwise it is preserved in object form (p. 154).

23. **Zap.** When a S' is complementary to an adjective which is itself predicate to a NP, if the S' contains the same NP, it is deleted (p. 161).

D. Conjoining Operations

24. **And so did**, motivated by conjoined sentences with identical VPs, transforms the second into the form *and so did Bill* or the equivalent. Details of the operation were not considered except as part of a question (p. 169).

25. **Respectively** condenses two conjoined sentences with identical verbs into one sentence with conjoined subjects and objects (p. 169).

26. **Zap.** When a second conjoined sentence expresses extra or unneeded information about some NP in the first sentence, the second may be inserted parenthetically directly after the NP in the first (p. 169).

Answers to Exercises

Exercise 1.11

1.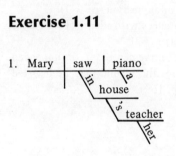

2.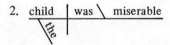

3.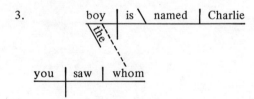

4.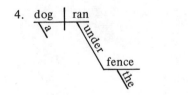

Exercise 1.12

1.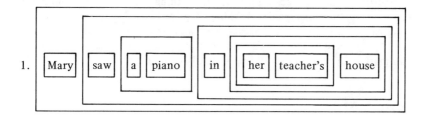

2.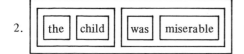

3.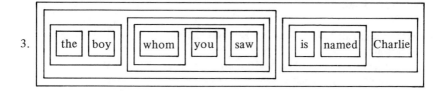

4.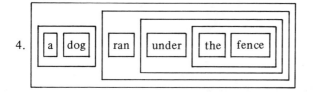

Exercise 1.13

1. /k, s/
2. No; /aw/ versus /ɔ/
3. No; a minimal spelling difference.
4. /yuw/ versus /uw/ or /y/ versus /∅/ ("nothing")
5. No. /ɪ/ versus /ay/; a minimal spelling difference.
6. /g, m/
7. /š, t/
8. /a, ɔ/
9. No; homonyms.
10. /t, θ/

Exercise 1.16

Traditionalist:	a noun, because a "cat" is a "thing," and of course nouns are "persons, places, or things."
Structuralist:	a Class I word, because *cat* can occur in a plural form (with *-s*), and can also occur in such frames as *The . . . is here.*
TG grammarian:	a noun. You just know that it's a noun.

Exercise 1.51

1., 2., and 4. involve paraphrases.
3. does not.
5. is, or is not, a set of paraphrases, depending on your preferred grammatical theory.

Exercise 1.52

1. is grammatically ambiguous: *tigers* may be either the subject or object of *hunt*.
2. is not ambiguous.
3. is ambiguous on lexical grounds: *lamb* may mean the animal or the meat.
4. is grammatically ambiguous: *pigs* may be the subject or object of *eat*.
5. is grammatically ambiguous: *it* may be the subject or object of *drink* or may be neither, that is, *it* may be the "expletive *it*."

Exercise 1.54

All are quasi-ambiguous.
1. *fall* is a verb, *interesting* is an adjective.
2. *candy* is the object of *eat*, *stars* is the subject of *fall*.
3. *the boy* is the subject of *drink*, *the toast* is the object of *eat*.
4. *up* is part of the verbal idiom, *call up*, *on* is acting as a normal preposition in the phrase *on the couch*.

Exercise 2.12

1. a. The boy has seen the girl.

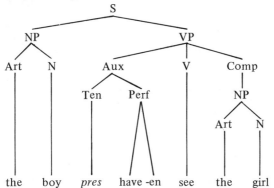

b. School was good.

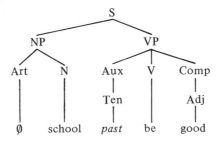

c. The girl was going to school.

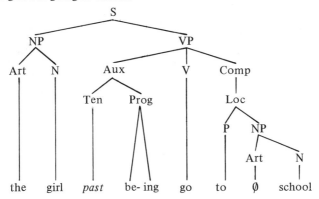

d. A girl can be seeing the stone.

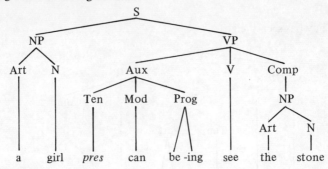

e. The boy will have been in the school.

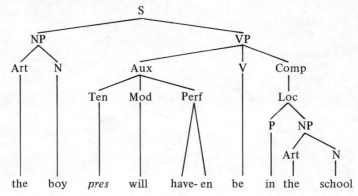

2. The easiest way is to alter rules 12 and 13 to read:

   12′ Perf → VCA + -en   (VCA: verb construct auxiliary)
   13′ Prog → VCA + -ing

A new lexical rule may then be added:

   16′ VCA → Lex [VCA]

and the lexicon itself may be augmented by the two words *have* [VCA] and *be* [VCA]. Attractive as this alternative may be, we shall continue to use the original formulation throughout the text.

Exercise 2.21

1. No. The new system simply shuffles information around; it does not add any new restrictions that were not there before, except as have already been discussed.

2. a. give [V], [Comp: NP + to NP] (that is, both direct and indirect objects required)
   b. three [Number] (or perhaps [Adj]), [Plural]
   c. happily [Adv], [Manner] (it's not any old adverb)
   d. sand [N], [Noncount]
   e. those [Art], (or perhaps [Demonstrative]), [Plural]

Exercise 2.22A

1. tree [N], [Count], (−*Animate*)
2. water [N], [Noncount], (−*Living*)
3. mother [N], [Count], (+*Human*)
4. music [N], [Noncount], (−*Concrete*)
5. lizard [N], [Count], (−*Human*)

Exercise 2.22B

1. The feature (*Liquid*) may fall below (−*Living*).

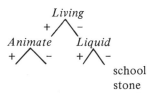

Now the lexical entry for *school* includes (− Liquid), and the feature for the adjective *liquid* includes (*subj: + Liquid*), with the result that *the school is liquid* would be marked as anomalous.
2. *Give* has three nouns associated with it: subject, direct object, and indirect object.

   The subject of give must always be at least animate, and probably human. Is it straightforward or metaphorical to say *The dog gave me his bone*? To be liberal, (*subj: + Animate*).

   The direct object can be anything concrete. Sentences like *he gave me an idea* are not (in my opinion) quite straightforward. (*direct object: + Concrete*).

   The indirect object is normally human, but can be animate. However, inanimate recipients are—to me—a little odd, and I do not regard *I gave a coat of paint to the house* as being straightforward. (indirect object: + *Animate*).

Exercise 2.41

1. a. John

D.S.   John
by **MF**   John

(In other words, the **Morphonemic** rule is not really necessary to make the appearance of the deep structure more comfortable for us.)

b. they

D.S.   they
by **MF**   they

(Ditto. However, it is a good idea to practice **MF** anyway, just to get into the groove of remembering to do it when it is necessary.)

c. water

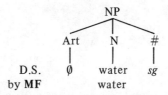

D.S.   ∅   water   *sg*
by **MF**   water

(Here, for example, **MF** disposes of ∅ and *sg*.)

d. the stone

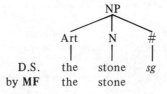

D.S.   the   stone   *sg*
by **MF**   the   stone

e. the men

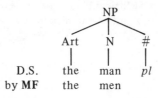

D.S.   the   man   *pl*
by **MF**   the   men

(And here, **MF** gives us the surface form *men*, from the sequence *man pl*.)

2. Probably not. However, defer the question until later, when your understanding of the grammar is richer—specifically, until Section 3.42 on expletive *it*.

Exercise 2.42

1. a friend

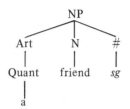

2. that dog

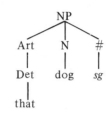

3. these women

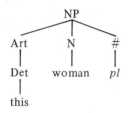

4. one of the girls

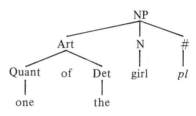

5. my brother's book   6. my brother's friend's book

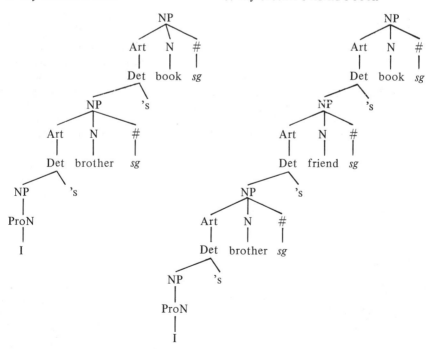

7. one of my brother's friends' books

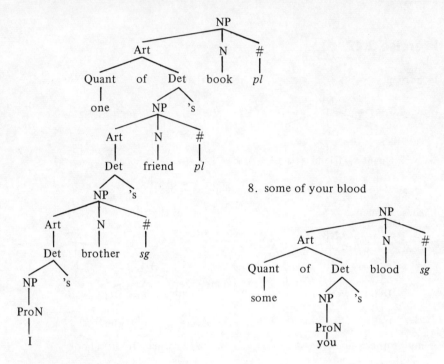

8. some of your blood

Exercise 2.44

1. While no two counts will be the same, it is expected that the most common category of *the* will be in the self-defining NP, which includes most cases of nouns followed by a modifying phrase, nouns that are modified by a superlative adjective or an ordinal numeral, and perhaps a few others. The next most common category is probably that of previously mentioned nouns following which we may find unique or universally known nouns (such as *the sun*), names, and finally an assortment of somewhat difficult to classify addenda.

2. When a countable noun is used without any article in the singular, it is most likely intended to indicate the *use* to which that noun is put: as food, as material, or whatever. The question remains whether *stone* in 2b is simply the mass noun *stone*, or a specialized use of the countable noun *stone*. I suspect the latter, as stone buildings are made of stones, not a mass of stone.

Exercise 2.52

It has been suggested (but not in print, to the best of my knowledge) that the construction with *will* may have connotations of determination and that the simple present and present progressive constructions carry implications of plans or schedules, such that the future is already determined. Of the four, the *be going to* future seems to have no additional connotations and so might be called the most neutral future.

Exercise 2.53

1. a. John may arrive tomorrow.

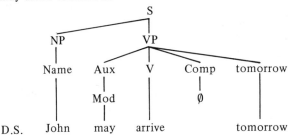

b. Mary must have left yesterday.

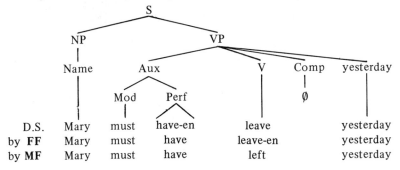

c. Those boys should be in school.

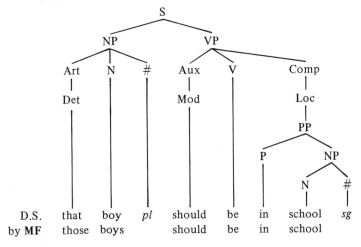

d. My cousin must read this book.

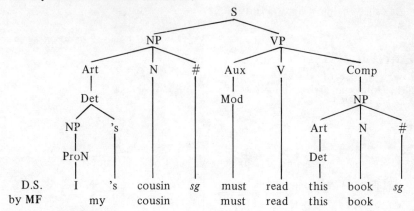

e. I could do it yesterday.

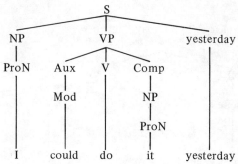

2. Because, unlike *must,* *have to* can be inflected for tense and number and is therefore more like *want to* in its grammar.

Exercise 2.56

1. a. John has been seeing Mary.

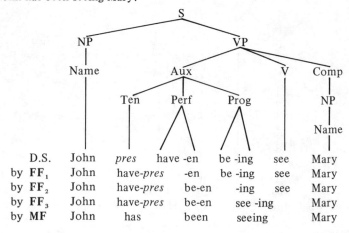

See would normally be marked Stative, suggesting that it cannot co-occur with the progressive construction. In this case it has occurred with it, suggesting that *see* (in this sentence, at least) is not Stative. In fact, in the sentence above, *see* is an Active verb with the meaning "meet," "date," or something along that line, rather than its usual (that is, Stative) meaning.

b. The dog was eating meat.

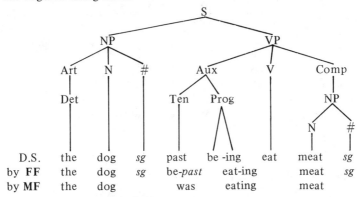

D.S.	the	dog	*sg*	past	be -ing	eat	meat	*sg*
by **FF**	the	dog	*sg*	be-*past*	eat-ing		meat	*sg*
by **MF**	the	dog		was	eating		meat	

c. He may have been telling a lie.

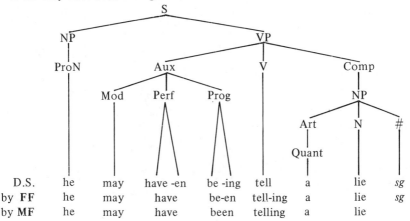

D.S.	he	may	have -en	be -ing	tell	a	lie	*sg*
by **FF**	he	may	have	be-en	tell-ing	a	lie	*sg*
by **MF**	he	may	have	been	telling	a	lie	

d. He is interesting.

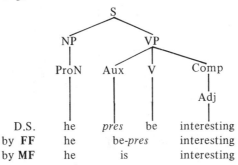

D.S.	he	*pres*	be	interesting
by **FF**	he	be-*pres*		interesting
by **MF**	he	is		interesting

(Let this teach you a lesson: you should have known that *interesting* is an adjective. That it has the appearance of a progressive construction is no excuse for describing it as a progressive.)

e. The stew smells funny.

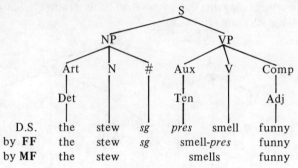

D.S.	the	stew	*sg*	*pres*	smell	funny
by **FF**	the	stew	*sg*	smell-*pres*		funny
by **MF**	the	stew		smells		funny

f. The man had been there.

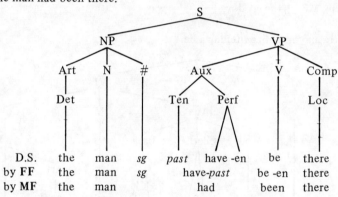

D.S.	the	man	*sg*	*past* have -en	be	there
by **FF**	the	man	*sg*	have-*past*	be -en	there
by **MF**	the	man		had	been	there

2. a. I have lived here since 1948.

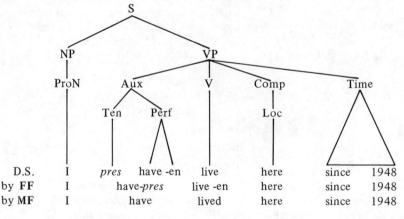

D.S.	I	*pres* have -en	live	here	since	1948
by **FF**	I	have-*pres*	live -en	here	since	1948
by **MF**	I	have	lived	here	since	1948

b. That woman has been sitting there for three hours.

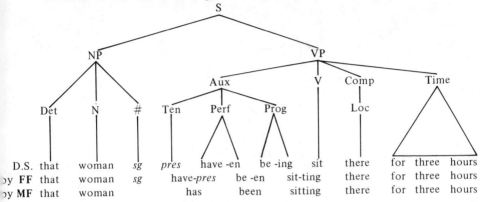

D.S.	that	woman	sg	pres	have -en	be -ing	sit	there	for three hours
ɔy FF	that	woman	sg	have-pres	be -en	sit-ting	there	for three hours
ɔy MF	that	woman			has	been	sitting	there	for three hours

3. One solution might be to have separate (and unrelated) verbs in the *lexicon* with the syntactic and semantic features [Comp: NP], (*subj*: + *Animate*) and [Comp: Adj], (*subj*: + *Concrete*), respectively. The two verbs would then be considered homonyms. A better solution would involve a composite of interlocking syntactic and semantic features in one entry for *smell*:

smell [Comp: $\begin{array}{l} \text{NP] ,(subj: +}Animate) \\ \text{Adj] ,(subj: +}Concrete) \end{array}$

This is "better" because both meanings would be associated with the single word *smell*, suggesting a meaningful relationship between them. Most lexicographers would prefer to treat *smell* as a case of polysemy rather than homonymy.

Exercise 2.6

1. Mary sent her mother a letter.

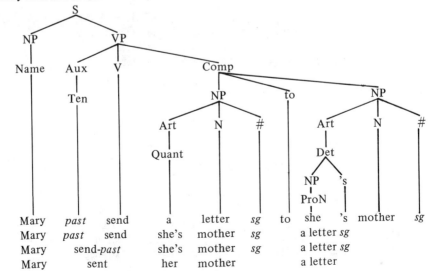

D.S.	Mary	past	send	a	letter	sg	to	she	's	mother	sg
by OS	Mary	past	send	she's	mother	sg		a letter sg			
by FF	Mary	send-past		she's	mother	sg		a letter sg			
by MF	Mary	sent		her	mother			a letter			

2. I put the ball in the closet.

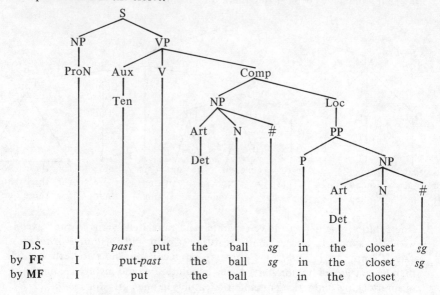

D.S.	I	*past* put	the	ball	*sg*	in	the	closet	*sg*
by **FF**	I	put-*past*	the	ball	*sg*	in	the	closet	*sg*
by **MF**	I	put	the	ball		in	the	closet	

3. They named Masters chief.

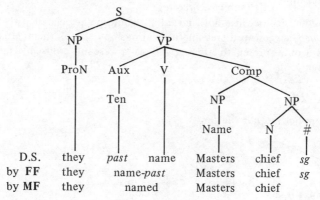

D.S.	they	*past* name	Masters	chief	*sg*
by **FF**	they	name-*past*	Masters	chief	*sg*
by **MF**	they	named	Masters	chief	

4. He looks strange.

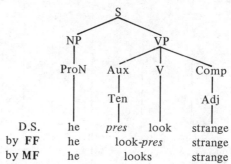

D.S.	he	*pres* look	strange
by **FF**	he	look-*pres*	strange
by **MF**	he	looks	strange

5. I kept it under a handkerchief.

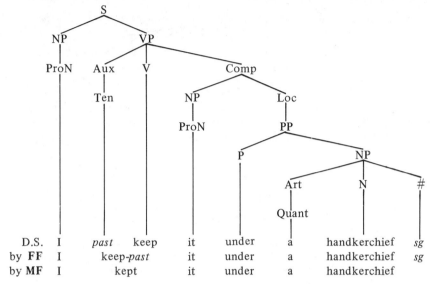

D.S.	I	*past* keep	it	under	a	handkerchief	*sg*
by **FF**	I	keep-*past*	it	under	a	handkerchief	*sg*
by **MF**	I	kept	it	under	a	handkerchief	

Exercise 2.7

1. a. He placed the book under the chair. (complement)

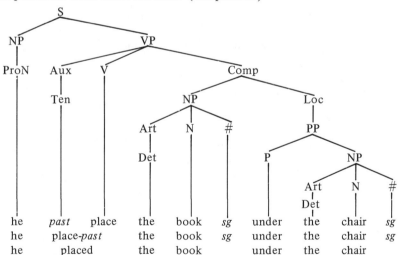

D.S.	he	*past* place	the	book	*sg*	under	the	chair	*sg*
by **FF**	he	place-*past*	the	book	*sg*	under	the	chair	*sg*
by **MF**	he	placed	the	book		under	the	chair	

    b. He's digging with a shovel. (VAP indicating instrument)
       According to the complementhood test, *with a shovel* is not part of the
       complement, indicating that it is a VAP. However, it is obviously not
       an adverb of frequency, manner, time, or place. Whenever this happens,
       feel free to invent another type of adverb. In this case, Instrument.

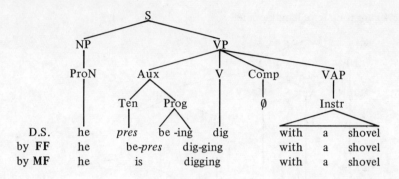

D.S.	he	*pres*	be -ing	dig	with	a	shovel
by **FF**	he	be-*pres*	dig-ging		with	a	shovel
by **MF**	he	is	digging		with	a	shovel

c. He bought a house for his mother. (VAP; would you believe Beneficiary?)

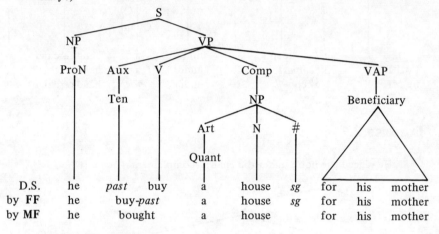

D.S.	he	*past* buy	a	house	*sg*	for	his	mother
by **FF**	he	buy-*past*	a	house	*sg*	for	his	mother
by **MF**	he	bought	a	house		for	his	mother

d. He handed the cat to me. (complement)

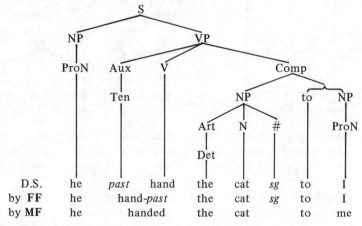

D.S.	he	*past* hand	the	cat	*sg*	to	I
by **FF**	he	hand-*past*	the	cat	*sg*	to	I
by **MF**	he	handed	the	cat		to	me

e. He usually hid the bottle in the desk. (VAP of Location)

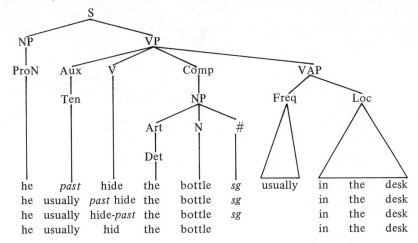

D.S.	he	*past*	hide	the	bottle	*sg*	usually	in	the	desk
by **Freq**[1]	he	usually	*past* hide	the	bottle	*sg*		in	the	desk
by **FF**	he	usually	hide-*past*	the	bottle	*sg*		in	the	desk
by **MF**	he	usually	hid	the	bottle			in	the	desk

2. a. Unfortunately, he got drunk.

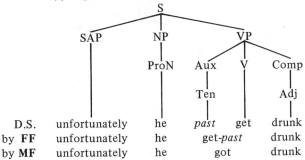

D.S.	unfortunately	he	*past*	get	drunk
by **FF**	unfortunately	he	get-*past*		drunk
by **MF**	unfortunately	he	got		drunk

b. We leave tomorrow at three o'clock.

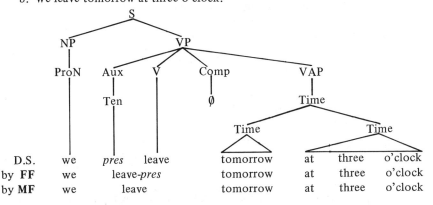

D.S.	we	*pres*	leave	tomorrow	at	three	o'clock
by **FF**	we	leave-*pres*		tomorrow	at	three	o'clock
by **MF**	we	leave		tomorrow	at	three	o'clock

[1] **Freq** moves frequency adverbs, of course, cf. p. 99.

c. He jumped awkwardly over the log.

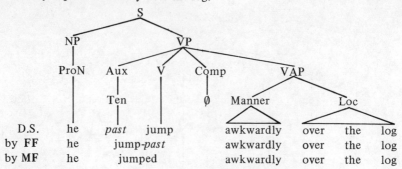

D.S.	he	*past*	jump	awkwardly	over	the	log
by **FF**	he	jump-*past*		awkwardly	over	the	log
by **MF**	he	jumped		awkwardly	over	the	log

Exercise 2.8

1. He turned the radio on.

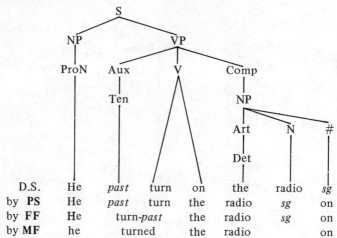

D.S.	He	*past*	turn	on	the	radio	*sg*
by **PS**	He	*past*	turn	the	radio	*sg*	on
by **FF**	He	turn-*past*		the	radio	*sg*	on
by **MF**	he	turned		the	radio		on

2. I made off with it.

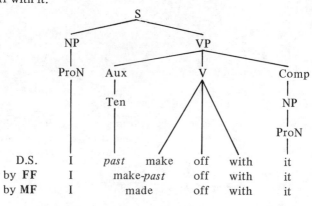

D.S.	I	*past*	make	off	with	it
by **FF**	I	make-*past*		off	with	it
by **MF**	I	made		off	with	it

3. She took off her gloves.

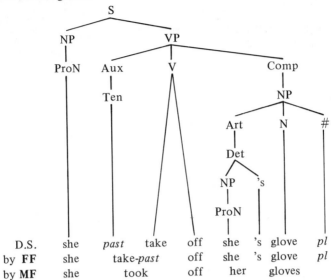

	D.S.	she	*past*	take	off	she	's	glove	*pl*
by **FF**	she	take-*past*	off	she	's	glove	*pl*
by **MF**	she	took	off	her	gloves

4. We called for her the next day.

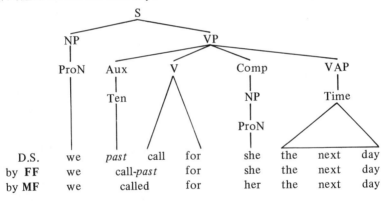

	D.S.	we	*past*	call	for	she	the	next	day
by **FF**	we	call-*past*	for	she	the	next	day
by **MF**	we	called	for	her	the	next	day

Exercise 2.9

1. a. Two of his brother's friends stomped him.

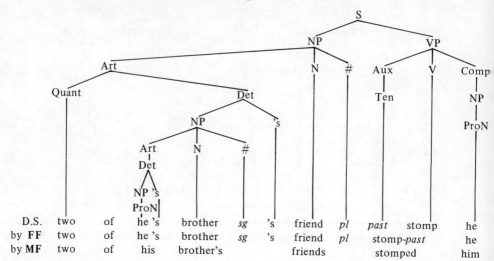

b. He must have gone there yesterday.

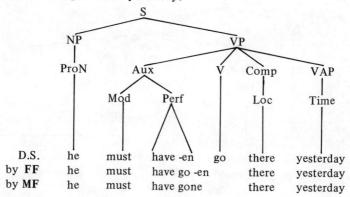

c. He's been feeling better since Monday.

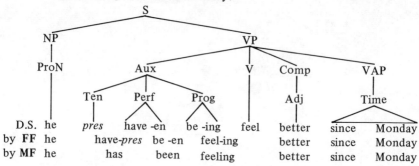

d. He keeps dingbats in the cellar.

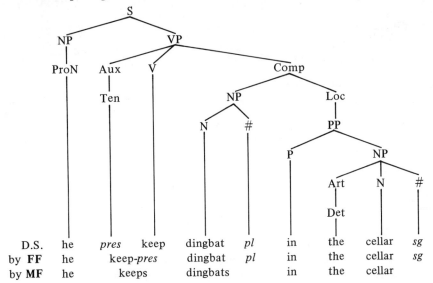

	D.S.	he	*pres*	keep	dingbat	*pl*	in	the	cellar	*sg*
by **FF**		he		keep-*pres*	dingbat	*pl*	in	the	cellar	*sg*
by **MF**		he		keeps	dingbats		in	the	cellar	

e. He's very interesting.

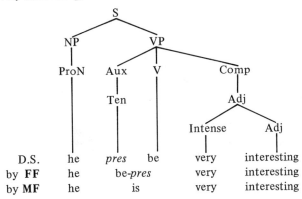

	D.S.	he	*pres*	be	very	interesting
by **FF**		he	be-*pres*		very	interesting
by **MF**		he	is		very	interesting

f. She may be studying in the library.

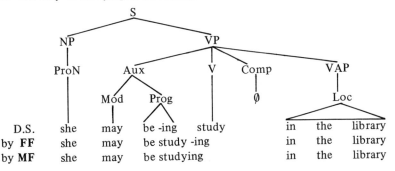

	D.S.	she	may	be -ing	study	in	the	library
by **FF**		she	may	be study -ing		in	the	library
by **MF**		she	may	be studying		in	the	library

g. Horribly, he ran a dog down with his car.

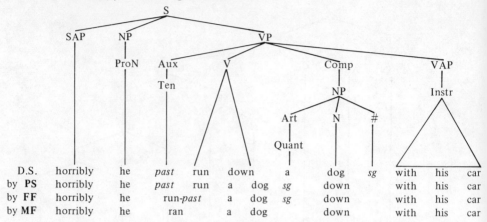

	SAP	NP	Aux	V		Comp		VAP
D.S.	horribly	he	*past*	run	down	a	dog	*sg*	with	his	car
by **PS**	horribly	he	*past*	run	a	dog	*sg*	down	with	his	car
by **FF**	horribly	he	run-*past*	a	dog	*sg*	down	with	his	car
by **MF**	horribly	he	ran	a	dog	down	with	his	car

2. They are paraphrases because they mean the same thing and the content words—the nouns and verbs—are the same.

3. *Answer* may take a direct object (*I answered the question*) or an indirect object (*I answered him*), but never both (**I answered him the question*).

Exercise 3.12

1. a. Is he helping you?

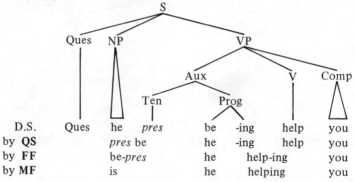

	Ques	NP		Aux		V	Comp
D.S.	Ques	he	*pres*	be	-ing	help	you
by **QS**		*pres* be		he	-ing	help	you
by **FF**		be-*pres*		he	help-ing		you
by **MF**		is		he	helping		you

b. Has John given the book to Mary?

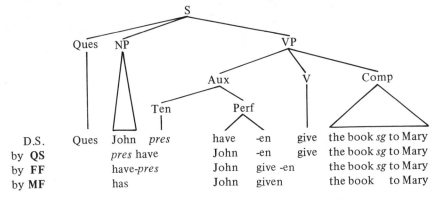

D.S.	Ques	John	*pres*	have	-en	give	the book *sg* to Mary
by **QS**			*pres* have	John	-en	give	the book *sg* to Mary
by **FF**			have-*pres*	John	give -en		the book *sg* to Mary
by **MF**			has	John	given		the book to Mary

c. Were the girls at school?

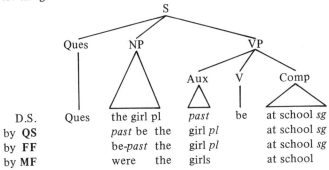

D.S.	Ques	the girl pl	*past*	be	at school *sg*
by **QS**		*past* be the	girl *pl*		at school *sg*
by **FF**		be-*past* the	girl *pl*		at school *sg*
by **MF**		were the	girls		at school

d. Did you fix my bicycle?

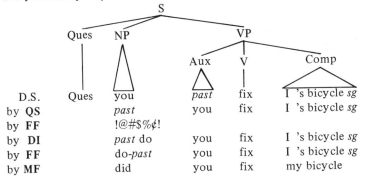

D.S.	Ques	you	*past*	fix	I 's bicycle *sg*
by **QS**		*past*	you	fix	I 's bicycle *sg*
by **FF**		!@#$%¢!			
by **DI**		*past* do	you	fix	I 's bicycle *sg*
by **FF**		do-*past*	you	fix	I 's bicycle *sg*
by **MF**		did	you	fix	my bicycle

e. Will you read it to me?

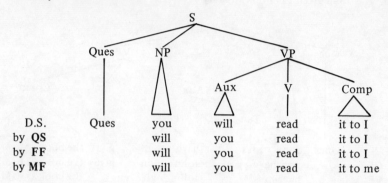

D.S.	Ques	you	will	read	it to I
by **QS**		will	you	read	it to I
by **FF**		will	you	read	it to I
by **MF**		will	you	read	it to me

(Strictly speaking, we could have skipped **FF**, but it's always good practice to cover all the bases.)

2. In Britain (where they regard our *Do you have* . . . as unstylish, if not downright primitive), the verb *have* in the meaning "possess" is grammatically similar to *be*. In the **Question Switch** and **Not Insertion** rules, which read:

QS   NP Tense (v) ⇒ Tense (v) NP
NI   Tense (v)   ⇒ Tense (v) not

v must be defined to include both *be* and *have* in Britain, whereas it includes only *be* in most American dialects.

Exercise 3.13

1. a. What did the man give to you?

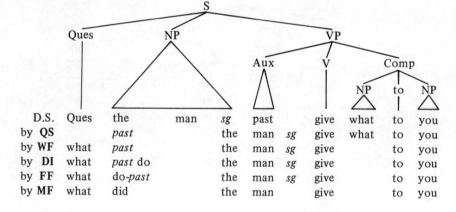

D.S.	Ques	the	man	*sg*	past	give	what	to	you
by **QS**		*past*			the	man *sg*	give	what	to	you
by **WF**	what	*past*			the	man *sg*	give		to	you
by **DI**	what	*past* do			the	man *sg*	give		to	you
by **FF**	what	do-*past*			the	man *sg*	give		to	you
by **MF**	what	did			the	man	give		to	you

b. Who has read the book?

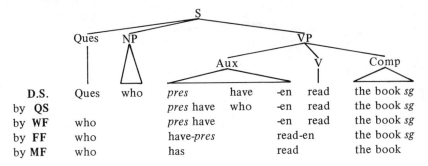

D.S.	Ques	who	*pres*	have	-en	read	the book *sg*
by **QS**			*pres* have	who	-en	read	the book *sg*
by **WF**	who		*pres* have		-en	read	the book *sg*
by **FF**	who		have-*pres*		read-en		the book *sg*
by **MF**	who		has		read		the book

c. When did he leave?

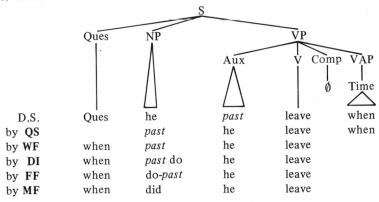

D.S.	Ques	he	*past*	leave		when
by **QS**			*past*	he	leave	when
by **WF**	when		*past*	he	leave	
by **DI**	when		*past* do	he	leave	
by **FF**	when		do-*past*	he	leave	
by **MF**	when		did	he	leave	

d. How many children were here?

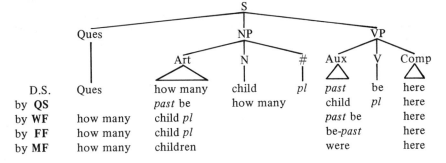

D.S.	Ques	how many	child	*pl*	*past*	be	here
by **QS**		*past* be	how many		child	*pl*	here
by **WF**	how many	child *pl*			*past* be		here
by **FF**	how many	child *pl*			be-*past*		here
by **MF**	how many	children			were		here

e. Whose friend are you?

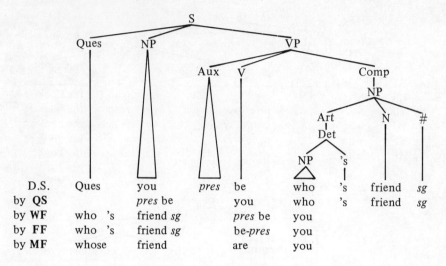

D.S.	Ques	you	*pres*	be	who	's	friend	*sg*
by **QS**		*pres* be		you	who	's	friend	*sg*
by **WF**	who 's	friend *sg*		*pres* be	you			
by **FF**	who 's	friend *sg*		be-*pres*	you			
by **MF**	whose	friend		are	you			

2. The "tag" question involves:
   (a) recognition of the auxiliary structure of the base sentence, and its reuse in the tag;
   (b) pronominalization of the base subject in the tag;
   (c) change of positive to negative (or vice versa) from base S to tag.
   One possible formulation may involve the **Tag** rule, which looks like this:

Tag   Tagques αNeg NP$_1$ Tense (v) . . .
   $\Rightarrow$ αNeg NP$_1$ Tense (v) . . . , Ques $-\alpha$Neg ProN$_1$ Tense (v)

which takes some explaining. αNeg and $-\alpha$Neg are the linguists' way of providing for opposite featurization, in this case Neg to positive and vice versa. α can be either + or −, and −α will be the opposite. (−Neg is assumed to be equivalent to positive in this case). ProN$_1$ is coreferencial to NP$_1$. One part of the **Tag** operation is the alteration of the constituent Tagques to Ques and its positional shift to the tag segment. For example,

John didn't go, did he?

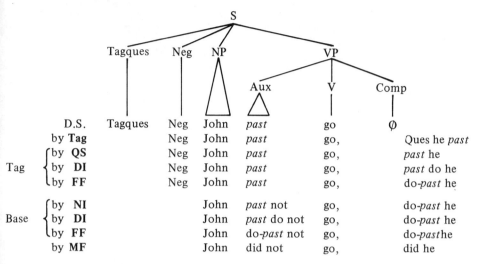

		D.S.	Tagques	Neg	John	*past*	go	$\emptyset$
		by **Tag**		Neg	John	*past*	go,	Ques he *past*
	⎧ by **QS**			Neg	John	*past*	go,	*past* he
Tag	⎨ by **DI**			Neg	John	*past*	go,	*past* do he
	⎩ by **FF**			Neg	John	*past*	go,	do-*past* he
	⎧ by **NI**				John	*past* not	go,	do-*past* he
Base	⎨ by **DI**				John	*past* do not	go,	do-*past* he
	⎩ by **FF**				John	do-*past* not	go,	do-*past*he
	by **MF**				John	did not	go,	did he

It is conventional (and sometimes necessary) to go through the transformational cycle for one sentence completely before going on to another. In this case, the tag qualifies (after a fashion) as a sentence different from the base.

Exercise 3.14

1. He can't help you.

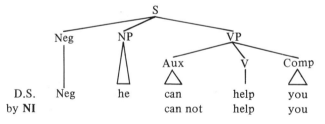

	Neg	NP	Aux	V	Comp
D.S.	Neg	he	can	help	you
by **NI**			can not	help	you

(The contraction of *can not* into *can't* is not normally considered a transformation because of its superficiality. Perhaps it could be considered one of a class of "output" transformational operations.)

2. He didn't see them.

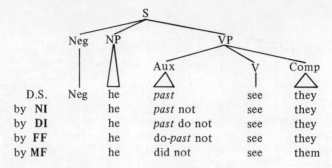

	Neg	NP	Aux	V	Comp
D.S.	Neg	he	*past*	see	they
by **NI**		he	*past* not	see	they
by **DI**		he	*past* do not	see	they
by **FF**		he	do-*past* not	see	they
by **MF**		he	did not	see	them

3. Won't John be angry?

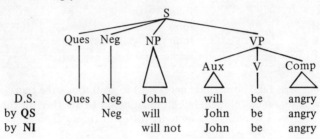

	Ques	Neg	NP	Aux	V	Comp
D.S.	Ques	Neg	John	will	be	angry
by **QS**		Neg	will	John	be	angry
by **NI**			will not	John	be	angry

4. Doesn't Mary look lovely?

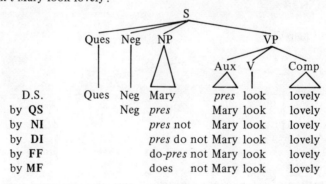

	Ques	Neg	NP	Aux	V	Comp
D.S.	Ques	Neg	Mary	*pres* look		lovely
by **QS**		Neg	*pres*	Mary look		lovely
by **NI**			*pres* not	Mary look		lovely
by **DI**			*pres* do not	Mary look		lovely
by **FF**			do-*pres* not	Mary look		lovely
by **MF**			does not	Mary look		lovely

Exercise 3.16

1. She has been given the prize.

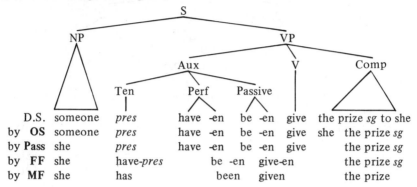

	NP	Ten	Perf	Passive	V	Comp
D.S.	someone	*pres*	have -en	be -en	give	the prize *sg* to she
by **OS**	someone	*pres*	have -en	be -en	give	she the prize *sg*
by **Pass**	she	*pres*	have -en	be -en	give	the prize *sg*
by **FF**	she	have-*pres*		be -en	give-en	the prize *sg*
by **MF**	she	has		been	given	the prize

2. Wasn't he seen there?

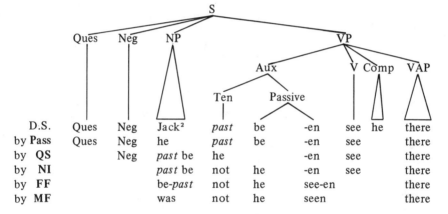

	Ques	Neg	NP	Ten	Passive	V	Comp	VAP
D.S.	Ques	Neg	Jack²	*past* be	-en	see	he	there
by **Pass**	Ques	Neg	he	*past* be	-en	see		there
by **QS**		Neg	*past* be	he	-en	see		there
by **NI**			*past* be	not he	-en	see		there
by **FF**			be-*past*	not he	see-en			there
by **MF**			was	not he	seen			there

3. Hasn't that been corrected?

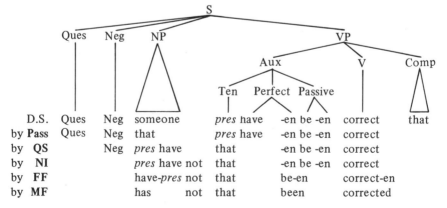

	Ques	Neg	NP	Ten	Perfect	Passive	V	Comp
D.S.	Ques	Neg	someone	*pres* have	-en be	-en	correct	that
by **Pass**	Ques	Neg	that	*pres* have	-en be	-en	correct	
by **QS**		Neg	*pres* have	that	-en be	-en	correct	
by **NI**			*pres* have not	that	-en be	-en	correct	
by **FF**			have-*pres* not	that	be-en		correct-en	
by **MF**			has	not	that		been	corrected

²*Jack?* This is to remind you that any and all NPs may be left out by the **Passive** option.
Not just *someone.*

4. Shouldn't it be destroyed immediately?

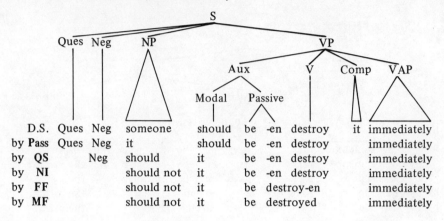

	Ques	Neg	NP	Modal	Passive	V	Comp	VAP
D.S.	Ques	Neg	someone	should	be -en	destroy	it	immediately
by **Pass**	Ques	Neg	it	should	be -en	destroy		immediately
by **QS**		Neg	should	it	be -en	destroy		immediately
by **NI**			should not	it	be -en	destroy		immediately
by **FF**			should not	it	be	destroy-en		immediately
by **MF**			should not	it	be	destroyed		immediately

5. The book must have been taken by Peter.

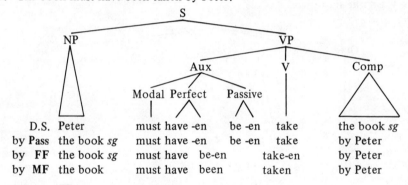

	NP	Modal Perfect	Passive	V	Comp
D.S.	Peter	must have -en	be -en	take	the book *sg*
by **Pass**	the book *sg*	must have -en	be -en	take	by Peter
by **FF**	the book *sg*	must have	be-en	take-en	by Peter
by **MF**	the book	must have	been	taken	by Peter

Exercise 3.18

1. a. Why shouldn't he be forgiven?

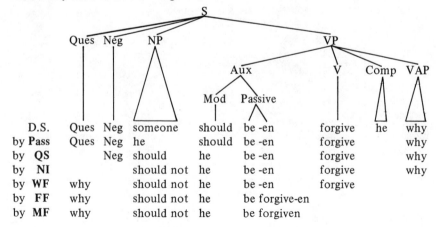

	Ques	Neg	NP	Mod	Passive	V	Comp	VAP
D.S.	Ques	Neg	someone	should	be -en	forgive	he	why
by **Pass**	Ques	Neg	he	should	be -en	forgive		why
by **QS**		Neg	should	he	be -en	forgive		why
by **NI**			should not	he	be -en	forgive		why
by **WF**	why		should not	he	be -en	forgive		
by **FF**	why		should not	he	be forgive-en			
by **MF**	why		should not	he	be forgiven			

b. Aren't they always being seen there?

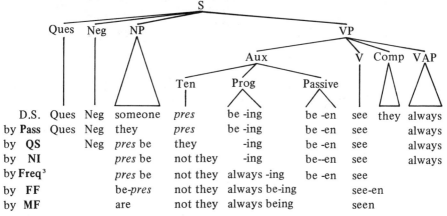

	Ques	Neg	NP	Ten	Prog	Passive	V	Comp	VAP
D.S.	Ques	Neg	someone	pres	be -ing	be -en	see	they	always
by Pass	Ques	Neg	they	pres	be -ing	be -en	see		always
by QS		Neg	pres be	they	-ing	be -en	see		always
by NI			pres be	not they	-ing	be--en	see		always
by Freq³			pres be	not they	always -ing	be -en	see		
by FF			be-*pres*	not they	always be-ing		see-en		
by MF			are	not they	always being		seen		

c. Wasn't Mary given those books?

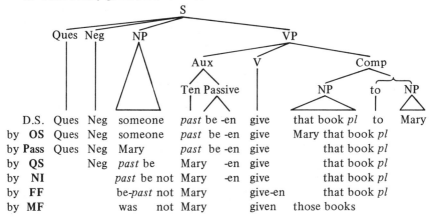

	Ques	Neg	NP	Ten Passive	V	Comp
D.S.	Ques	Neg	someone	*past* be -en	give	that book *pl* to Mary
by OS	Ques	Neg	someone	*past* be -en	give	Mary that book *pl*
by Pass	Ques	Neg	Mary	*past* be -en	give	that book *pl*
by QS		Neg	*past* be	Mary	-en give	that book *pl*
by NI			*past* be not	Mary	-en give	that book *pl*
by FF			be-*past* not	Mary	give-en	that book *pl*
by MF			was	not Mary	given	those books

d. How many men were sent that letter?

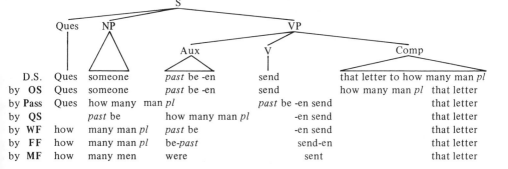

	Ques	NP	Aux	V	Comp
D.S.	Ques	someone	*past* be -en	send	that letter to how many man *pl*
by OS	Ques	someone	*past* be -en	send	how many man *pl* that letter
by Pass	Ques	how many man *pl*		*past* be -en send	that letter
by QS		*past* be	how many man *pl*	-en send	that letter
by WF	how	many man *pl*	*past* be	-en send	that letter
by FF	how	many man *pl*	be-*past*	send-en	that letter
by MF	how	many men	were	sent	that letter

³ **Freq** moves the frequency adverb into position.

e. Who did they speak to?

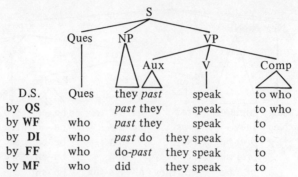

D.S.	Ques	they *past*	speak	to who
by **QS**		*past* they	speak	to who
by **WF**	who	*past* they	speak	to
by **DI**	who	*past* do they speak		to
by **FF**	who	do-*past* they speak		to
by **MF**	who	did they speak		to

2. One way would be to have the constituent **Imp** off to the left, like Ques. **Imp** might then trigger the **Imperative** operation:

Imp   you will V . . . ⇒ V . . .

in which the subject (always *you*) and the modal *will* (I don't want to explain that; look it up) are deleted. The negative imperative requires a special rule of its own:

Neg-imp   you will V . . . ⇒ do not V

in which *you* and *will* are deleted as before, and *do* and *not* are inserted. Why *do*? I don't know. *Do* is not motivated here by the same considerations that motivate the **DI** rule.

3. One possible explanation for the inability to apply the passive operation to *The slipper fit Cinderella* lies in the suggestion (that comes to us via Case Grammar, cf. Fillmore, 1968) that *the slipper* is itself not the deep structure subject of the sentence, but the deep structure object, and that *Cinderella* is a sort of indirect object. There is no deep structure subject (or agent) in the sentence, a circumstance that effectively blocks normal statement or passive development, and instead obligates an operation that results in the sentence as given.

The notion that a sentence might not have a deep structure subject is not entirely alien if you define the subject to be the agent of the sentence or the causer of the events in the predicate. The operation that results might be called the **Middle** operation, for it would certainly be involved in all cases of what used to be called the "middle voice." For example, *The glass broke* might be said to have the following derivation:

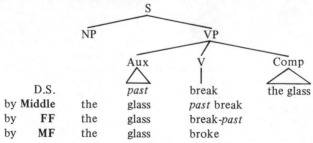

D.S.		*past*	break	the glass
by **Middle**	the	glass	*past* break	
by **FF**	the	glass	break-*past*	
by **MF**	the	glass	broke	

Exercise 3.22

1. a. The dog that bit me was examined.

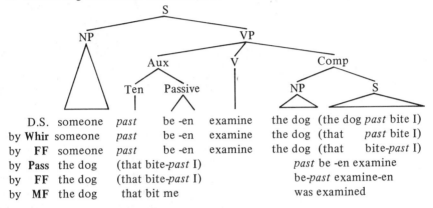

b. The student who didn't pass the exam failed.

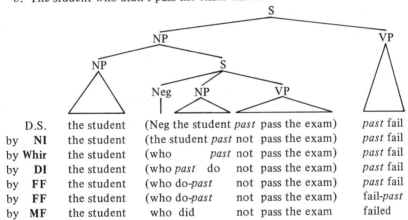

c. The girl I bought the ring for returned it. (anaphoric it!)

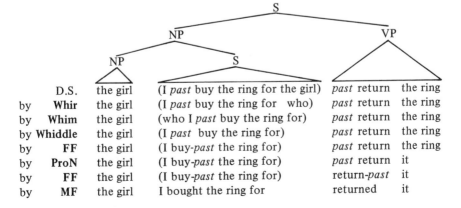

d. Wasn't the girl who didn't come your sister?

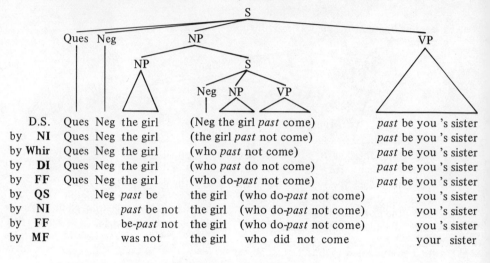

D.S.	Ques Neg the girl	(Neg the girl *past* come)			*past* be you 's sister
by NI	Ques Neg the girl	(the girl *past* not come)			*past* be you 's sister
by Whir	Ques Neg the girl	(who *past* not come)			*past* be you 's sister
by DI	Ques Neg the girl	(who *past* do not come)			*past* be you 's sister
by FF	Ques Neg the girl	(who do-*past* not come)			*past* be you 's sister
by QS	Neg *past* be	the girl	(who do-*past* not come)		you 's sister
by NI	*past* be not	the girl	(who do-*past* not come)		you 's sister
by FF	be-*past* not	the girl	(who do-*past* not come)		you 's sister
by MF	was not	the girl	who did not come		your sister

e. The girl who was given an F didn't graduate.

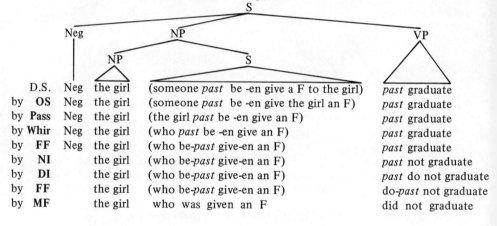

D.S.	Neg the girl	(someone *past* be -en give a F to the girl)	*past* graduate
by OS	Neg the girl	(someone *past* be -en give the girl an F)	*past* graduate
by Pass	Neg the girl	(the girl *past* be -en give an F)	*past* graduate
by Whir	Neg the girl	(who *past* be -en give an F)	*past* graduate
by FF	Neg the girl	(who be-*past* give-en an F)	*past* graduate
by NI	the girl	(who be-*past* give-en an F)	*past* not graduate
by DI	the girl	(who be-*past* give-en an F)	*past* do not graduate
by FF	the girl	(who be-*past* give-en an F)	do-*past* not graduate
by MF	the girl	who was given an F	did not graduate

2. The deep structure is:

Someone examined the dog that I was bitten by.

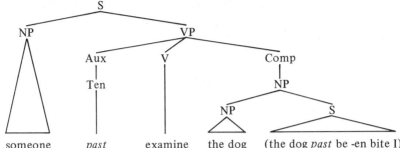

	D.S.	someone	*past*	examine	the dog	(the dog *past* be -en bite I)
by	**Pass**	someone	*past*	examine	the dog	(I *past* be -en bite by the dog)
by	**Whir**	someone	*past*	examine	the dog	(I *past* be -en bite by that)
by	**Whim**	someone	*past*	examine	the dog	(that I *past* be -en bite by)
by	**FF**	someone	*past*	examine	the dog	(that I be-*past* bite-en by)

(With **Whir, Whim** first)

	D.S.	someone	*past*	examine	the dog	(the dog *past* be -en bite I)
by	**Whir**	someone	*past*	examine	the dog	(that *past* be -en bite I)
by	**Whim**	(vacuous)				
by	**Pass**	someone	*past*	examine	the dog	(I *past* be -en bite by that)
by	**FF**	someone	*past*	examine	the dog	(I be-*past* bite-en by that)

At this point, it should be clear that the word order in the latter relative clause is not the desired one. Since **Whim** has already applied (vacuously), there is no way to return *that* to its proper position. Ergo, **Passive** must come before **Whim**. 3. Probably the most efficient way of getting rid of the *wh-* is to suggest an **Equi-NP deletion (End)** rule, which will delete the repeated NP entirely, but only if it is not contiguous with the modified NP (that is, as long as it isn't in subject position).

Compare: **Whir, Whim, Whiddle**   **End**

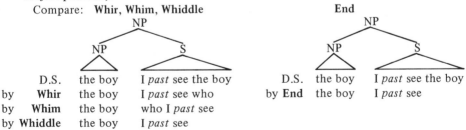

	D.S.	the boy	I *past* see the boy		D.S.	the boy	I *past* see the boy
by	**Whir**	the boy	I *past* see who	by	**End**	the boy	I *past* see
by	**Whim**	the boy	who I *past* see				
by	**Whiddle**	the boy	I *past* see				

Efficiency, nevertheless, is not the principal purpose of a grammar. It happens that I, for one, believe that **Whir, Whim,** and **Whiddle** are closer to the truth of the matter than **End**, that is, that there is an "understood" relative pronoun *in its proper place*. With this belief hanging about my neck like a millstone, I have no choice but to reject **End** despite its attractions. However, **End** should not be entirely discounted, as a use for it is found in a structure similar to the one above—see p. 234.

Exercise 3.23

1. a. The lady walking her dog is not a lady.

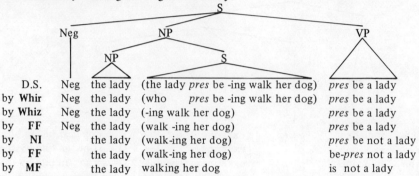

	Neg	NP	S	VP
D.S.	Neg	the lady	(the lady *pres* be -ing walk her dog)	*pres* be a lady
by **Whir**	Neg	the lady	(who *pres* be -ing walk her dog)	*pres* be a lady
by **Whiz**	Neg	the lady	(-ing walk her dog)	*pres* be a lady
by **FF**	Neg	the lady	(walk -ing her dog)	*pres* be a lady
by **NI**		the lady	(walk-ing her dog)	*pres* be not a lady
by **FF**		the lady	(walk-ing her dog)	be-*pres* not a lady
by **MF**		the lady	walking her dog	is not a lady

b. The boy at the door is a Boy Scout.

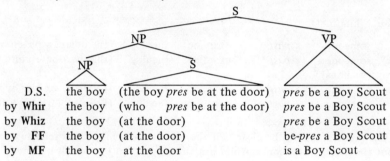

	NP	S	VP
D.S.	the boy	(the boy *pres* be at the door)	*pres* be a Boy Scout
by **Whir**	the boy	(who *pres* be at the door)	*pres* be a Boy Scout
by **Whiz**	the boy	(at the door)	*pres* be a Boy Scout
by **FF**	the boy	(at the door)	be-*pres* a Boy Scout
by **MF**	the boy	at the door	is a Boy Scout

c. The theory proposed by Chomsky was revolutionary.

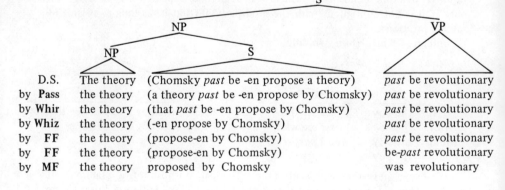

	NP	S	VP
D.S.	The theory	(Chomsky *past* be -en propose a theory)	*past* be revolutionary
by **Pass**	the theory	(a theory *past* be -en propose by Chomsky)	*past* be revolutionary
by **Whir**	the theory	(that *past* be -en propose by Chomsky)	*past* be revolutionary
by **Whiz**	the theory	(-en propose by Chomsky)	*past* be revolutionary
by **FF**	the theory	(propose-en by Chomsky)	*past* be revolutionary
by **FF**	the theory	(propose-en by Chomsky)	be-*past* revolutionary
by **MF**	the theory	proposed by Chomsky	was revolutionary

Exercise 3.26

1. a. the clever fox that ate the stupid chicken...

Standard

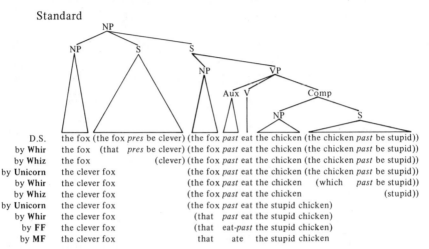

D.S.	the fox (the fox *pres* be clever)	(the fox *past* eat the chicken (the chicken *past* be stupid))
by Whir	the fox (that *pres* be clever)	(the fox *past* eat the chicken (the chicken *past* be stupid))
by Whiz	the fox	(clever) (the fox *past* eat the chicken (the chicken *past* be stupid))
by Unicorn	the clever fox	(the fox *past* eat the chicken (the chicken *past* be stupid))
by Whir	the clever fox	(the fox *past* eat the chicken (which *past* be stupid))
by Whiz	the clever fox	(the fox *past* eat the chicken (stupid))
by Unicorn	the clever fox	(the fox *past* eat the stupid chicken)
by Whir	the clever fox	(that *past* eat the stupid chicken)
by FF	the clever fox	(that eat-*past* the stupid chicken)
by MF	the clever fox	that ate the stupid chicken

Nonstandard

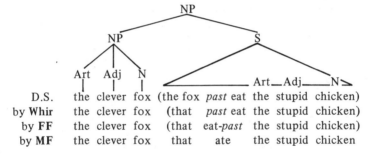

D.S.	the clever fox	(the fox *past* eat the stupid chicken)
by Whir	the clever fox	(that *past* eat the stupid chicken)
by FF	the clever fox	(that eat-*past* the stupid chicken)
by MF	the clever fox	that ate the stupid chicken

b. the ripe red apple on the tree...

Standard

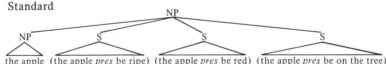

D.S.   the apple   (the apple *pres* be ripe) (the apple *pres* be red) (the apple *pres* be on the tree)

Nonstandard

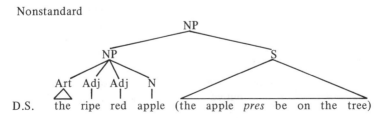

D.S.   the ripe red apple (the apple *pres* be on the tree)

c. one of the two trees...

Standard

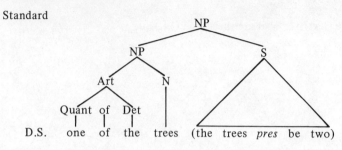

D.S.   one   of   the   trees   (the   trees   *pres*   be   two)

Nonstandard

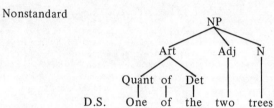

D.S.   One   of   the   two   trees

2. *Floating* is an adjective derived from the verb *float* and describes the activity of the *pole*. *Fishing* is a nominal, describing the purpose of the pole. If you consult Table 3.1, p. 140, it is evident that the adjective must precede the noun. That some *-ing* forms are adjectival and some nominal has been known for a long time by traditional grammarians, who coined the terms *gerundive* and *gerund*, respectively, for the two concepts.

Exercise 3.32

1.   a.   Did he tell you that Mary wouldn't go?

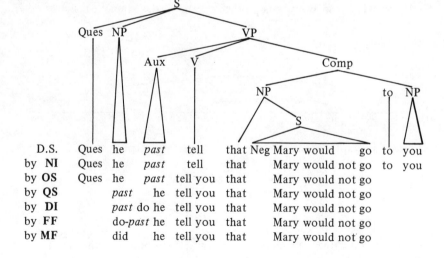

D.S.	Ques	he	*past*	tell	that Neg Mary would	go	to	you
by **NI**	Ques	he	*past*	tell	that	Mary would not go	to	you
by **OS**	Ques	he	*past*	tell you	that	Mary would not go		
by **QS**		*past*	he	tell you	that	Mary would not go		
by **DI**		*past* do he	tell you	that	Mary would not go			
by **FF**		do-*past* he	tell you	that	Mary would not go			
by **MF**		did	he	tell you	that	Mary would not go		

b. John didn't know who was caught.

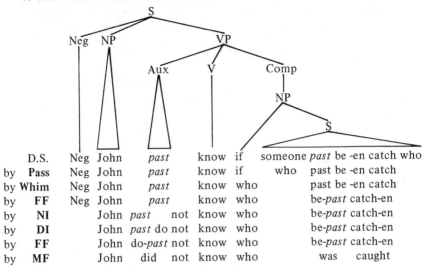

D.S.	Neg John	*past*	know	if	someone	*past* be -en catch who
by **Pass**	Neg John	*past*	know	if	who	past be -en catch
by **Whim**	Neg John	*past*	know	who		past be -en catch
by **FF**	Neg John	*past*	know	who		be-*past* catch-en
by **NI**	John *past*	not	know	who		be-*past* catch-en
by **DI**	John *past* do	not	know	who		be-*past* catch-en
by **FF**	John do-*past*	not	know	who		be-*past* catch-en
by **MF**	John did	not	know	who		was caught

c. Where do you think they will go?

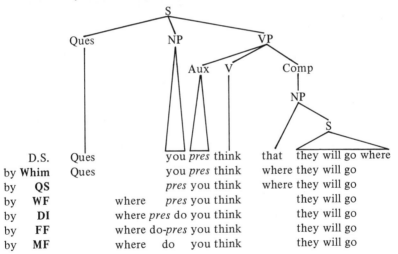

D.S.	Ques	you *pres* think	that	they will go where
by **Whim**	Ques	you *pres* think	where	they will go
by **QS**		*pres* you think	where	they will go
by **WF**		where *pres* you think		they will go
by **DI**		where *pres* do you think		they will go
by **FF**		where do-*pres* you think		they will go
by **MF**		where do you think		they will go

2. This class of sentences is actually dependent on the class of verbs *demand*, *insist, suggest, require*, etc., which are followed by the "plain" or "dictionary" form of the verb in the RNS. It used to be said that this was the subjunctive form of the verb—and in fact if you want to call it a subjunctive, that's fine with me. These verbs (*demand*, etc.) are marked in the lexicon as "taking" the subjunctive, in that case, where the subjunctive is defined as the dictionary form of the verb. It is something of a puzzle, however, to explain what happens to tense. Another approach is to forget about the form of the

verb in the RNS and to concentrate on what happens to tense. Let us say that *demand* is marked [+Shazam] in the lexicon, and that *Shazam* triggers an operation that deletes tense in the following RNS (the **Shazam** transformation).

D.S.   I *pres* demand that he *pres* be here by noon
by **Shazam**   I *pres* demand that he   be here by noon

The results will be those desired with the minimum operational complexity. Moreover, it becomes clear that *demand* does not "take" a form of the verb (whether "subjunctive" or "dictionary"), it is followed by tenseless verb phrases.

3. One means for doing so is to allow for an optional inclusion within the NP rule generating factive sentences. That is,

NP → (the fact) that + S

Another way is to add another rule to the NP rules,

NP → NP + NP

which would be equivalent to the traditionalist's appositive noun phrase, and already previously encountered in the discussion of NP + NP complements. This suggests that the *that + S* part is appositive to *the fact*, in the structure

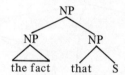

The ambiguity of the sentence is easily accounted for in either of the above formulations, for neither is like the modifying structure that underlies one of the meanings.

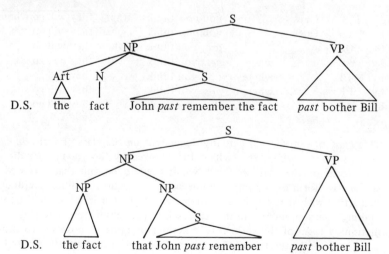

4. To begin with, it should be recognized that the foreign student is being quite logical. *Whom* is supposedly appropriate for nonsubject relative or interrogative pronouns, and this one is assuredly the object of the verb *see*. Although *whom* is perfectly acceptable when generated in the uppermost sentence or in a relative clause (for example, *Whom did he see?*, *The man whom he saw . . .* , etc.), it does not seem to be so good when generated in an RNS. Most people indicate some doubt about the grammaticality of *I don't know whom he saw* and *Whom do you think he saw?* However, how do you explain this to a foreign student? Frankly, I would prefer just to tell him to avoid *whom* entirely and have done with it.

Exercise 3.42

1. a. For you to lie to me is what hurts most!

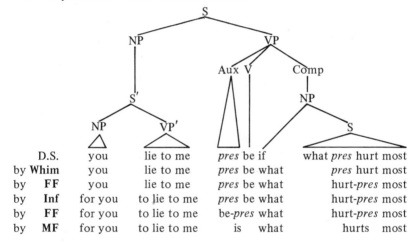

D.S.	you	lie to me	*pres* be if	what *pres* hurt most
by **Whim**	you	lie to me	*pres* be what	*pres* hurt most
by **FF**	you	lie to me	*pres* be what	hurt-*pres* most
by **Inf**	for you	to lie to me	*pres* be what	hurt-*pres* most
by **FF**	for you	to lie to me	be-*pres* what	hurt-*pres* most
by **MF**	for you	to lie to me	is what	hurts most

b. His arguing won't help him.

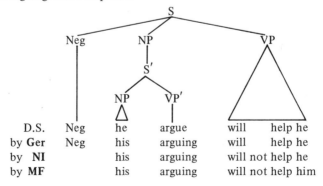

D.S.	Neg	he	argue	will help he
by **Ger**	Neg	his	arguing	will help he
by **NI**		his	arguing	will not help he
by **MF**		his	arguing	will not help him

c. It won't matter what he does.

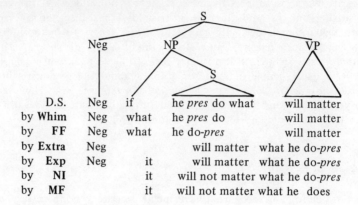

D.S.	Neg	if	he *pres* do what	will matter
by **Whim**	Neg	what	he *pres* do	will matter
by **FF**	Neg	what	he do-*pres*	will matter
by **Extra**	Neg		will matter	what he do-*pres*
by **Exp**	Neg	it	will matter	what he do-*pres*
by **NI**		it	will not matter	what he do-*pres*
by **MF**		it	will not matter	what he does

d. The pin may be difficult to find.

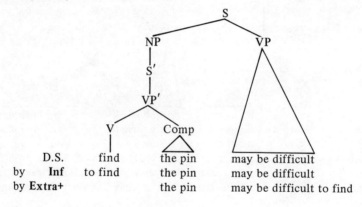

D.S.		find	the pin	may be difficult
by **Inf**	to find	the pin	may be difficult
by **Extra+**		the pin	may be difficult to find

e. It is his desire to be recognized.

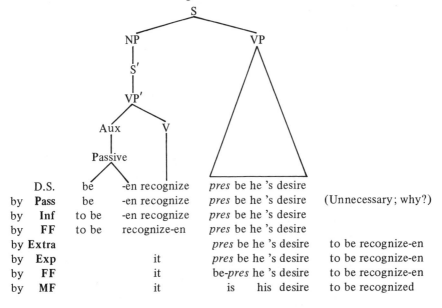

D.S.	be	-en recognize	*pres* be he 's desire		
by **Pass**	be	-en recognize	*pres* be he 's desire	(Unnecessary; why?)	
by **Inf**	to be	-en recognize	*pres* be he 's desire		
by **FF**	to be	recognize-en	*pres* be he 's desire		
by **Extra**			*pres* be he 's desire	to be recognize-en	
by **Exp**		it	*pres* be he 's desire	to be recognize-en	
by **FF**		it	be-*pres* he 's desire	to be recognize-en	
by **MF**		it	is his desire	to be recognized	

2. The expletive *there* occurs only in sentences whose verb is the existential *be* (that is, *be* meaning, roughly, "exist"). Moreover, in virtually all such sentences, there are two elements found in the complement of the verb: a noun and a location, as in the example given, *there are two chairs in the room*. While the complement type NP + Loc exists with verbs like *put*, etc., (see p. 92), it does not seem compelling that *be* should be classified in this category. Instead, we might do better to seize on the paraphrase, *two chairs are in the room*, as more closely reflecting the deep structure of both sentences. A form of extraposition can give us the intermediate structure in which *two chairs* follows *be*, and a form of the expletive rule can then generate *there*.

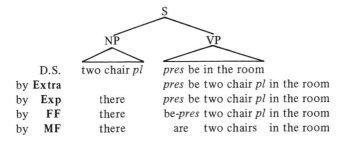

D.S.	two chair *pl*	*pres* be in the room	
by **Extra**		*pres* be two chair *pl* in the room	
by **Exp**	there	*pres* be two chair *pl* in the room	
by **FF**	there	be-*pres* two chair *pl* in the room	
by **MF**	there	are two chairs in the room	

Exercise 3.43

1. a. John asked me to consider allowing him to do it.

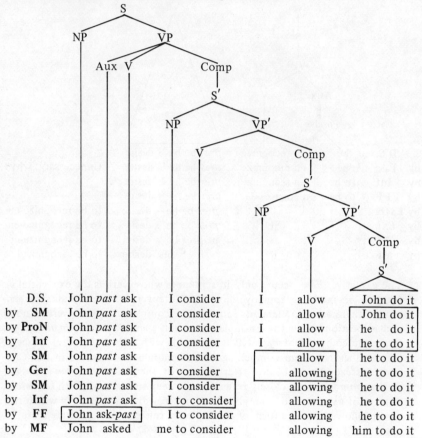

	D.S.	John *past* ask	I consider	I	allow	John do it
by	**SM**	John *past* ask	I consider	I	allow	John do it
by	**ProN**	John *past* ask	I consider	I	allow	he do it
by	**Inf**	John *past* ask	I consider	I	allow	he to do it
by	**SM**	John *past* ask	I consider		allow	he to do it
by	**Ger**	John *past* ask	I consider		allowing	he to do it
by	**SM**	John *past* ask	I consider		allowing	he to do it
by	**Inf**	John *past* ask	I to consider		allowing	he to do it
by	**FF**	John ask-*past*	I to consider		allowing	he to do it
by	**MF**	John asked	me to consider		allowing	him to do it

b. She hated not being told who did it.

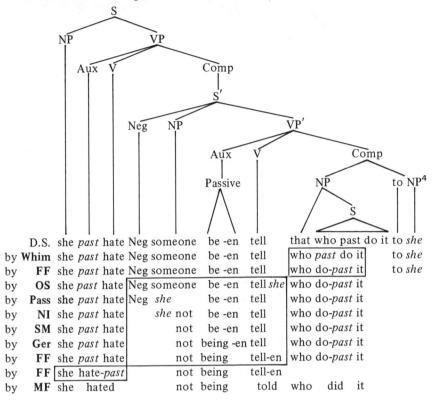

	D.S.	she	*past*	hate	Neg	someone	be -en	tell	that who past do it	to *she*
by	**Whim**	she	*past*	hate	Neg	someone	be -en	tell	who *past* do it	to *she*
by	**FF**	she	*past*	hate	Neg	someone	be -en	tell	who do-*past* it	to *she*
by	**OS**	she	*past*	hate	Neg someone		be -en	tell *she*	who do-*past* it	
by	**Pass**	she	*past*	hate	Neg *she*		be -en	tell	who do-*past* it	
by	**NI**	she	*past*	hate		*she* not	be -en	tell	who do-*past* it	
by	**SM**	she	*past*	hate		not	be -en	tell	who do-*past* it	
by	**Ger**	she	*past*	hate		not	being -en	tell	who do-*past* it	
by	**FF**	she	*past*	hate		not	being	tell-en	who do-*past* it	
by	**FF**	she hate-*past*				not	being	tell-en		
by	**MF**	she	hated			not	being	told	who did it	

[4] Note that *to she* is in the conventional indirect object position (cf. p. 94), i.e., following the direct object (of the verb *tell*). *She* is italicized in this example to make it easier to follow her progress through **OS** and **Pass** to her ultimate extinction at the hands of **SM**.

c. Who do you think will be told to go?

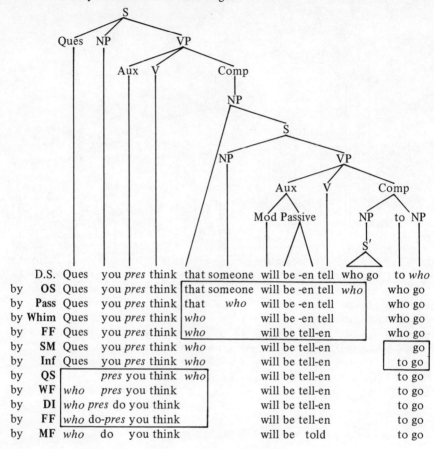

	D.S.	Ques	you *pres* think	that someone	will be -en tell	who go	to *who*
by	OS	Ques	you *pres* think	that someone	will be -en tell	*who*	who go
by	Pass	Ques	you *pres* think	that *who*	will be -en tell		who go
by Whim	Ques	you *pres* think	*who*	will be -en tell		who go
by	FF	Ques	you *pres* think	*who*	will be tell-en		who go
by	SM	Ques	you *pres* think	*who*	will be tell-en		go
by	Inf	Ques	you *pres* think	*who*	will be tell-en		to go
by	QS		*pres* you think	*who*	will be tell-en		to go
by	WF	*who*	*pres* you think		will be tell-en		to go
by	DI	*who pres* do you think		will be tell-en		to go
by	FF	*who* do-*pres* you think		will be tell-en		to go
by	MF	*who* do you think		will be told		to go

If we begin, as usual, with the lowest sentence, the first operation is the **Subject-matching** operation. *Someone* and *who* being different, *who* is preserved, and we are stuck with two *who*'s with no way to get rid of one of them. At the same time, we have no choice about the deep structure, as may be seen if we use a known NP in place of *who*, such as *Sam was told to go*, since *tell* must have an indirect object. The only way to get rid of the extra *who* is to get the upper *who* into subject position (via **OS** and **Pass**) so that **SM** will delete the lower *who*. This means, however, that operations begin on a higher sentence rather than the lowest. There are, apparently, exceptions to even the most sacrosanct rules! For your convenience in keeping track of *who* as it is shuffled across the length of the sentence, it is italicized.

d. What would you like me to admit having done?

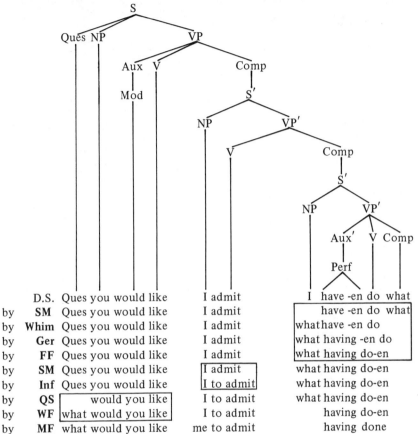

	D.S.	Ques you would like	I admit	I have -en do what
by	**SM**	Ques you would like	I admit	have -en do what
by	**Whim**	Ques you would like	I admit	what have -en do
by	**Ger**	Ques you would like	I admit	what having -en do
by	**FF**	Ques you would like	I admit	what having do-en
by	**SM**	Ques you would like	I admit	what having do-en
by	**Inf**	Ques you would like	I to admit	what having do-en
by	**QS**	would you like	I to admit	what having do-en
by	**WF**	what would you like	I to admit	what having do-en
by	**MF**	what would you like	me to admit	having done

Exercise 3.47

1. a. I'll have him paint the barn.

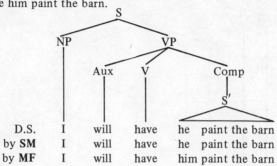

D.S.	I	will	have	he	paint the barn
by **SM**	I	will	have	he	paint the barn
by **MF**	I	will	have	him	paint the barn

b. I have to sell my Jaguar.

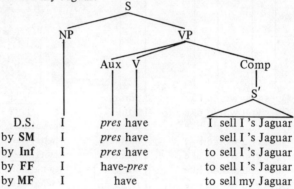

D.S.	I	*pres* have	I sell I 's Jaguar
by **SM**	I	*pres* have	sell I 's Jaguar
by **Inf**	I	*pres* have	to sell I 's Jaguar
by **FF**	I	have-*pres*	to sell I 's Jaguar
by **MF**	I	have	to sell my Jaguar

c. Will you have something to eat?

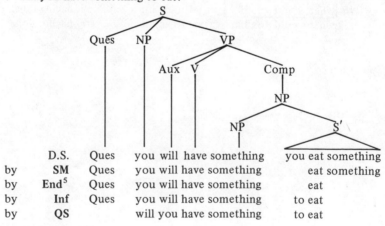

	D.S.	Ques	you will have something	you eat something
by	**SM**	Ques	you will have something	eat something
by	**End**[5]	Ques	you will have something	eat
by	**Inf**	Ques	you will have something	to eat
by	**QS**		will you have something	to eat

---

[5] See answer 3, p. 221. **End** here, however, is unrestricted: the equi-NP of the modifying S′ may be subject or object. Note the family resemblance of **End** to **Zap** of Exercises 2a and 2c, p. 235.

2. a. I've been anxious to meet you.

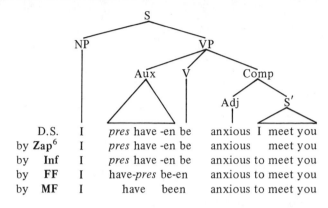

D.S.	I	*pres* have -en be	anxious	I	meet you
by **Zap**[6]	I	*pres* have -en be	anxious		meet you
by **Inf**	I	*pres* have -en be	anxious to		meet you
by **FF**	I	have-*pres* be-en	anxious to		meet you
by **MF**	I	have been	anxious to		meet you

b. It's too hot to drink coffee.

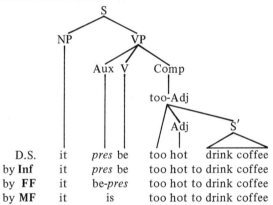

D.S.	it	*pres* be	too hot	drink coffee
by **Inf**	it	*pres* be	too hot to	drink coffee
by **FF**	it	be-*pres*	too hot to	drink coffee
by **MF**	it	is	too hot to	drink coffee

c. That dress is too small for you to wear.

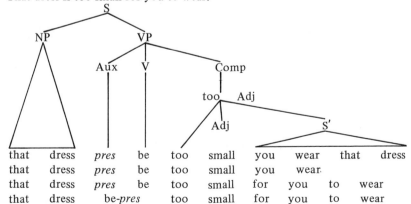

D.S.	that	dress	*pres*	be	too	small	you	wear	that	dress
by **Zap**[6]	that	dress	*pres*	be	too	small	you	wear.	
by **Inf**	that	dress	*pres*	be	too	small	for	you	to	wear
by **FF**	that	dress	be-*pres*		too	small	for	you	to	wear
by **MF**	that	dress	is		too	small	for	you	to	wear

[6]See p. 161. Note also comments in footnote on p. 234.

d. I heard myself say something.

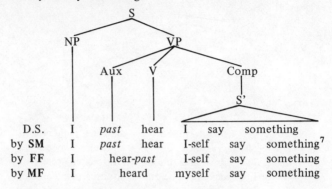

D.S.	I	*past*	hear	I	say	something
by **SM**	I	*past*	hear	I-self	say	something[7]
by **FF**	I	hear-*past*		I-self	say	something
by **MF**	I	heard		myself	say	something

3. Using the features [+Fact] and [−Fact] (for lack of any better) we may designate which verbs take the **Gerund** operation by keying them [+Fact] in the lexicon, etc. Note that [+Fact] and [−Fact] are grammatical, not semantic features, for they relate to the selection of grammatical operations.

Exercise 3.5

1. John kissed his wife and so did Bill.

On the assumption that **and so did. . .** derives from conjoined sentences with identical VPs, the deep structure appears as

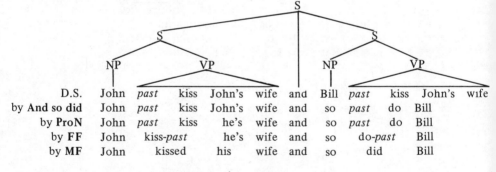

D.S.	John	*past*	kiss	John's	wife	and	Bill	*past*	kiss	John's	wife
by **And so did**	John	*past*	kiss	John's	wife	and	so	*past*	do	Bill	
by **ProN**	John	*past*	kiss	he's	wife	and	so	*past*	do	Bill	
by **FF**	John	kiss-*past*		he's	wife	and	so	do-*past*		Bill	
by **MF**	John	kissed		his	wife	and	so	did		Bill	

In this case, Bill definitely kissed John's wife, for only then are the underlying VPs really identical. If we want Bill to have kissed his own wife, then we must relax the restrictions on the **And so did** operation, allowing it to operate on any identical intermediate structure, not just on identical deep structures. In this case, **And so did** may work just after pronominalization has occurred:

---

[7]Cf. Exercise 3.43, No. 2, p. 157.

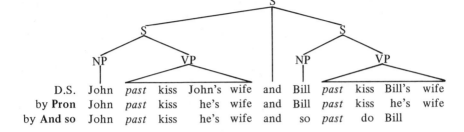

D.S.	John	*past*	kiss	John's	wife	and	Bill	*past*	kiss	Bill's	wife
by **Pron**	John	*past*	kiss	he's	wife	and	Bill	*past*	kiss	he's	wife
by **And so**	John	*past*	kiss	he's	wife	and	so	*past*	do	Bill	

The chances are that the rule "prefers" to work on identical deep structures, but that the restriction will relax to allow for other possibilities when circumstances suggest that such an interpretation is unreasonable or unlikely.

2. I put the box down where he told me to.

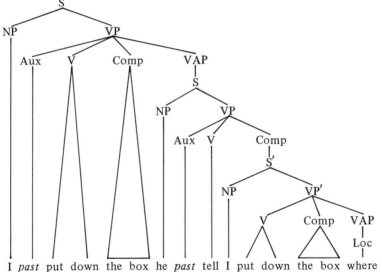

D.S.	I	*past*	put	down	the	box	he	*past*	tell	I	put	down	the	box	where
by **WF**	I	*past*	put	down	the	box	he	*past*	tell	where	I	put	down	the	box
by **SM**	I	*past*	put	down	the	box	he	*past*	tell	where	me	put	down	the	box
by **Inf**	I	*past*	put	down	the	box	he	*past*	tell	where	me	to	put	down	the box
by **Zap**	I	*past*	put	down	the	box	he	*past*	tell	where	me	to			
by **WF**	I	*past*	put	down	the	box	where	he	*past*	tell	me	to			
by **FF**	I	*past*	put	down	the	box	where	he	tell-*past*	me	to				
by **PS**	I	*past*	put	the	box	down	where	he	tell-*past*	me	to				
by **FF**	I	put-*past*	the	box	down	where	he	tell-*past*	me	to					
by **MF**	I	put	the	box	down	where	he	told	me	to					

There are several new points about this example, the most obvious of which is a new operation **Zap**, which deletes the infinitival verb phrase (saving the *to*) if it is identical to a higher **VP**. This operation is optional, as we may also say *I put* *the box down where he told me to put it down*, in which, of course, **ProN** is obligatory. The other point is the repetition of **WF**. We do **WF** twice because we get the wrong answer otherwise. The need to move *wh-* words has come to our attention previously (p. 156, and in the exercises on p. 157), solved then by invoking separately **WF** and **Whim**. In this case, it does not seem to be amenable to the same solution. The issue of multiple and selective *wh-* movements is still something of a puzzle.

3.   This text, which I have slaved over, has come to an end.

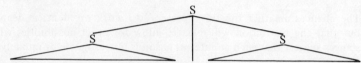

D.S.	this	text	has	come	to	an	end	and	I	have	slaved	over	this text
by **Zap**[8]	this	text	(I	have	slaved	over	this	text)	has	come	to	an	end
by **Whir**	this	text	(I	have	slaved over		which)		has	come	to	an	end
by **Whim**	this	text	(which	I	have	slaved	over)	has	come	to	an	end
by **Comma**	this	text,	which	I	have	slaved	over,	has	come	to	an	end

4. Since he asked me to, I helped John wash and wax his car.

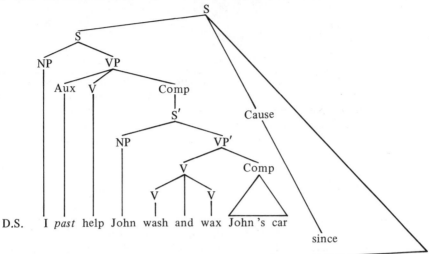

D.S.   I *past* help John wash and wax John's car   since

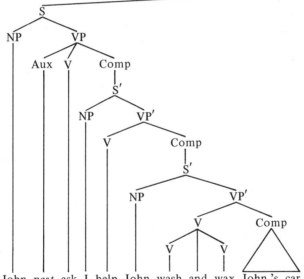

	John *past* ask I help John wash and wax John's car
by **SM**	John *past* ask *I* help *John* wash and wax John's car
by **SM**	*John* *past* ask *I* help John wash and wax John's car
by **Inf**	John *past* ask I to help John wash and wax John's car
by **Zap**	John *past* ask I to
by **FF**	John ask-*past* I to

D.S.	I *past* help John wash and wax John's car since John ask-*past* I to
by **Pron**	I *past* help John wash and wax he's car since he ask-*past* I to
by **SM**	*I* past help *John* wash and wax he's car since he ask-*past* I to
by **FF**	I help-*past* John wash and wax he's car since he ask-*past* I to
by **Zap**	since he ask-*past* I to I help-*past* John wash and wax he's car
by **MF**	since he asked me to I helped John wash and wax his car

5. John kissed and kicked his wife and his dog, respectively.

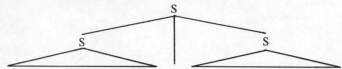

D.S.	John	*past*	kiss	John's	wife	and	John	past	kick	John's dog
by **ProN**	John	*past*	kiss	he's	wife	and	John	past	kick	he's dog
by **Respectively**	John	*past*	kiss	and	*past*	kick	he's	wife	and	he's dog
by **FF**	John	kiss-*past*	and	kick-*past*		he's	wife	and	he's	dog
by **MF**	John	kissed	and	kicked		his	wife	and	his	dog

Exercise 3.6

1. By a convention established previously (p. 123), **Passive** precedes **NI**, although more for convenience than anything else. **Passive** must precede **SM**, for **SM** matches the final subject brought forward by **Passive**. **SM** precedes **Gerund** by virtue of the fact that the **Gerund** rule sometimes operates on the subject, whose determination by **SM** should then be already completed. **NI** could actually be sequenced anywhere with respect to the other three without any attendant distortions of the syntax. However, since **NI** is an operation that relates strictly to the deep structure of the sentence node itself, it should precede operations that draw on information in the higher sentence and that fit the lower sentence into the higher sentence—that is, **SM** and **Gerund**. Thus: **Passive, NI, SM, Gerund**.
2. Sentences a, b, and c are awkward because there is only one change in the second clause; sentence d is awkward because there are three changes. One of the semantic/syntactic aspects of *but*-conjunction is an apparent preference for two changes in the second clause with respect to the first.
3. **And so did** is motivated by the fact that the VPs of two conjoined sentences are identical. The major point to embody in the rule is a preservation of the auxiliary verb:

    NP Tense v ⇒ so Tense v NP

    where v is defined as the first verbal in the auxiliary, or the verb *be*. If there is no v, then a *do* is inserted by **DI** in normal fashion.
4. *Unless* can be used in place of *if . . . not* only so long as the condition is factual.

Index